COLUMBIA UNIVERSITY GERMANIC STUDIES
EDITED BY ROBERT HERNDON FIFE
New Series

NUMBER SIX

LITERARY CRITICISM IN THE WORK OF LUDWIG ACHIM VON ARNIM

LITERARY CRITICISM AND ROMANTIC THEORY IN THE WORK OF ACHIM VON ARNIM

BY HERBERT R. LIEDKE
COLLEGE OF THE CITY OF NEW YORK

AMS PRESS, INC.
NEW YORK
1966

Copyright 1937, Columbia University Press,
New York

Reprinted with the permission of the
Original Publisher, 1966

AMS PRESS, INC.
New York, N.Y. 10003
1966

Manufactured in the United States of America

To
K.B.L. and F.K.

PREFACE

The completion of this study is due largely to Professor Robert Herndon Fife, at whose suggestion I started the work and for whose invaluable guidance and constant encouragement I wish to express my sincerest gratitude. I am indebted for kind advice and continued interest to Professor Edwin C. Roedder of the College of the City of New York, to Director Dr. Ernst Beutler, and to Dr. Franz Götting of the Goethe Museum in Frankfort for the permission to avail myself of hitherto unpublished material. I also wish to express my gratitude for pertinent information given by the von Arnim family, by Dr. Otto Mallon, and Mr. Ernst Henrici. From the Columbia University Library, the Goethe Museum in Frankfort, the Goethe-Schiller Archiv in Weimar, the Universitätsbibliothek in Heidelberg, and the administration of the Preussische Staatsbibliothek in Berlin I have received many courtesies which I wish to acknowledge.

ABBREVIATIONS

Arnim-Bettina	Reinhold Steig, *Achim von Arnim und die ihm nahe standen*, Bd. II. *Achim von Arnim und Bettina Brentano.* Stuttgart, 1913.
Arnim-Brentano	Reinhold Steig, *Achim von Arnim und die ihm nahe standen*, Bd. I. *Achim von Arnim und Clemens Brentano.* Stuttgart, 1894.
Arnim-Grimm	Reinhold Steig, *Achim von Arnim und die ihm nahe standen*, Bd. III. *Achim von Arnim und Jacob und Wilhelm Grimm.* Berlin, 1904.
Bettina-Goethe	Reinhold Steig, *Bettinas Briefwechsel mit Goethe.* Berlin, 1922.
DNL, CXLVI, I.	*Deutsche National-Literatur.* Bd. CXLVI. *Arnim, Klemens und Bettina Brentano, J. Görres.* Teil I. Hrsg. v. Max Koch, Stuttgart.
HeidelbJbb.	*Heidelbergische Jahrbücher der Literatur.*
NHeidelbJbb.	*Neue Heidelberger Jahrbücher.*
Werke	*Ludwig Achim's v. Arnim sämtliche Werke.* Neue Ausgabe. Berlin, 1857.

CONTENTS

V. OLDER ROMANTIC CONTEMPORARIES 87

Friedrich Schlegel's *Gedichte.*—August W. Schlegel's *Poetische Werke.*—Novalis' *Heinrich von Ofterdingen.*—Hölderlin's *Hyperion.*—Arnim's essay, "Ausflüge mit Hölderlin."—Zacharias Werner's "system," *Attila, Die Weihe der Unkraft.*

VI. CLASSICISM 105

National genius versus mastership of the antique.—Arnim's "Scherzendes Gedicht von der Nachahmung des Heiligen."—Arnim's "Träume."—Goethe's *Iphigenie* and A. W. Schlegel's *Ion.*—Goethe's attitude towards the *Wunderhorn* and *Zeitung für Einsiedler.*—*Die Wahlverwandtschaften.*—Goethe's breach with Arnim.—Arnim's "Wunder über Wunder" and Goethe's *Wilhelm Meister.*—*Faust.*—*Dichtung und Wahrheit.*—Schiller.

VII. THE RISE OF NATIONALISM 136

Berlin 1810.—The "Nordstern" circle, *Die Versuche und Hindernisse Karls.*—Kleist and the *Berliner Abendblätter.*—E. M. Arndt, *Das Preussiche Volk und Heer 1813, Der Rhein, Teutschlands Strom aber nicht Teutschlands Grenze.*—The *Preussiche Correspondent.*—Fouqué's *Gedichte vor und während dem Kriege.*—Fichte.—Arnim's political disillusionment.

VIII. THE DRIFT TOWARD REALISM (1815-1831) 152

Realistic tendencies.—*Der Gesellschafter.*—Henriette Schubart's *Schottische Lieder und Balladen von Sir Walter Scott.*—Translations and imitations of Scott's novels.—"Über eine Theater-Kritik."—*Blätter für literarische Unterhaltung.*—Varnhagen von Ense's biographical writings.

IX. ARNIM'S POSITION IN THE HISTORY OF CRITICISM 174

BIBLIOGRAPHY 179

INDEX 183

ABBREVIATIONS

Arnim-Bettina	Reinhold Steig, *Achim von Arnim und die ihm nahe standen*, Bd. II. *Achim von Arnim und Bettina Brentano*. Stuttgart, 1913.
Arnim-Brentano	Reinhold Steig, *Achim von Arnim und die ihm nahe standen*, Bd. I. *Achim von Arnim und Clemens Brentano*. Stuttgart, 1894.
Arnim-Grimm	Reinhold Steig, *Achim von Arnim und die ihm nahe standen*, Bd. III. *Achim von Arnim und Jacob und Wilhelm Grimm*. Berlin, 1904.
Bettina-Goethe	Reinhold Steig, *Bettinas Briefwechsel mit Goethe*. Berlin, 1922.
DNL, CXLVI, I.	*Deutsche National-Literatur.* Bd. CXLVI. *Arnim, Klemens und Bettina Brentano, J. Görres.* Teil I. Hrsg. v. Max Koch, Stuttgart.
HeidelbJbb.	*Heidelbergische Jahrbücher der Literatur.*
NHeidelbJbb.	*Neue Heidelberger Jahrbücher.*
Werke	*Ludwig Achim's v. Arnim sämtliche Werke.* Neue Ausgabe. Berlin, 1857.

INTRODUCTION

In this study an attempt has been made to explore Arnim's activities and attitude as a literary critic, a field that has heretofore been almost completely neglected. The material for such an investigation is not easily accessible. None can be found in the three editions of Arnim's *Sämtliche Werke*, published by his widow with the help of Wilhelm Grimm between 1839 and 1857. These editions lack all of Arnim's reviews, essays, anecdotes, and short stories, as well as his correspondence. Only minor attempts have been made to collect and to reprint Arnim's extensive journalistic writings, which originally appeared in about forty different periodicals.[1] The wealth and quality of the material on which this study is based has become known only recently through the publication in 1925 of Otto Mallon's scholarly *Arnim-Bibliographie*, which furnishes an excellent reference work in the field. Furthermore, the auction of Arnim-Brentano manuscripts and posthumous works from the family archives in Wiepersdorf in 1929-30 brought to light additional and important material.

For the present work all of the published writings of Arnim have been examined. In addition a certain number of unpublished essays and fragments, found chiefly in the Goethe Museum in Frankfort, have been read. A further important expression of Arnim's critical views is that which is found in his correspondence. The letters to Clemens Brentano, to Joseph Görres, and especially to Jacob and Wilhelm Grimm contain much that is necessary for an understanding of his views on literature, particularly for his ideas concerning popular poetry. These are in the main accessible in the volumes of Reinhold Steig (*Achim von Arnim und die ihm nahe standen*), which have contributed much to Chapters IV and V of this investigation. Some unpublished letters from Arnim and

[1] Ludwig Geiger, "A. v. Arnim's Beiträge zum Literatur-Blatt", *Zeitschrift für vergl. Literaturgeschichte*, XII; Ludwig Geiger, *L. A. v. Arnim, Unbekannte Aufsätze und Gedichte*, Berlin, 1892 (cited below as *Unbekannte Aufsätze*), contains selected reprints of Arnim's contributions to *Der Gessellschafter;* Otto Mallon, "A. v. Arnims Beiträge zum literarischen Conversationsblatt", *Preussische Jahrbücher*, 1931.

others, in part also in the Frankfort Goethe Museum, have been used, as will appear in the following pages.

The scope of such a study as this cannot, however, be limited to a discussion of the reviews, essays, pronouncements, notes, and letters, or the other purely critical material that flowed so easily from Arnim's pen. By his very nature he was obliged to stamp whatever he wrote with the quality and force of his own personality. All of his writings, published and unpublished, are the expression of a *Weltanschauung* that struggled for utterance. All that he put before the public was a challenge to the literary and social world of his time. Obviously, his critical position and his contribution to literary criticism cannot be understood unless we widen the boundary of our investigation to include aspects of personality and characteristic productions in other fields than the critical. The explanation and the excuse for such an extension of our discussion are to be found in Arnim's nature and in the totalitarian character of the romantic spirit.

The conceptions which form the basis of Arnim's critical work are to be sought in the spiritual legacy which the younger romantic generation received from that immediately preceding it, and also in the unique personality of young Arnim. Our investigation begins, therefore, with these aspects. The first chapter tries to survey and define the critical approach to literature which Arnim found in his predecessors, chiefly in Herder, and the form and interpretation which he gave to the idea of "spirit" (*Geist*) in its historical and popular expressions. The second chapter traces the background of family tradition and character development that throws light on the peculiar soul structure of Arnim. With the third chapter we enter, then, on an examination of his critical activities. The history of these may be divided roughly into four periods. The first includes his student days at Halle, beginning in 1799, and at Göttingen, and the years of his "grand tour." Here again the boundaries of our study must be widened to include his interest in the natural sciences. This was his first field of scholarly activity and an understanding of his attitude toward it throws light on his approach to literature. It has also been felt necessary to trace the relation of Arnim to the scientific and pseudo-scientific literature of the time with some care for the reason that this side of his work has heretofore received rather insufficient treatment. Coincident with the development of this critical interest in the natural sciences, came the beginning of a critical interest in literature, evidenced as early as 1803 in his contributions to Friedrich Schlegel's *Europa* and confirmed in the spring of 1804 by his confession to Clemens that he would like to make journalism his life career.

The maturing of his work as a literary critic follows, from 1808 to 1810. This is treated in our fourth chapter, which deals with his writings for the *Heidelbergische Jahrbücher* and the *Einsiedler-Zeitung,* and includes the important discussions of critical questions which he carried on with members of the group of Heidelberg romanticists. The third period of his critical activity falls, then, in Berlin, beginning in 1810, and embraces the nationalistic propaganda that preceded the War of Liberation, the period of his association with Heinrich von Kleist's *Berliner Abendblätter* (1810-1811) and with the *Preussische Correspondent* (1813-1814). The fourth and last period, which is characterized by a wider range of critical interest, covers the years from 1814, when he withdrew from public affairs to live on his estate at Wiepersdorf, to his death in 1831. In these years his more important critical work appeared in Gubitz' *Gesellschafter* and Brockhaus' *Blätter für literarische Unterhaltung.*

This periodization furnishes, in the main, a framework for the organization of the results of our investigation. However, a strictly chronological treatment of the material was found to be impracticable. Arnim's interest in natural sciences overlapped his development as literary critic; indeed, it will be noted below that it experienced a revival in 1810 and reappeared here and there in the later decades of his life. Equally important with any chronological arrangement for a complete view of his critical work is an investigation of his relationship to literary groups. To his attitude toward older romantic contemporaries and toward Goethe special chapters have been devoted. Particularly his relation to the Weimar master has been treated extensively. Its importance for an understanding of his ideas concerning literature will be obvious.

Nowhere, not even in the interchanges with Brentano, do the literary aspirations and views of Arnim stand out more clearly than in his contacts with Goethe.

It will be apparent from the foregoing that the present work has been obliged to go somewhat further than its title indicates. Any investigation of Arnim's literary criticism must soon overstep the commonly recognized boundaries both of literature and of criticism. The reasons for this lie in the character of the man and his epoch. Arnim regarded the works that came into his hand as subject matter for the expression of ideas that were not bounded by considerations of literary history or convention, genre or style. In such matters as these, in the field of aesthetic discrimination, he was certainly inferior to Brentano and possibly to Görres. Nevertheless, it cannot be denied that Arnim had a feeling for works of literature and a talent for discussing them. Journalistic essays and studies, notes of the most varied content flowed even more readily from his pen than from that of any other member of the Heidelberg group, even including Görres. He brought to his critical work a spirit that was peculiar to himself. This appears even in essays on insignificant topics. It can best be described as a spirit of consecration. He felt himself called to a mission: to change the spiritual attitude of his people. As will appear below, he wrote only on those books that interested him positively or negatively, and the spiritual and patriotic ground-tone of his critical purpose can be noted everywhere. It is this that gives to his literary criticism a certain consistent seriousness and an essential dignity.

I

THE ROMANTIC APPROACH TO LITERARY CRITICISM

The object of early Romanticism was to arouse the literary world and to create new idealistic standards. It opposed the utilitarian rationalism of men like Nicolai and turned against the philistine spirit of Kotzebue and Iffland. It turned at first with enthusiasm to the classical harmony and perfection idealized by Goethe, but speedily passed on to new fields of speculation and literary and artistic interest. The generation of early romanticists had experienced during the most impressionable years of youth the emergence of new ideas in natural science, and the new development of idealistic philosophy, and it was now to carry its theorizing to unlimited extremes. In the political field the last decade of the Eighteenth Century was comparatively quiet in Germany, and the petty bourgeois mind was little affected by the revolutionary ideas which held sway on the other side of the Rhine. Political and politico-social questions, such as Rousseau's interpretation of the relation between the individual and society, did not interest the great men of letters, or at most, only as a stimulus for aesthetic and ethical theorizing. National sentiment, as the Nineteenth Century understood it, did not enter into their range of ideas. In this "peaceful" atmosphere the early romanticists spun their thoughts regarding the individual and the universe. Fichte carried this system of idealistic philosophy to a dazzling height. Novalis surpassed him with his "magical idealism," and in literature Friedrich Schlegel created the concept of "progressive universal poetry."

Ten years later men of letters were facing an entirely different situation. The French Revolution had failed to bring about the "Golden Age," men were looking more realistically into prevalent concepts, such as "innate goodness of man," "*liberté, egalité et fraternité.*" Napoleon had appeared on the political horizon, and Germany had begun to realize the danger of the French imperialistic policy. Not German territory alone, German "Kultur" also was to be defended against a foreign invasion.

Particularly the younger generation of Romanticists, the group of young poets and scholars which embraced Arnim, Brentano, Görres, and their friends from Cassel, the Grimm brothers, were among the first to awaken to this danger, while older, well-known leaders in literature, like Goethe and Voss, realized more slowly the changed situation. Following the path opened by Herder, the Heidelberg group began to emphasize actively the cultural tradition of Germany and the hidden treasures in her art and literature. It was their feeling that if the German people could be led back to this wealth, the present would be enriched, and art and literature would receive an impetus hitherto undreamed of. They cherished the belief that the senility of the age had almost killed the delicate flower of true creative art, and that it had to be revived through a reawakening of the spirit of the people. On the one hand, unassimilated forms of expression from abroad had smothered native endeavors; on the other, a narrow-minded philistinism and a love of bombastic display still held the attention of the public as they had since the Thirty Years' War. To the mind of the young men of Heidelberg the nation was waiting for a reappearance of creative genius such as it once possessed in the Nibelungenlied, in the Minnesang, and in Hans Sachs. It is understandable that this absorbing quest for *Volkspoesie* was sometimes exaggerated and pursued with a disregard of the aesthetic standards erected by the preceding generation. Thus Arnim, with the unbounded spirit of youth, wrote that in folklore he liked that which was most free and liberal and did not even mind the burlesque.[1]

Very early in the new century, therefore, the cultural consciousness and historical-philosophical thinking of Romanticism in Germany had struck out in two directions. The earlier of these expounded the cult of the individual, of the ego, as a supreme, incomparable entity in its relation to society (*Allgemeinheit*). The second, more concretely historical in attitude, was absorbed in a wealth of historical material, and was endeavoring to formulate a literary-historical philosophy in the train of Herder. Single phenomena like nature, man, history, and society were viewed as the

[1] Arnim-Brentano, p. 169: "Mir gefällt auch das Freieste, auch das Burleskeste."

expression of a dynamic world organism moved by spirit. Spirituality became the sole basis for the interpretation of all life.

Romantic historical thinking built upon a not entirely unprepared soil. The transition from the principle of reason to that of spirit, the tendency to emphasize the rôle of history in the concept of the universe had been long under way. In the preceding century Johann Jakob Winkelmann and Justus Möser approached the historical organism in a manner that was intuitive and emotional.[2] Hamann's philosophy opened the way for the disintegration of German rationalism. Sensitivity and emotion took the place of reason; art was no longer a literal and rational reflection of nature, but rather of the artist's soul and feelings. "It is the spirit that creates life; the letter is flesh, and your dictionaries are rubbish!"[3] The spiritual element was emphasized especially in the evolution of history.[4] Herder, and later Schelling, gave a new impetus to the recognition of the metaphysical basis of existence and to the spirit as a force in life. The former in his treatise "Vom Geist des Christentums" found the *spirit* to be the essence of religious consciousness, and in his philosophical essays on mankind he regarded the *spirit* as the universal basis of all human endeavors. The peculiarity or essence of every phenomenon Herder designated as "spirit," "genius," or "character."[5] For the philosophers of the Enlightenment these concepts had individualistic, structural meanings, while Herder applied them to collectivistic ideas. The Heidelberg Romanticists and the romantic historical school employed the term *spirit* to explain an historical reality. They assumed an autonomous rule by the spirit of the people (*Volksgeist*).[6]

In accordance with these ideas, art must necessarily become the

[2] Wilhelm Dilthey, *Das 18. Jahrhundert und die geschichtliche Welt;* also Josef Heimann, *Möser und Herder* (Diss. München 1924), p. 372.

[3] *Hamanns Schriften*, hrsg. von Friedrich Roth, Berlin, 1823, IV, 146.

[4] *Ibid.*, p. 50: "Jede Geschichte trägt das Ebenbild des Menschen, einen Leib, der Erde und Asche und nichtig ist, den sinnlichen Buchstaben, aber auch eine Seele, den Hauch Gottes."

[5] Herder thus speaks of "Geist der Sprache, Geist der Poesie, Geist der Erdichtung, Geist der Literatur."

[6] The concept of "Volksgeist" may be traced to the philosophers of the French Revolution, especially Montesquieu. Herder used the following terms: "Volksgeist", "Nationalgeist", "Zeitgeist"; cf. Herders *Werke*, hrsg. von Suphan, III, 30; XVII, 80; XX, 117; also Rothacker, *Einleitung in die Geisteswissenschaft*, 1930.

expression of the creative spirit of a people, not an individualistic expression. Thus Herder spoke of the *Volksgeist* as the creator of the folk-song as well as of all other poetry.[7] Many of the Heidelberg romanticists were disciples and friends of Schelling and Savigny, who had enlarged and built upon Herder's ideas. The idealistic-historic *Weltanschauung* which they held looked upon the spirit as the ultimate force behind all matter. Schelling's theory of the unconscious evolution of the absolute spirit was the climax of Herder's ideas. In Savigny's philosophy of history and the state and in Hegel's system one finds a further elaboration of the idea *Volksgeist*.

One looks in vain for frequent references to Herder in the writings of Arnim, Görres, Brentano, or the Grimm brothers. For this circle, however, his concepts and phraseology had become accepted facts and presuppositions of general usage. "Did I write the same once before?"[8] asks Jacob Grimm naïvely, referring to Herder's "Zerstreute Blätter." Arnim also must be regarded as one of the chief sponsors of the theory of the spirit. Throughout his writings the word "Geist," meaning genius or spirit, occurs frequently in many contexts and combinations, such as *Volksgeist, Zeitgeist, aufgeregter Geist*, etc.[9]

In addition to "spirit" (*Geist*) one must note also the frequent occurrence of *Genius* and *Genie* in the works of the romanticists. These words had already an interesting history in Germany.[10] As foreign words, *Genius* and *Genie* became in German Eighteenth Century usage identical with *Geist*, just as in English "genius" became synonymous with "wit" and "spirit," and in French with

[7] Cf. Herder's summons to collect folksongs in 1767, also in 1773 his "Briefwechsel über Ossian und die Lieder alter Völker."
[8] *Briefwechsel zwischen Jacob und Wilhelm Grimm aus der Jugendzeit*, 1881, p. 43.
[9] No check-up on the frequency of the word *Geist* or *Genius* is possible, because an index is lacking, but in Oehlke's Bettina edition it ranks first in frequency. In Bettina's "Königsbuch" one finds an elaboration of Arnim's concept *Geist*, i.e., *Volksgeist*.
[10] Cf. Rudolf Hildebrand's discussion of *Geist* in Grimms' *Deutsches Wörterbuch* Bd. I. Teil II, Spalte 2623-2741. Also Herman Wolf, *Versuch einer Geschichte des Geniebegriffs in der Ästhetik des XVIII. Jahrhunderts*, Bd. I, Heidelberg 1923; also Hellmuth Sudheimer, *Der Geniebegriff des jungen Goethe*, "Germanische Studien," Heft 167, Berlin, 1935; Julius Ernst, *Der Geniebegriff der Stürmer und Dränger und der Frühromantiker*, Zürich, 1906.

"esprit."[11] With the advent of a flourishing German literature *Genius* was so extensively misused that Immanuel Kant once suggested—though in vain—*eigentümlicher Geist* as a good German substitute. Nevertheless the word continued to be in great vogue, and various philosophical movements interpreted it each in accord with its peculiar *Weltanschauung*.[12] To the *Kraftgenies* of Storm and Stress genius was divine. Its creations were intuitive visions. Herder used the word *Genius* as identical with "being original and inventive." However, Herman Wolf in his "Die Genielehre des jungen Herder" admits that any clear-cut definition of the nature of genius is hardly found in young Herder's works.[13]

In the important essay "Von Volksliedern" Arnim wondered respecting the proper meaning of the term *Genius* and suggested the study of all the different contexts:

> The habit of playing with words in our times has put art and genius at opposite poles; in poor imitations one speaks of much art and little genius, although many works are without genius. . . . If genius is the creative force, then art is the mode of appearance of this creation.[14]

He distinguished between *Genius* and *Genialität*, however. A great poet possesses *Genius;* the dry sophisticated scholar who just manages to show off and glitter and fails to create anything of lasting spiritual value is possessed of *Genialität*. In Arnim's *Wintergarten* the woman of genius is his mouthpiece: "Stop speaking of *Genialität*," she cries, "this empty expression which is meaningless in our time."[15] In one of his letters he remarks: "What the mob calls *Genialität*, I call devil. I appreciate all originality, but I am a solid rock against that so-called originality which wants to rule the world as if it were law."[16] The originality which he does appreciate, Arnim generally designates as "spirit" (*Geist*) or "genius," following the customary terminology. He is as ready as his predecessors to use the word in combinations and compounds. In general he prefers the German word *Geist* to the foreign *Genius*

---

[11] Benedetto Croce, *Estetica*, 4th edition 1912, pp. 189-190, translated into English by Douglas Ainslie, London 1922.

[12] B. Rosenthal, *Der Geniebegriff des Aufklärungszeitalters*, Berlin, 1932.

[13] Herman Wolf, "Die Genielehre des jungen Herder", *Vierteljahresschrift für Literaturwissenschaft und Geistesgeschichte*, Bd. III, 1925 H. 3, pp. 401-430; especially page 406.

[14] DNL, CXLVI, I, 57-8.   [15] Werke, V, 77.   [16] Arnim-Bettina, p. 203.

and *Genie,* yet is inclined to use the terms without distinction in meaning.

Like Herder, Arnim regarded the creative spirit as the fundamental basis of all art. "Art without genius," he says, "is comparable to a point without dimensions;" and again, "art is only the visible appearance of the genius."[17] He supports Goethe's profound observation that the nature of poetry is the truthful expression of the aroused spirit (*Divan,* p. 378).[18] In July, 1805, in the essay on the folksong, referred to above, when speaking of the interdependence of the future, past, and present,[19] Arnim emphasizes the eternal continuity of the rule of the spirit: "The world is spirit and does not need us,"[20] he writes to Wilhelm Grimm. Arnim's "Lehrgedicht an die Jugend" is an exhortation to pay heed to the good spirits.[21] In his poem "Träume" he identifies "words" as human spirits, to be esteemed and cultivated, because spirits are holy.[22] In Arnim's opinion the manifestations of the spirit are quiet, unobtrusive, and unnoticeable, and are revealed in their full importance only later by history. Man is but a tool of the spirit, predestined to fulfill his fate, to follow unknowingly the spirits, and thus to become, like Frederick the Great, a *tool* of the *Volksgeist.*[23]

A summons to exaltation of the spirit, a sincere plea for the spiritualization of his age, he voiced most emphatically in the introductory chapter to the *Kronenwächter.* One may justly call this chapter "a hymn to the spirit."[24] Here Arnim declares that

[17] Werke, XIII, 453; cf. also DNL, CXLVI, I, 57-8, Arnim's essay "Von Volksliedern."

[18] Ludwig Achim von Arnim. *Unbekannte Aufsätze und Gedichte.* Hrsg. von Ludwig Geiger, cited below as *Unbekannte Aufsätze,* p. 53.

[19] Cf. DNL, CXLVI, I, 78.

[20] Arnim-Grimm, p. 12.

[21] Werke, XXI, 68.

[22] *Ibid.,* V, p. 92;

"Was die Worte nur sind?
Es sind die Geister der Menschen,
Und ich achte das Wort,
Weil mir heilig der Geist."

[23] *Monatliche Beiträge zur Geschichte dramatischer Kunst und Literatur,* hrsg. von K. v. Holtei, Berlin, 1812, II, 1-42; cf. Arnim's "Sammlung zur Theatergeschichte": "Er (Frederick the Great) aber mußte hier, wie in so vielen Fällen tun und erfüllen, wozu er bestimmt war, ohne diese seine Bestimmung zu kennen."

[24] Werke, XV, 3-9.

in the writings of former centuries we have documents which cannot be made our own without effort: "Genius loves its finite creations as a symbol of eternity which we can attain neither through our earthly activities nor by reasoning." The evaluation of these documents differs according to the trend and interests of different periods. There is no absolute standard for the productions of genius in its spiritual realm: "Who honors the boundary lines he drew? Who recognizes the originality of his ideas? . . . There exists no law to protect works of the spirit against sacrilege." The spiritual holds within itself the ultimate secret of the universe, more precious in its wisdom than anything voiced in history. Contemporaries may not grasp the significance of its workings, but true history ("Geschichte in höchster Wahrheit") will transmit visions of them. It is only poetry which has an insight into this secret of the universe. Poetry is the knowledge of this secret, born of spirit and truth, communicated from the past to the present.

With Arnim the word "spirit" (*Geist*) was a concept of mood and feeling (*Stimmungsbegriff*). Thus it appears in *Volksgeist,* the "soul of the people." Herder had said of the *soul of the people:* "What a mysterious and peculiar phenomenon the soul and character of a people are, unexplainable and indestructible, as old as nature, as old as the country."[25] Arnim uses the expression *Volksgeist* as early as 1805 in his essay "Von Volksliedern," likewise such words as *Zeitgeist, Gemeingeist, Volkstätigkeit.* In one place he contradicts the philosophers who make it their task to oppose sentimentalism, defined by Arnim as the imitation and exploration of emotion. He hoped that the living *Volksgeist* would terminate their activities. The country lacks *Volkstätigkeit.* Only when the poet has become the *"spiritus familiaris"* (*Gemeingeist*) in the community of the world, will it be possible to live in true poetic enjoyment.[26]

The most interesting discussion and definition of the *Volksgeist* is found in Arnim's *Wintergarten,* where he compares this force to a slumbering giant, who must be awakened by the people themselves. The *Volksgeist* is of divine origin and becomes potent

[25] Herder's Werke, hrsg. von Suphan, XX, 181.
[26] DNL, CXLVI, I, 50.

through divine grace. Then "he will stand, free, a strong, pious hero, looking up above to where the hopeful days of the new earth glow in a thousand colors."[27]

The belief of Arnim in the awakened giant (potent *Volksgeist*) looking forward to hopeful days must be compared to Novalis' and Hölderlin's ideas of the Golden Age. While their version was more romantically abstract, Arnim introduced political and national ideas. In this connection he tried to formulate in an idealistic manner his conception of the real mission of the nobility, a question much discussed in his day. This appears in the poems "Der Götter Adel" and "Adel."

> Nicht die Geister zu vertreiben
> Stand des Volkes Geist einst auf,
> Nein, daß jedem freier Lauf,
> Jedem Haus ein Geist soll bleiben,
> Nein, daß adlich all' auf Erden,
> Muß der Adel Märtrer werden.[28]

> Die neuen Zeiten
> Sie nennen Adel
> Was ohne Tadel
> Die Geister leiten.
> Der Schein, die Plage
> Versinkt am Tage.[29]

Allusion to this role of the nobility may be found in others of his poems and in the *Gräfin Dolores*. In this work Graf Karl is the protagonist of Arnim's vision. Karl is morally superior to the Gräfin. He strives for one lofty ideal, namely, to lead the people to a higher moral plane. Arnim's preoccupation with ideas for the spiritual rejuvenation of the nation was shown repeatedly during the War of Liberation, 1813-14. To Clemens he wrote in August, 1814: "My soul is bound for hours by the enchantment of ponder-

[27] Werke, V, 251.
[28] Ibid., XXI, 172; "Lieder aus einem ungeschriebenem Roman," also the interesting version of this stanza in the poem entitled "Still bewahr' es in Gedanken":
> Nicht die Geister zu vertreiben,
> Steht des Volkes Geist jetzt auf,
> Nein, daß jedem freier Lauf,
> Jedem Haus ein Geist soll bleiben:
> Nein, daß adlich all'auf Erden,
> Muß der Adel Bürger werden.   (Werke, XXI, pp. 232-3)
[29] Ibid., XXI, 177.

ing over the tower of Babel; how all may be united which I consider of profound value in the Germans."³⁰ After the war, however, a more pessimistic note is struck in his letters to Görres: "We expected fine times for Germany and worked hard, thinking she would unite the world like a wonderful many-sided mirror."³¹

Unlike Herder, Arnim and his circle used the concept *Zeitgeist* to denote something undesirable and even despicable. They saw it manifest itself in Germany in arrogant intellectualism, rooted, in their opinion, in the cult of reason of the French Revolution. The *Zeitgeist* also appeared to them in the philistinism of the petty German bourgeoisie. Arnim charged that the *Zeitgeist* "belittles everything magnificent" and that empty arrogance and boasting prevails among the educated classes.³² A result of the *Zeitgeist* appears in the miserable productions in literature betraying a lack of talent and of imagination, such as occasional poems without a real underlying experience or cause.³³ He pitied contemporary Germany for "silencing beauty, forgetting excellence, and desecrating sincerity."³⁴ Two contemporary works dealing with the *Zeitgeist* did not remain unnoticed by Arnim. They are Ernst Moritz Arndt's *Geist der Zeit* (1805) and Madame de Staël's posthumous work, *Considérations sur les principaux événements de la révolution française*, (1818). He disagreed with both writers, particularly with Arndt's pessimism about his own day and about the future of Germany. To be sure, the author's fruitless efforts, Arnim admits, may well have brought him to the verge of despair, but in spite of this he has not lost faith in the greatness of his fatherland. Arndt's denunciation of Prussia he considered most unjust,³⁵ as he wrote to Clemens in July, 1806.

Madame de Staël's book was discussed at length in a review in Gubitz' *Gesellschafter* in 1818.³⁶ While acknowledging the

---

³⁰ Arnim-Brentano p. 338.

³¹ Joseph von Görres, *Gesammelte Briefe*, hrsg. von Marie von Görres; letter of January 23, 1816; cf. *Werke*, VIII, 481-4.

³² Cf. Arnim-Brentano, pp. 262, 280, 338; Arnim-Bettina, p. 333; Herder's "Was ist der Geist der Zeit," Werke, XVII, 77-81.

³³ Arnim-Brentano, p. 238.

³⁴ *Ibid.*, p. 238.

³⁵ *Ibid.*, p. 184.

³⁶ *Der Gesellschafter oder Blätter für Geist und Herz*, hrsg. von F. W. Gubitz, Berlin; cited below as *Ges.* 1818; Arnim's "Frau von Staël und Herr von Haller", pp. 734-738. Republished in *Unbekannte Aufsätze*, pp. 38-43.

excellence of her portrayal of the spirit of the French Revolution, particularly its noble and heroic element, Arnim criticizes and pities her for her failure to understand the true origin of a state and for her hostility to feudalism. It is evident that Arnim shared here Karl von Haller's point of view as set forth in his *Restauration der Staatswissenschaft*. According to Haller, the state owes its origin and existence to the feudal system and to private ownership of land. Feudal forms tie the spirit of the present with that of the past and future. The spiritual element in the origin of a state Haller sees in family life, while possession of land constitutes the material element; the state is an historic organism in which the spiritual dominates the material. However, Arnim shared only Haller's historical, not his political views. He rejected Haller's theory, which derived all civic rights from land ownership and endowed the church with considerable political control, as just as impractical as Rousseau's *contrat social*. Haller's conception of the state as the creation of the spirit of a people in its historical development was accepted by Arnim and by other members of the German nobility united under his leadership in the *Christlich-deutsche Tischgesellschaft*.[37] These were men who had lost much through Napoleon's ascendancy and his invasion of Germany. However, they wanted to solve the German question by a progressive movement and not by un-German or reactionary methods based on outworn traditions, such as became the program of Metternich and of the Prussian government during the ascendancy of Hardenberg.

Arnim endeavored not to be submerged by the *Zeitgeist*, to avoid infection by the poisonous trend of the time, and to preserve his own individuality. He wanted, as he says, to blow away the noxious spirit like "the smoke of a strange pipe."[38] In his efforts to escape from the *Zeitgeist*, however, he went to such extremes of eccentricity that Wilhelm von Humboldt in 1809 would not recommend him for service in the government. Humboldt felt

[37] In an essay "Ein Wort über die jetzige Gesetzmacherei", Leopold von Gerlach, another member of the *Tischgesellschaft*, compares the predominating spirit of the time to that of the French Revolution, "which abolished with one stroke many honorable institutions without consideration of historic events, yet history is the greatest teacher of the human race and dreadful prophet of the fate of nations."

[38] Arnim-Brentano, p. 159; Arnim's letter to Clemens, January 25, 1806.

sorry he could not do something for the *"Wunderhorn* man." It was out of the question, as he said, "because this man who quarrels rudely with Voss and Jacobi, wears an impossible fur cap, and has similarly impossible whiskers, is in ill-repute."[39] The loss of many promising and valuable contemporaries Arnim attributed to the deadening effects of, or the strenuous struggle against, the *Zeitgeist*. One of the victims was his friend August Winkelmann, taken away in the prime of life: "The times killed him," Arnim wrote to Brentano.[40] Eight years later, the great Fichte succumbed to the *Zeitgeist*, in Arnim's opinion. This he affirms in the poem which concludes his eulogy of Fichte in *Der Preussische Correspondent*:

> Auch Dich hat uns die Pest der Zeit entrissen,
> Dich mutigsten Bestreiter schlechter Zeit,
> Du hattest Dich als Opfer ihr geweiht,
> Als Du ihr strafend riefest ins Gewissen.
> Bekämpft die Zeit in EUCH mit heiligem Willen!
> So riefest Du.—Den Bogen spannt im Stillen
> Die tück'sche Zeit—auch Du mußt ihr erliegen.[41]

This new attitude toward the world and life as an expression of the spirit necessitated a new direction in art and literature. This meant a new criticism, which had its roots likewise in Herder's spiritual and historical approach to literature. Productive criticism in Germany had found its first champion in Lessing. However, Lessing's methodical, standardized, and regulated procedure had been rejected by Hamann and Herder, for genius hates classification and comparison.[42] Both objected to limitation in literature and to comparison as a critical method. Instead of using classical antiquity as a standard for modern poetry, the method in vogue among the critics of the Enlightenment, they advocated another approach, namely, to regard each poet as a product of his age, his people and his environment. Bearing this in mind, the reader should try to penetrate, understand, and appre-

---

[39] Wilhelm von Humboldt to Caroline, February 28, 1809; *Wilhelm und Caroline von Humboldt in ihren Briefen 1808-1810*, hrsg. von Anna von Sydow, 1909, pp. 101-2.
[40] August Winkelmann died in February, 1806.
[41] Quoted by R. Steig, Arnim-Brentano, p. 324.
[42] Herder's *Werke*, hrsg. von B. Suphan, XIII, 138.

ciate the work of art. In this manner intuitive criticism, often assuming the form of characterization, was pitted against analytical criticism. Herder advanced and deepened interpretative criticism (*Auslegergeist*),[43] which has also been called "apocalyptic criticism."[44] He distinguished between objective and subjective, or "higher" and "lower" criticism. Only genius is capable of objective criticism of high standing. Herder went one step farther in his innovations, so important for future generations, and emphasized the national and historical elements as factors to be considered in criticism: "To pass judgment without taking into account time, country, and language," he declares, "is stupid"....[45] "Sound criticism the world over demands that one enter into the spirit of the author, his public, his nationality, and last but not least, into the spirit of his creation, in order to appreciate fully a piece of literature."[46]

These views entered into conflict with the destructive, narrow-minded criticism which had dominated during most of the Eighteenth Century, and gradually won their way. This was due in large measure to the wide range of Herder's influence, which extended to Goethe and the romanticists. During the last decade of the century a progressive criticism in art, with the slogans: understanding, interpretation, intuition, and characterization, had supplanted the former subjective method. The romanticists had taken cognizance of Herder's views on aesthetics. They emphasized even more than he the inter-relationship between literature and history. All phenomena were to be explained in their dependency on time and civilization. According to Friedrich Schlegel, criticism was to be the link between the solitude of the literary world on its lofty heights of idealism and active, realistic, national life.[47]

Even as a youth Arnim was well acquainted with the aesthetic currents of his age, and with most of the leading advocates of these ideas. He could not but accept the principles of Herder's

[43] *Ibid.*, I, 41.
[44] Cf. Sigmund von Lempicki, *Geschichte der deutschen Literaturwissenschaft*, 1920, p. 369.
[45] Herder's *Werke*, III, 232.
[46] *Ibid.*, VI, 234.
[47] HeidelbJbb., 1808. I, Abt. 5, p. 379.

criticism as broadened by Goethe, Tieck, Schelling, and the Schlegel brothers. The great mission of literary criticism in his day as he saw and interpreted it was to acquaint the reader with the "remote and forgotten in literature."[48] The task of the critic was thus to be educational and constructive. Furthermore, he wanted to curb unnecessary so-called learned discussion. Criticism was not the primary thing; it was only a necessary tool to purify the spirit.[49] Art, he declared, should never be subjugated by criticism, as it unfortunately was in his day. These views were bound, sooner or later, to come into conflict with another attitude that developed simultaneously out of the romantic movement, the scientific approach to the past. A method of criticism like Arnim's, which endeavors to acquaint the reader with the "remote and unknown," will often overstep the boundary line of literary historical research. As Lempicki says, "Jacob Grimm's opposition to Brentano and Arnim reveals the line of demarcation between the literary criticism historically oriented and scientific research in literature."[50]

Arnim's essay "Von Volksliedern"[51] must be regarded as the first document in the development of his critical style. It takes the form of a characterization and description of the history of civilization, written in an entertaining and stimulating manner. Here he presents, not only his observations of different countries, districts, and ages, but also a cultural program which was to form the basis for his later activities. This is centered around the creation of a new spiritual life of the people. He believed that culture had degenerated during the preceding centuries because, since the ending of the Middle Ages, one had looked askance at the simple enjoyment of life. Unhealthy materialism, gluttony, fear of death were substituted. Only an awakening of the people to an active communal life could lead humanity back to a higher

---

[48] Arnim's letter to Goethe, April 1, 1808 in *Schriften der Goethe-Gesellschaft*, Weimar, XIV, 126; cited below as *Schriften der Goethe-Ges.*

[49] *Briefe an L. Tieck,* hrsg. von Karl von Holtei, I, 12; Arnim's letter to Tieck, December 3, 1807.

[50] Sigmund von Lempicki, "Über literarische Kritik und die Probleme ihrer Erforschung," *Euphorion,* XXV, 501-517.

[51] This essay had been partly published as early as 1805 in the *Berliner Musikalische Zeitung*, and appeared in completed form in 1806 as appendix to the first volume of *Des Knaben Wunderhorn*.

plane of living, prepare the ground for a new poetry of the people (*Volkspoesie*) and usher in a new era of understanding and reconciliation. *Volkspoesie* will inspire people to a noble and deep understanding of each other and put an end to disputes such as those about Christian and heathen, Hellenic, and Romantic.[52] In further development of this idea he proceeds to expose and attack what he regards as harmful elements in the art and literature of the nation, dwelling especially on pseudo-originality, *Genialität*, as mentioned above, and on the wretched state of contemporary criticism. This kind of critical gossip, he says, is not of German origin, but has become the fashion. In the eyes of the people these pedantic critics do nothing but spin sophisms and throw dirt at everything for the sole purpose of gathering questionable laurels for themselves.[53]

This then was Arnim's entry into the field of literary criticism and this was the spirit and the program which marked his work throughout life.

[52] Cf. DNL, CXLVI, I, 70.
[53] *Ibid.*, p. 76, footnote.

II
THE BACKGROUND OF FAMILY TRADITION AND CHARACTER DEVELOPMENT

If we glance through a list of the poets and other writers in Germany at the beginning of the Nineteenth Century, we discover many aristocratic patronymics. Most of the bearers of these betray their noble origin in their writings. There is none for whose work family tradition and background were more important than for Ludwig Achim von Arnim's; none whose literary conceptions were more strongly moulded by such forces. It is surprising that such a small amount of biographical data should have come down to us from a man of such a prominent family and of such poetic importance.[1] Max Koch declares, "there is scarcely a modern German poet about whose early years we have so little information as about those of Arnim."[2] We have, however, a good deal of information about his forefathers, their way of living, and their personalities.[3] From these sources we may venture some deductions as to the part played by heritage and milieu in the formation of Arnim's attitude toward life and art.

In analyzing Arnim's background, three elements are very striking. These are, first, the connection of the Arnim family with its native district, the Mark Brandenburg, and with the Prussian ruling house during many centuries; second, the intelligent, objective outlook on life characteristic of the family; and third, the artistic inclinations of Achim von Arnim's father and his maternal grandfather. Ludwig Achim von Arnim was first of all "a genuine squire of the *Mark*."[4] The tradition of the family, which had for seven hundred years lived on the soil of Brandenburg, was powerful within him. He felt himself to be a link in the chain of his ancestors and a part of the great historical events in which they

---
[1] Both Max Koch and Reinhold Steig deplore this fact.
[2] Cf. DNL, CXLVI, I, p. V; Arnim-Brentano, p. 10.
[3] Otto Devrient, *Das Geschlecht von Arnim*, Vol. I, Leipzig, 1914; Arnim-Crieven, *Beiträge zur Geschichte des Arnimschen Geschlechts*. 1. Teil, Berlin, 1883.
[4] Josef Nadler, *Die Berliner Romantik*, p. 154.

had played a rôle, as well as of national customs and life that had surrounded them. Love for his native land was born in him. The wide expanse of the North German plains and the rugged folk who dwelt there were dear to his heart. In contrast to his great master Goethe and his best friend Clemens Brentano, he was not of urban stock. In rural life he found always invigorating strength and peace of mind.

Thus the attachment to homeland and to family and local tradition held him with unbreakable bonds. He regarded it as one of his chief tasks to cultivate the past, which had for him "a peculiar austerity and sanctity."[5] Yet he did not want to live for the past alone. To him it was merely the source for a better understanding of the present and future, a fixed point from which to spin threads of the historical web further on to his German people and his fatherland. His master, Goethe, was almost entirely independent of local or national limitations. He was not merely the great poet of his native town or of Weimer, but a great world genius and an internationally minded artist. To Arnim, on the other hand, poetry, fatherland, and nation were one. He does not say, "I want to build a castle dedicated to art on German soil"; his goal is more restricted: he wants to build this structure on the sturdy soil of the *Mark*.[6] This love and admiration for his Prussian fatherland and his own people may always be found as the underlying note of his critical approach. Even when he steps into the "beautiful, simple, free Greek temple," he is in his thoughts still in the oak forests of Eastern Germany.[7]

However, in Arnim there was not merely the heritage of an old Prussian, land-owning family. In him there was also a strong artistic element which made him one of the most ardent of the romanticists. Furthermore, he revealed himself as an outstanding student and scholar, with a broad horizon, taking an interest in almost all fields of intellectual endeavor. The scholarly bent was especially strong in his youth, and it is noticeable again at the end of his career: "He is too diligent, too prone to versatility; he shows a thirst for knowledge and a wide reading in all fields."

[5] Arnim-Brentano, p. 270.
[6] *Ibid.*, p. 67.   [7] *Ibid.*, p. 35.

Thus a school report describes him.[8] This universality of intellectual interest permeated all his writings, especially his essays and reviews. Arnim feels himself compelled to bring his accumulated wealth of knowledge into relation with his own ideas; and it reappears sometimes clothed in fantastic garb, in his artistic creations.[9]

As a young student in Halle, Arnim's first interest was in the founding of a scientific club, and immediately thereafter, he prepared a series of articles for Gilbert's *Annalen der Physik*. These articles show a more objective attitude of mind than would be expected of the author of his fantastic poetic creations. He bases his discussions on Kant, Volta, and Priestley and opposes the pseudo-scientific notions so common at this period. The impression which we get of Arnim in his later period is similar to this early one. Interest in the factual and practical is a strongly marked characteristic and persisted throughout life. In the depressing years after 1806 he is the typical North German Junker, worrying incessantly about his financial and administrative obligations and always struggling to make ends meet. His interest in these days was of necessity concentrated much more on political and economic than on artistic problems. In his later years he saw the political sluggishness of his fatherland reappear, as well as the dull trends in literature against which he had fought so vigorously for over a decade. A certain resignation took possession of him. He came to realize more and more that he had lost in the struggle for the great cause to which he had dedicated his life, and he wearied of preaching his literary and political gospel to deaf ears.

This practical side of Arnim was in strong contrast to his romanticism.[10] Both combined in a dual personality, and he endeavored

---

[8] Ibid., pp. 7-8.

[9] Reinhold Steig in "L. A. v. Arnim als Tagesschriftsteller", *Nationalzeitung*, 427 (Berlin 1892), makes the following comment: "Dieser Trieb nach praktischer Betätigung dessen was er geistig empfand, führte ihn früh dazu an der Tagesschriftstellerei Teil zu nehmen."

[10] This contrast is best pictured by young Adolf Friedrich von Schack, who met Arnim in 1829: "Ich dachte, alle seine Reden müßten außergewöhnlich und von denen der gewöhnlichen Sterblichen verschieden sein. Aber bald fand ich mich sehr enttäuscht, da Alles, was er sagte, so einfach und schlicht wie möglich war . . . zu meinem großen Verdruß sprach er meistens von Landwirtschaft, welcher er sich mit großem Eifer widmete, und hie und da von Politik. Über Literatur hingegen floß auch nicht die kleinste Äußerung von seinen Lippen. Ich selbst wagte

all his life to reconcile the one with the other. As a child he was, he declares, highly romantic: "When I was a child, I thought as a child and believed in everything I thought. At that time, I was sure that I saw many marvellous things both in heaven and on earth."[11] But the romantic urge in him was checked through many years by various influences: after the early death of his parents, the strict, prosaic upbringing in the house of his grandmother, the Baroness von Labes, and the rationalism prevailing in the school system to which he was subjected. He mentions "the early artificial measures of the Roman school poets who were the torment of my youth."[12] Nevertheless an enthusiasm for poetry and romance was too essential a part of his character to be smothered by a rationalistic education. Indeed, an artistic strain lay in the family. His father was *directeur des spectacles* at the Berlin court from 1776 to 1778, and on terms of close friendship with the musician and composer, Johann Friedrich Reichardt. To his maternal grandfather Arnim ascribes "a soul of a very peculiar sort, an odd mixture of broad, liberal experiences and of the narrow attitude of his day, a distinctive personality with a great deal of eccentricity."[13] This description might apply almost as well to Arnim's own personality.

The only contact Arnim had with art and journalism in his youthful years in Berlin was at the home of Reichardt.[14] A close

---

nicht von diesem Thema anzufangen, und so habe ich denn von dem Urheber der 'Isabella von Aegypten' und so vieler phantastischen Erfindungen keinen anderen Eindruck erhalten, als von manchen sonstigen Landedelleuten, deren geistiger Horizont sich nicht weit über ihre Roggen- und Weizenfelder hinaus erstreckt . . . Der literarische und persönliche Charakter müssen bei Arnim in auffallender Weise im Widerspruch gestanden haben. Denn mein Vater, der nach damaliger Studentensitte mit ihm das nämliche Zimmer bewohnt hatte, versicherte mir wiederholt, er sei schon in seiner Jugend, wie immer nachher, ein praktischer, keineswegs überspannter Mensch gewesen. . . ." Adolf Friedrich Graf von Schack, *Ein halbes Jahrhundert. Erinnerungen und Aufzeichnungen* (Stuttgart, 1889), I, 14-16.

[11] Werke, I, p. XVII; Anrede an meine Zuhörer, im Herbst, 1811.

[12] *Ibid.*, p. XIX, cf. also in Arnim's essay "Von Volksliedern" (DNL, CXLVI, I, 62, footnote), "Wenn ich es verkehrt nenne, wie die Alten in vielen Schulen betrieben, so ist es meine Erfahrung. An allen Orten des Altdeutschen war nichts, des Lateins zuviel, des Griechischen zu wenig. Verkehrt nenne ich der Annäherung-Schulen nationale Geschichte, das Eigenste des Volks, den Alten nachzubilden, da doch diese nur wegen dieser erschöpfenden Nationalität vortrefflich sind."

[13] Arnim-Brentano, p. 1.

[14] Reichardt published the periodical *Deutschland*, beginning 1796, and the *Berlinische Musikalische Zeitung* from 1805.

friendship united him with this family all his life. It was Reichardt who first called Arnim's attention to Herder and to many collections of folksongs, and some of Arnim's critical writings were published in Reichardt's *Musikalische Zeitung*.[15] However, it was men like Tieck, Schelling, and especially Clemens Brentano who first aroused Arnim's artistic temper. Once awakened it soon mounted to fantastic heights. When he met Arnim at Göttingen in May, 1801, Brentano had just passed through three years of intimate association with the Jena romantic group. Years of rare friendship were to follow on this first meeting. During this time Arnim's literary critical ideas were subjected and conformed to Brentano's. When this bond of friendship gradually loosened, however, it seems that Arnim's somewhat cooler nature gained the upper hand. Brentano's share in shaping Arnim's critical point of view should not be overestimated. He had had, it is true, a longer literary experience. They had a common interest in folklore and a similar attitude toward their contemporaries. However, before Arnim came to Göttingen he had gone through a thorough training in the scientific and philosophical thinking of his age. Here Brentano was never able to follow him, nor into the realm of nationalistic enthusiasm, which is such a vital element in Arnim's criticism. Their opinions differed also with regard to Goethe and on religious matters.

At the end of July, 1801, Arnim left Brentano and Göttingen and went on his "grand tour." This was his first experience of travelling into greater Germany, away from his immediate Prussian surroundings. From early childhood, love of the Mark Brandenburg and his *engere Heimat* was strong in him; now for the first time he experienced the color and variety of the many different German states and their varying landscape. Still, different as they were, a similar culture united them; and he found the same folksongs and legends in Prussia and on the Rhine, in Switzerland and in Austria. He was much impressed by Munich and Vienna, both larger and more distinctly cultural centers than Berlin at this time. Here he found the old German traditions united with a new artistic life. He regretted much that cultural unity was divided

[15] Cf. Otto Mallon, *Arnim Bibliographie*, pp. 10, 23; cited below as "Mallon."

by political boundary lines, and expressed the hope that North and South Germany might be united in the future. The solitude of the Swiss mountains inspired his fantastic plan for the conservation, revival, and world-wide dispersion of German lyrical poetry. He was not enthusiastic about France, sharing the attitude of most of his German contemporaries, who disapproved of French culture and especially of Paris, the cosmopolitan center, with its artificial modes of life. He criticized French art in an article, "Erzählungen von Schauspielen," published at this time in Friedrich Schlegel's *Europa*.[16] It was his conviction that French forms of art were unsuitable for Germany and would lead only to pretense and bombast. In Paris longing for home seized him: "Oh, my hallowed fatherland, here among strangers I still feel the breath of thy inspiration!"[17]

His "grand tour" also took him to England, in the summer of 1803. Here also he could not feel at home, in spite of many beautiful scenic impressions and his admiration for the English people. He shared the great enthusiasm of his time for Shakespeare. While in London he found that tragedy was still presented in great perfection and still enjoyed great popularity.[18] Above all, he was interested in Walter Scott's Scottish ballads and romances.[19]

In the fall of 1804 Arnim returned from his tour. Though still a young man, he had already seen and experienced much, and had associated with many distinguished people. He had also won his spurs as an author, having published his first novel, *Hollins Liebeleben* in 1802, and in 1804, *Ariels Offenbarungen*. By this time he had also had his first experience as a literary critic. Following his many contributions as a student of natural science to Gilbert's *Annalen der Physik* after 1799, Arnim had now found recognition as a critic of literature from no less an authority than Friedrich Schlegel. His "Erzählungen von Schauspielen," had been published, as we have seen, in Schlegel's *Europa*. The three years which he had spent abroad were not without results in the shaping of his character. We might have expected him to return home

---
[16] *Europa*, hrsg. von Friedrich Schlegel, 1803, pp. 140-192.
[17] Arnim-Brentano, p. 68.
[18] *Ibid.*, p. 95.
[19] *Ibid.*, p. 95.

equipped with cosmopolitan ideas. On the contrary, his stay abroad had made him more German than before. His interest in folklore had increased through his correspondence with Clemens Brentano and the attainment of a deeper insight into the writings of Walter Scott, Percy, and Macpherson.

Arnim came back to Germany with a fixed resolve to do for his fatherland in the field of folklore that which had already been accomplished for England and Scotland. He went about this task with dauntless optimism, supreme confidence in himself and in a better future for Germany, and with a complete faith in divine providence. This confidence in the future of the fatherland remains characteristic of him throughout his whole life; it is expressed in all his writings on cultural and political questions concerning Germany. In the program for his planned weekly *Der Preusse, ein Volksblatt,* announced in 1806 Arnim says with characteristic optimism:

We shall call this paper *Der Deutsche* as soon as Germany has recovered from the long illness which destroys all individual and collective strength which we had gathered and cultivated silently and joyfully.[20]

The quality of his optimism is expressed in the lines of Goethe, which Arnim quotes in his introduction to *Wunder über Wunder:*

> Liegt dir Gestern klar und offen,
> Wirkst du heute kräftig frei;
> Kannst auch auf ein Morgen hoffen,
> Das nicht minder glücklich sei.[21]

Even in the depressing years after 1806, when Ernst Moritz Arndt struck a very pessimistic note in the first volume of his *Geist der Zeit,* and when a well-known publicist, Archenholtz,[22] expressed the fear that the German language would die out, Arnim still believed in the future greatness of Germany, a result, however, which could come only through the cultivation of the treasures to be found in folk-art and folk-literature. It is this faith that gave the impulse for the rise of the historical school in language and

---

[20] *Ibid.,* p. 191; Mallon, pp. 22, 23.
[21] Werke, XIX, 266; *Landhausleben, Wunder über Wunder, indisches Mährchen, Mittwochs-Erzählung des Direktors der Theaterschule.*
[22] Johann Wilhelm von Archenholtz, 1743-1812, published in Hamburg from 1792-1812 the periodical *Minerva, ein Journal historischen und politischen Inhalts.*

literature and for publications such as the *Wunderhorn* and the *Zeitung für Einsiedler*.

In Arnim this optimism goes hand in hand with an absolute faith in God. He was a convinced Protestant and believed confidently in "a heart of eternal love that throbs through the entire world." God, he felt, would not permit His own destruction, for the love of God is the will of the world. If mankind has to suffer, it is because mankind has failed in recognizing the divine will.[23] Beginning with early childhood, Arnim had a very strict religious education, both in his grandmother's home and during his school and student days at Berlin and Halle. From these years dates his admiration for Luther. His romantic nature was later to draw him in a mystical direction similar to that of Jung-Stilling and young Zacharias Werner.

Such, broadly, was Arnim's background when he started out on his critical activities. In Heidelberg he hoped that the *Zeitung für Einsiedler* would become his "Opera omnia," and he took a very active part in the beginning of the *Heidelbergische Jahrbücher*. Nevertheless, the former, his own periodical, survived less than half a year, and he soon had to withdraw as collaborator from the *Heidelbergische Jahrbücher* in the face of a rising antagonism towards him on the part of members of the university circle. In Berlin, his critical activities, his association with the *Abendblätter* and with the *Preussische Correspondent*, were all short-lived. These failures show conclusively that he was not popular as a critic and journalist.

To understand the reason for this failure it is necessary to analyze some additional features of his personality. Arnim was throughout life the simple, forthright *Junker*. He was not really born to become an acute and subtle critic. Nature seems to have intended him rather to be an officer in the king's army. The inner conflict between the desire for the free life of the soldier and the urge to take part in the tedious struggle for the spiritual rejuvenation of his country came particularly to the fore during Napoleon's rule in Prussia. At that time he deplored that his weapon had to

---

[23] Werke, XX, 278; Arnim's favorite maxim was, "Gott ist die Liebe, und wer in der Liebe lebt, lebt in Gott." Cf. Arnim-Bettina p. 362.

be the pen instead of the sword. During this conflict with himself he writes to Bettina:

> Again the same old regret takes hold of me that tormented me in Königsberg, the feeling that perhaps I have taken the wrong course. Instead of letters, I ought to have taken the sword. Now it is too late, habit with its millions of invisible threads has bound me so firmly that I can never free myself entirely from it.[24]

These profound contradictions within his personality made it difficult for him to achieve the inner harmony and balance so necessary for the exercise of the critic's office. There were also other reasons. Arnim lived and wrote only in and for his own idealistic world. He never wrote merely for pecuniary reward.[25] Often he clung to his opinions in an obstinate and uncompromising manner. Theories, schools, or literary groups had little meaning for him. "He kept away from all literary cliques," says Reinhold Steig,

> His concern was ever with the matter itself, never with disputes about it. In judging the work of others, he fixed his attention first of all on what had actually been accomplished, in order to be able the more easily to overlook any weakness. Not a single one of his reviews or observations contains anything to wound the feelings. He had too rich and noble a soul for that.[26]

[24] Arnim-Bettina, p. 268; March 10, 1809; cf. also *Ariel*, autobiographical sketch of the *Siebente Winterabend:* "Ich stamme aus rühmlichem und reichem Geschlechte; meine erste Neigung würde mich zum Soldaten gemacht haben, doch das läppische Wesen, das durch lange Friedenszeit in diesen Stand gekommen, machte ihn mir verächtlich; ich wählte das Buch statt des Schwertes. Was mich ergreift, dem ergebe ich mich ganz, meine ganze Lebensweise entwickelte sich darnach, meinen Büchern, dieser lieben Gesellschaft aus alter Zeit zu leben, alle Wissenschaften und Künste suchte ich mir nach möglicher Kraft anzueignen. Bald genügte es mir nicht, dies allein in mir zu treiben, ich fühlte einen Drang andre damit zu ergreifen und zu durchdringen, ich knüpfte reisend mit Unzähligen an, wir hofften auf eine schöne Zeit für Deutschland, und arbeiteten fleißig, es sollte wie ein wunderbarer allseitiger Spiegel die Welt vereinigen. Schnell über und fort, wie eine wilde Taube im Sturm, der Krieg brach ein, zerschlug den Spiegel; wohl recht sagt Sophokles, er raubt die Guten nur. Ich hätte gern mitgefochten aber ich konnte das Schwert nicht führen; tausend Gewohnheiten hielten mich gefangen, die eben darum sich hielten, weil sie nicht leer, sondern in würdigen Zwecken erworben, doch fühle ich, wenn ich auch meinen Sinn und meine Bemühung achten mußte, daß ich etwas Verkehrtes getrieben, was in der verderblichen Zeit nicht paßte, ich trauerte tief und hoffte dann wieder abwechselnd mit aller Torheit." Werke, V, 110-14.

[25] Arnim-Bettina, p. 308: "Die Schriftstellerei für Geld ist einmal mir verhaßt ... von anderer Gnade zu leben wäre mein Tod."

[26] "Achim von Arnim als Tagesschriftsteller," *Nationalzeitung*, Nr. 427, Berlin, 1892.

This nobility of mind was not entirely advantageous to his career as a critic. Often his friends in Heidelberg complained that he was too lenient in the quarrel with Voss and the *Jenaer Literaturzeitung*. Wilhelm Budde, while a young student in Heidelberg, gives us in his diary a sketch of Arnim in those days, as "a man of noble and self-contained nature. His intelligent face wears an expression of youthful, good-natured irony."[27] Arnim himself recognized this trait, and declared that his worst fault was too great softness of character.[28]

In addition to these characteristics, it must also be emphasized that Arnim lacked completely a sense of order and form. He neither co-ordinated nor systematized the facts, ideas, and outer form of his writings. He wrote as the spirit moved him. He would often incorporate into his writings symbolical comparisons and farfetched ideas. He liked to interpolate anecdotes and sententious remarks. His basic trait of character, his hatred for any kind of system, fostered this manner of writing. Brentano bemoaned the great confusion in Arnim's papers. He wanted to live near him in order to help him organize his ideas and his work.[29] In his criticisms Arnim almost never discusses form, style, or other external characteristics; only the spirit and the thought of a work attract him. He prefers to deal with writers and ideas close to his heart and of his own way of thinking. He sympathizes with poets "whose only purpose is to express their ideas," and he contrasts them with those who value ideas only when clothed in perfect form.[30] This one-sided and undisciplined approach to literature sometimes impaired his perception of literary values and hampered his objective judgment. In this respect he was unlike Brentano, who possessed excellent critical faculties.[31] In Arnim's writings one searches in vain for analytical discussions, but one finds abundant expressions of feeling and many hasty, subjective conclusions. His entire critical production is an *Erlebniskritik* based on *Tendenz*

---

[27] H. Wilhelm Budde, 1786-1858, studied in Heidelberg for two semesters, beginning Easter, 1807. *Heidelberger Tagebuch,* p. 267, 1807-8.

[28] Arnim-Bettina, p. 269.

[29] Arnim-Brentano, p. 105.

[30] HeidelbJbb., Abtlg. I, 153, 1810; Arnim's review of *Friedrich Schlege's Gedichte,* Berlin, 1809.

[31] Cf. Arnim-Brentano, p. 354 (Anm. 188).

and thus constitutes a continuation of the method of approach of Hamann and Herder, who looked upon such topics as nature, spirit, mankind, the nation in literature subjectively, uniting them monadically into a great harmony of the *All*.

It was for the realization of this great harmony in literature and art that Arnim struggled. For him it was exemplified in the creations of the Middle Ages and the old German past generally. He desired also that this harmony might enter into his personal life. He tried to put an end to the conflict between life and art inherent in almost all of the younger Romanticists. He wished to attain to the lofty height of a romantic monism and to the full unity of spirit and nature found in Goethe.

His *Lebensgefühl* is definitely in this direction and is therefore positivistic and joyfully optimistic.[32] He wished to overcome obstacles and conflicts in a grand manner, to let his literary creations spring from the wealth of his overflowing soul and the richness of life itself. It was his aim to grasp the "sublime life":

> Es trägt nur freie Kraft durchs hohe Leben
> Vertrauend soll sich jeder ihr ergeben.[33]

The same thought when applied to literature is expressed in a passage in the *Zeitung für Einsiedler:* "The blind conflict between the Romanticists and the so-called Classicists is coming to an end: what remains is life itself."[34] At the same time he strove to retain a popular appeal, the ability to be understood by all social classes, something that he always admired in other writers. What he valued and sought to attain was, as he expresses it, the ability to give distinction to ordinary things in such a way as to make what is sublime appear as nothing unusual or out of the ordinary.[35]

---

[32] Even though Arnim appeared as a happy, carefree human being, there was a deep seriousness hidden in his nature. But he preferred to express himself often in a jesting manner. When critical, he inclines to good-natured irony of an entirely different character from Tieck's romantic irony. Thus, in announcing the *Zeitung für Einsiedler,* Arnim admonished the reading public: "Nehmt alles ernsthafter, als wir es Euch sagen, und Ihr werdet den Sinn fassen." *Arnim's Tröst Einsamkeit. Hrsg. von Fridrich Pfaff* (Frieburg i.B. und Tübingen 1883), p. 4, cited below as *Tröst Einsamkeit.* Similarly he confided to Bettina that behind the comic mask of his journal a more serious face was concealed. Arnim-Bettina, p. 91.

[33] Werke, I, p. XXI; "Anrede an meine Zuhörer."

[34] *Tröst Einsamkeit,* p. 71, Anmerkung.

[35] Arnim-Bettina, p. 239.

A prerequisite for the attainment of this *hohe Leben* was the spiritual rejuvenation of his fatherland, for life in his age was too prosaic to inspire a poet: "In our time one cannot be a poet, one can only do something for poetry," Clemens wrote him.[36] To the Count in his *Gräfin Dolores* Arnim assigned one purpose in life: service to his fellow-countrymen.[37]

However, it was not given to Arnim to reach these lofty heights of spirit and nature, of desire and accomplishment in life. Comparatively early in his life he had to realize that his hopes and capacity did not balance. Shortly before his marriage to Bettina he cautioned her not to look for too much that was good in him: "I know better than anyone how much I have wanted to do and how little I have accomplished".[38] His *Spiegelmensch*, against which he struggled in vain all his life long, is a Wilhelm Meister type. In a discussion of *Wilhelm Meister* in his later years he gives unconsciously a fine bit of self-analysis which emphasizes the conflicting elements in his own soul:

> Wilhelm's goodheartedness and weakness, his great aspirations and his pliant nature, his desire for development and his continual talk about it, and the constant interruption of this development by capriciousness, his isolation from the world and then his attachment to it, his doubts of himself, although he is always falling back on himself,—all this makes him a faithful though intellectualized image of gifted young men in a period which ended with the Revolution. He makes only a pretense of contact with the life of the middle classes; public life arouses his disgust and suspicion. He is only persistent in the effort for his own development and he sticks to that like a bird to a lime twig . . . he is endowed with all the admirable powers of his time and is subject to all the evil temptations, with no force to urge toward a goal selected by his own genius.[39]

Like Wilhelm Meister, Arnim lacked the determination and driving force of the genius who is able to master the contrasts in himself and those of his age.[40]

---

[36] Arnim-Brentano, p. 106.
[37] Werke, XVIII, p. 455.
[38] Arnim-Brentano, p. 401; letter of July 29, 1810.
[39] Werke, XIX, 267/8; Arnim-Brentano, p. 54: "Lies einmal im Wilhelm Meister . . .das dritte Capitel des fünften Teils, Wilhelms Brief an Werner, und Du hast was Savigny und Winkelmann über mich urteilen. . . "
[40] Arnim-Brentano, p. 54; Klinger's *Weltmann und Dichter* likewise reminded Arnim of the two realms which he could not reconcile.

But although Arnim never could attain to the greatness and wisdom of Goethe, he was spared the fate of many of his contemporaries who, like Brentano, for instance, became the fragile toys of their romantic whims. The whirlwind of romantic sentiment, the wild intoxication of spirit never entirely gained the upper hand in Arnim, because his Mark Brandenburg tradition kept his feet on the ground. Hence in his critical writings one encounters a novel accent which distinguishes him from contemporary thought and throws light on the transition to, first, a national and later, a realistic outlook on life.

In conclusion, one may say that like his other works, his critical writings are the outgrowth of a vague, groping idealism. His philosophy and his art did not appeal to his contemporaries, and Arnim died lonely and misunderstood. Nor was he appreciated by the next generation, with the exception of a chosen few. Among these was Heinrich Heine, who praised Arnim's writings very highly in his *Romantische Schule*,[41] and paved the way for his subsequent fame. There are many interesting comments on Arnim's personality by those who knew him,[42] but none of these describes the conglomerate which formed the basis for his critical work more strikingly or more aptly than that by Wilhelm Grimm his most faithful and understanding friend:

> He was a man of decision, but of mild temper; to even the most insignificant person he would give sunshine and warmth. Thoroughly nonpartisan in character, he maintained a noble attitude of detachment amid the dissensions of the time. He was not a poet of despair revelling in the agony caused by the dissonances of his own soul. He rose superior to turmoil and prejudice. With hope for the future he brought the most extraordinary and astounding things without hesitation into close companionship with those of general acceptance, the simplest songs that appeal to every human heart with those mysterious ones whose meaning he alone might fathom. He seemed like one who could suddenly leave a party and surrender himself to his own thoughts in the depths of a forest.[43]

[41] *Heines Sämtliche Werke,* Insel Ausgabe, VII, 128-136.

[42] Goethe to Reichardt, October 10, 1810; Wilhelm von Humboldt to Caroline, *Briefe,* III, 101-2; Immermann, *Jahrbücher für wissenschaftliche Kritik,* pp. 760-6, 1827; K. A. Varnhagen von Ense, *Tagebücher* X, 414, 14-16.

[43] Introduction to *Arnims Sämtliche Werke,* I, VIII.

III
FROM SCIENCE TO LITERATURE

Arnim was relatively late in discovering the field of literature. Not until his twenty-first year, in 1802, did he begin to look at poetry as "the focus of life and affairs."[1] As a student of eighteen, however, he had found the path to critical journalism in the field of science. In May, 1798, he matriculated at the University of Halle as a student of law but felt himself attracted by the field of natural science. On July 15 of the same year he presided at the organization of the "Freunde freier Untersuchungen,"[2] a student society devoted to the cultivation of research. The results of his studies were embodied in the following year in a book, *Versuch einer Theorie der elektrischen Erscheinungen,*[3] and in sixteen contributions to Gilbert's *Annalen der Physik.*[4] It was the age of revolutionary discoveries in the field of science. The startling problems of electricity and magnetism occupied the leading minds; but metaphysics and mysticism were also strongly in vogue. The relationship between experiment and deductive reasoning in the approach to nature was by no means clear. Scientific and poetic activities had their origin in the same soil. In Middle Germany the universities particularly engaged in scientific speculation were Jena, Halle, Göttingen, and Würzburg. These centers were becoming widely known through the activities of men like Fichte, Schelling, Ritter, and Novalis.

While Arnim was a student at Halle, a strictly scientific attitude toward nature was prevalent there. The dominating figure in scientific circles was Ludwig Wilhelm Gilbert (1769-1824), who had been professor of mathematics and physics at Halle since 1795. He was Arnim's teacher and was chief editor of the *Annalen der Physik,* founded by Albert Carl Gren. This journal was much

[1] Arnim-Brentano, p. 38.
[2] *Ibid.*, p. 8.
[3] Mallon, p. 1.
[4] *Ibid.*, pp. 1-3; also Ernst Darmstaedter, "Achim von Arnim und die Naturwissenschaft"; *Euphorion,* 1931, pp. 454-76.

concerned with polemics against the pseudo-scientific mysticism fashionable in those days. This attitude is emphasized in the concluding paragraphs of Editor Gilbert's preface to the first volume of the *Annalen* (1799):

> Nothing in my opinion is more incompatible with true science than the passion for novelties and the snatching at sensational news, instead of being satisfied with thorough studies and research. I am concerned only about the promotion and propagation of true science and disdain this passion for sensational pseudo-scientific novelties.[5]

Influenced by the point of view of his teacher, Arnim in his first published work warns against an unscientific, unsystematic spirit:

> I would not advise the acceptance of any mere semblance of knowledge in the field of natural science where there is an illegible passage in the book of nature, nor would I, like the freebooter in Homer, be satisfied to show my tracks in reverse, leaving the reader in uncertainty as to what path had led me to the goal.[6]

This objective attitude was strikingly in contrast with that of Arnim's mystical Romantic contemporaries. One of these, Christian Brentano, some years later accuses him of a too materialistic approach to physics. "Men on earth," he writes Arnim, "have to seek refuge with God and his religion, not with mechanism or philosophy or whatever it may be."[7]

The *Versuch einer Theorie der elektrischen Erscheinungen,* from which the quotation in the foregoing paragraph is taken, is based on Kant's dynamic conception of nature. Arnim rejects all mechanistic materialism and adopts as a working hypothesis the principle of a formative force (*gestaltende Kraft*).[8] His briefer contributions to the *Annalen* are partly translations and announcements drawn from French scientific publications, and partly reports on the author's own researches, or critical reviews of other

---

[5] *Annalen der Physik,* hrsg. von Ludwig Wilhelm Gilbert. Vol. I, Vorwort, Halle, 1799.

[6] "Ich würde raten, in der Naturlehre weder den Schein des Wissens anzunehmen, wo im Buche der Natur eine unleserliche Stelle ist, noch, wie jener Homerische Freibeuter, die Fußtapfen umgekehrt zu zeigen, und die Leser bei dem erreichten Ziele über den zurückgelegten Weg in Ungewißheit lassen." *Versuch einer Theorie der elektrischen Erscheinungen,* p. 3, also DNL, CXLVI, 11.

[7] Christian Brentano's letter to Arnim (unpublished), July 23, 1805, quoted partly in K. E. Henrici, *Auktions-Katalog* 149, p. 31.

[8] Moritz Carriere, *Achim von Arnim,* p. 13.

publications. These and Arnim's later articles on scientific subjects are clear and objective, and are therefore quite in contrast with the writings of certain contemporary students of the natural sciences, like the famous Jena physicist, J. W. Ritter, whose works make a very mystical and confusing impression. A glance at Arnim's topics reveals that he did not choose pseudo-scientific subjects.[9] The significance of his scientific contributions has recently been confirmed in a paper by Ernst Darmstaedter.[10]

Important and interesting in this connection is a closer study of Arnim's relationship to the two men who played such an important rôle in formulating the philosophic conception of this romantic period, Johann Wilhelm Ritter (1776-1810) and Friedrich Wilhelm Schelling. The names of Ritter and Arnim have been mentioned together very often.[11] August Winkelmann, who was in close contact with Ritter in Jena, wrote in the preface to his *Einleitung in die dynamische Physiologie,* published in 1803, a dedication to "his friends," Ritter and Arnim.[12] If Bettina may be relied on, Clemens Brentano in a letter of May, 1801, referred to Arnim as Ritter's great rival in the field of physics.[13] Such references to Arnim's relation to Ritter are especially noteworthy if one recalls the leading position young Ritter held among his romantic contemporaries in that field. The brilliant career of the self-

[9] Mallon, pp. 1-5.

[10] Ernst Darmstaedter, "Achim von Arnim und die Naturwissenschaft," *Euphorion,* XXXII (1931), 454-476. Unlike Schönemann, who maintains that Arnim was ill prepared to discuss philosophically the results and problems of scientific research (L. A. von *Arnims geistige Entwicklung an seinem Drama "Halle und Jerusalem" erläutert*), Darmstaedter comes to the conclusion that young Arnim displayed a rare independence in scientific thinking (p. 47).

[11] The only article I have found on Arnim's relations with Ritter, that of Paul Hoffmann, "Achim von Arnim über J. W. Ritter" (*Archiv f. Gesch. d. Mathematik, Naturwiss. u. Technik,* X, 357), is misleading. Apparently Hoffmann overlooked completely two publications containing valuable information: R. Steig, "Zeugnisse zur Pflege der deutschen Literatur in den Heidelbergischen Jahrbüchern" (NHeidelbJbb., 1902), and Alfred Kloss, *Die Heidelbergischen Jahrbücher der Litteratur,* 1918. From Hoffmann one gets the impression that Arnim reviewed Ritter's book in dutiful compliance with the editor's wishes, while as a matter of fact, the review was Arnim's choice. Furthermore Arnim's attitude toward Ritter was essentially different from Hoffmann's view of it. He quite misinterprets Arnim's statement, "den Ritter habe ich mit Lust und Liebe und ganz in allgemeiner menschlicher Beziehung geschrieben," NHeidelbJbb. (1902), p. 247; quoted from Arnim's letter to August Böckh, March 12, 1810.

[12] Arnim-Brentano, p. 9.

[13] *Frühlingskranz,* p. 246; letter to Bettina, May, 1801.

educated young peasant was the result of strenuous and intensive effort; indeed, overwork, accompanied by a dissolute life, was responsible for his untimely death. Arnim was familiar with Ritter's queer habits of living and working, and describes them vividly in a letter to Clemens Brentano:

> Intensive work for a few days; hunger, then sleep, drink, and gluttony for the next days; love making, despair, artificial stimulation, interspersed with insult and truth, absurd and futile literary endeavors.[14]

Arnim and Ritter were interested in similar questions, chiefly galvanism and magnetism, and they influenced each other mutually, as is apparent in their writings. Arnim wrote two reviews of Ritter's early scientific papers, his *Beweis, daß ein beständiger Galvanismus den Lebensprozeß im Tierreiche begleite* (Weimar, 1798) and his *Beiträge zur Kenntnis des Galvanismus* (Bd. I, Jena, 1802).[15] Ritter, likewise, noticed Arnim's scientific contributions published in the *Annalen der Physik* in 1800[16] and discussed them in his *Beiträge* (II, 17). Here he contended that some of Arnim's hypotheses had become antiquated. Arnim was offended by this criticism and in a letter to Gilbert, October 29, 1801, maintained his views with youthful stubbornness.[17] Furthermore, in his "Versuche und Bemerkungen über den Galvanismus der Voltaischen Batterie," a series of letters addressed to the editor of the *Annalen der Physik,* Ritter criticized severely Arnim's paper "Bemerkungen über Voltas Säule," published in the *Annalen* in 1801,[18] and expressed his surprise that Arnim, otherwise so well acquainted with the laws of electricity, should overestimate the importance of wet bodies.[19]

While Ritter was a great rival of young Arnim, Schelling, the

---

[14] *Arnim-Brentano*, p. 187. Here Arnim compares Winkelmann's life with that of Ritter: "Er (Winkelmann) ist an einem Typhus gestorben, den seine Art von wilder Praxis gefährlicher gemacht hatte. Er hat sich auch eigentlich nicht durch Liederlichkeit geschwächt—denn das soll mehr Redensart gewesen sein—sondern durch sein altes, Ritter nachgebildetes ungewöhnliches Leben: langes Arbeiten für einige Tage, Hungern, dann Schlafen, Trinken, Fressen für den folgenden, Verliebttun, Verzweifeln, eine künstliche Empfindungsmanege. . . ."

[15] These two reviews appeared in the *Annalen der chemischen Literatur,* hrsg. von Friedrich Wolff, I, 197-399, Berlin, 1803. Cf. Mallon, Nr. 20.

[16] Mallon, No. 4.

[17] *Annalen der Physik,* IX, 494-496.

[18] Mallon, No. 10.

[19] *Annalen der Physik,* IX, 212-262, esp. 238, 239.

greatest nature philosopher of his generation, was a stimulus to him, and was probably responsible for his abandoning science and entering the field of literature. Arnim and Schelling never met. Intermediaries between the two were the Reichardt family, who during Arnim's student years resided at Giebichenstein Castle at Halle. Here many of the prominent figures of the day were accustomed to meet. Later on, in 1808, Bettina, while visiting in Munich, seems to have started a short-lived correspondence between Arnim and Schelling, of which only one letter, from Arnim to Schelling, is available.[20] Arnim had an intimate knowledge of Schelling's writings. In his *Versuch einer Theorie der elektrischen Erscheinungen* he discussed them critically, and Schelling took favorable notice of young Arnim's scientific articles in his *Zeitschrift für spekulative Physik*, 1801-1802.[21]

The common ground of interest in these earlier exchanges was the phenomenon of electricity. In the *Versuch* Arnim felt obliged to inform his readers that he had not found any novel point of view in his study of Schelling.[22] This youthful approach of Arnim to the problem of electrical manifestation is purely scientific (in the modern sense), taking as its basis only the actual physical data and paying no heed to the universal character of the thought of Schelling, who endeavored to find the "all" behind single phenomena of nature. Only when he began a study of Schelling's *Weltseele* and *Ideen zu einer Philosophie der Natur* did Arnim begin to realize the importance of relating spiritual life and art to science.

The *Ideen zu einer Philosophie der Natur,* published in 1797, and the study *Von der Weltseele, eine Hypothese der höheren Physik zur Erklärung des allgemeinen Organismus,* published a year later (in the spring of 1798), were two brilliant works on natural philosophy. They gave, indeed, an entirely new, transcendental outlook on the world. In the *Ideen* Schelling expounded the thesis that scientific achievements are of secondary importance and can not explain the wonders of the world. It is rather the task

[20] Partly published by K. Henrici, *Auktions-Katalog* 149, p. 15; not mentioned in Arnim Bibliography.
[21] Jena, 1800, Vol. I, 142-8, 1801, Vol. II, 152-3.
[22] *Versuch einer Theorie,* p. 120.

of philosophy, the instrument of the spirit, to interpret scientific facts.[23] Chemistry furnishes only information on the elements, physics only such as concerns formulas (*Silben*), mathematics only details with respect to nature, while philosophy alone is able to synthesize and expound the data. In *Von der Weltseele* Schelling departed still further from logical, scientific thinking and empirical procedure and delved deeper into metaphysics and mysticism. He declared that behind the antagonism of forces and the yawning dualism of nature, in the last analysis a single natural principle manifests itself, namely the "World Soul," as the ancient Greeks called it without being able to define it more adequately.[24] From both these works, the *Ideen* and the *Weltseele*, extensive quotations are found in Arnim's *Versuch* of 1799. Four years later, in the essay "Erzählungen von Schauspielen," published in Friedrich Schlegel's *Europa*,[25] we find Arnim making use of expressions and ideas drawn from Schelling, such as "World Soul," and the "inner essence of all nature."

Of the greatest influence on Arnim's conception of art was a third work of Schelling, his *System des transzendentalen Idealismus* (1800). This was the book which forced Goethe to declare that he would have to depart from the traditional method of science.[26] In the sixth chapter of his *System* Schelling declares that art is the pattern of science and that science must associate itself with art;[27] for art, which can spring from genius alone, is "the sole and eternal revelation."[28] These ideas must have stirred Arnim deeply, as one can readily see in the "Lebensplan," which he submitted to Clemens in a confidential letter of July 9, 1802.[29] In other letters which he wrote in the following years on his

[23] *Schellings Werke*, hrsg. von K. A. Schelling, Abt. I, Bd. II, 6: "Aus der Innerlichkeit des Geistes soll die Natur gedeutet werden."
[24] *Ibid.*, p. 562.
[25] *Europa*, II, 163, 173; Frankfurt, 1803. Here Arnim says: "Die Weltseele scheint noch wie ein unerzogenes Mädchen in ihren Bildungen aus Erdschollen zu spielen, sie hängt immer einen gewaltigen Geist und ein gewaltiges Schicksal einem schwachen Körper zum Schabernack an."
[26] In April, 1800, Goethe wrote to Schelling: "Ich glaube in dieser Vorstellungsart sehr viele Vorteile für denjenigen zu entdecken, dessen Neigung es ist, die Kunst auszuüben und die Natur zu betrachten."
[27] *System*, pp. 460, 468, 469.
[28] *System*, pp. 460, 468, 469.   [29] Arnim-Brentano, pp. 38-9.

grand tour, particularly those written during the time when he felt most strongly the conflict between the call to a scientific career and to an artistic one, Arnim echoes Schelling's statement that even science has to serve art.[30] In the letter to Clemens just referred to he had declared that "everything that occurs in the world is on account of poetry."[31] Similarly, Schelling's emphasis on the sacredness of art inspires Arnim's appeal to the poet not to show pride, but the greatest virtue.

Very early in Arnim's letters we note an inclination to approach literature through nature. His attitude was similar to Goethe's: "to practice art and observe nature." In 1802 he proclaims that a mighty spirit of poetry breathes throughout all nature, revealing itself at one time as history, at another as a phenomenon of nature. The poet need only catch a few faint echoes of this spirit in order to see clearly into the profoundest depths of the emotions.[32] Schelling maintained that perfection (*das Vollendete*) can be reached only by genius.[33] With a truly romantic egotism Arnim feels that he is a genius according to Schelling's definition, and in the somewhat turgid language characteristic of Schelling, he declares that he recognizes in himself the "pole," e.g., the focal center of all languages, "without which nature must of necessity fade into indefiniteness."[34]

Arnim was attracted to Schelling because of the latter's very broad definition of poetry and art. In his "transcendental idealism" Schelling considered poetry and art as the main-spring of life. Arnim felt that genuine greatness and glory were attained only by creative artists, such as Goethe, Tieck, and his friend Brentano when he gave to the world his *Godwi*. He held it to be his immediate task to bring new life to humanity through poetry: "Art must take a hand in the transformation of the world," he declared many years later in the *Kronenwächter*.[35] This was to be the

[30] *System*, p. 468.
[31] Arnim-Brentano, p. 38.
[32] *Ibid.*, p. 35. Schelling expressed this idea as follows, "Nature and history are the two poles proper which combine to a new third unity, namely art."
[33] Schelling interprets poetry (*Poesie*) as "the realistic element by means of which the infinite is moulded into the finite." *Werke*, I, V, 479, 468. Cf. also Heinrich Knittermeyer, *Schelling und die romantische Schule*, p. 345.
[34] Arnim-Brentano, p. 32.
[35] *Kronenwächter*, II, 387.

poetizing of reality for which Novalis, Hölderlin, and Tieck had struggled; yet Arnim set for it more immediate goals. As early as December 1803, he came to believe that he could thus render a service to mankind which would never be possible in the natural sciences. In retrospect he now views his work in physics as useless. He does not want to write for bookworms: "My mind stood open like a chalice to the light of poetry."[36]

Appreciating this philosophy of Arnim in the light of Schelling's "transcendental idealism," one can understand now fully his "plan of life," (*Lebensplan*). The framework of this romantic universalism contained, however, definite goals which Arnim pursued seriously in succeeding years. National boundaries were not to put a limitation on these goals. In the first place, a *Sprach- und Singschule* was to be founded, where a standard modern German language was to be created which would soon be accepted by all people in Germany and later also by all nations of the world. This would bring about at once a closer association and more intimate unity among Germans of all tribes. All the agitation and quarreling of their princes would cease, for Germans would not fight against their brethren. Even the foreigners, no longer supported by selfish individual German princes, would ally themselves with united Germany. Thus Arnim hoped that Germany would become the "lightning rod of the world."[37] It is evident that these ideas of Arnim's can be traced ultimately to Schelling's romantic monism.

Romantic monism presupposed thinking and planning on a grand scale with the final purpose of integrating the individual with the universe. Thus Friedrich Schlegel advocated a world revolution; Novalis, a universal church; and Arnim, a Golden Age, to be realized by the "poetizing" of the world. Direct references to romantic monism cannot be found in Arnim's writings, as he generally seems to abhor philosophical discussions. He hardly mentions Spinoza and Leibnitz. However, he was well acquainted with the works of Hamann and Herder, whose philosophy, emphasizing feeling and nature, he adopted. With Herder he recognized the bond between the individual and the universe

---
[36] Arnim's letter to Clemens Brentano, Christmas, 1803, Arnim-Brentano, p. 104.
[37] *Ibid.*, p. 39.

which led finally to the concept of the "folk-soul." Arnim, like Herder before him, listened intently to the expressions of the "soul of the people," and he believed that he saw it reflected in the history of mankind throughout the ages. Leibnitz' monad, e.g., the original force (*Urkraft*), became for both of them the national force (*Volkskraft*), manifesting itself in the national spirit (*Volksgeist*).[38] These ideas not only stimulated literature and art, but also led Arnim's contemporaries to productive research in universal history and comparative linguistics. With the men engaged in these studies Arnim kept in close touch.

Monistic thinking can be traced throughout Arnim's life. It is found especially in his literary theories. The idea of the totality of expression and of literature as an organism, an organic unit, he expounded in great detail in his correspondence with Jacob Grimm on the problem of "nature-poetry" and "art-poetry." "You will understand," he writes to Jacob on April 5, 1811, "that I deny the assumption that poetry, history, and life in general are to be set off in contrast with each other," a practice, he goes on to say, for which contemporary philosophy has a predilection.[39] To contrast nature and art appeared ridiculous; he wanted rather to derive the whole universe, including art, from nature. He regarded Goethe as the living example for this thesis:

> It is not possible to trace in Goethe the boundary between art and nature. Often the intuitive character of his personality takes him by surprise; the expression of this is then called art.[40]

As appears from the foregoing, Arnim's transition from science to art seems to have been rather sudden. In reality he remained for many years in close contact with science. Nevertheless, as soon as he becomes interested in art, he begins with youthful arrogance to ridicule science and theoretical thinking. He now has the "courage" to describe an idealistic philosophy of life. He now believes he has overcome the "fear and laziness" of the days when he saw the only salvation in science.[41] Satirizing the too

---

[38] Compare paragraph on *Volksgeist, Zeitgeist* in Chapter I.
[39] Arnim-Grimm, p. 110.
[40] *Ibid.*, p. 109.
[41] Arnim-Brentano, p. 52. Arnim's youthful, somewhat dry, scholarly inclinations can be partly explained as an after-effect of his Berlin school days. He wrote to Goethe from Berlin, February, 1806, "Es steht hier noch wie eine Mauer, die trübe

abstract theories in Fichte's and Schelling's philosophy, he writes to Clemens in November, 1802:

> You probably know the subject of the quarrel between Fichte und Schelling. The former says: the ego = the universe; the latter, the universe = the ego. Mathematically speaking, both equations amount to the same. But Schelling, proud of his ego and productivity, emphasizes that he bases his ideas on productivity; Fichte, on reflection.[42]

Clemens, answering this letter from Düsseldorf, Christmas, 1802, notes that Schelling's lectures have lately become rather unpopular because of his obscure barbarism.[43] Arnim turned away from the natural science of those days chiefly because he detested its scholastic disputes and the resultant theoretic confusion. He felt that working in this field was too remote from life and reality. He hoped to find the true well of life in art and poetry.[44] There was still another reason for his desertion of the sciences. He declares that "success came too slowly in this field." He recognized that he had not enough original ideas. At Christmas, 1803, he wrote to Clemens: "I did not discover anything in physics which was not published at the same time by Ritter, Schelling, or others; indeed, many papers I have torn to pieces because the others were ahead of me."[45]

However, as noted above, Arnim's scientific interests and activities did not terminate suddenly and forever. When the concentrated efforts ceased which the publication of the *Wunderhorn* had required, and he again settled down to a quieter life, we notice a revival of his scientific activities. The very year which witnessed

---

gepreßte Luft einer zwangvollen Kinderstube, aus der ich mich in verzweifelnder Langeweile in allerlei Gelehrsamkkeit stürzte, die nachher in wärmerer Sonne bis auf wenige Neigen rein verdampfte." *Schriften der Goethe-Ges.*, XIV, 83.

[42] Arnim-Brentano, p. 53.

[43] *Ibid.*, p. 59.

[44] What Friedrich von Raumer, at eighty years of age, recorded in his memoirs about Arnim's transition from science to literature can hardly be taken seriously. He and Arnim had been schoolmates at the Joachimsthaler Gymnasium and also studied together at Halle und Göttingen. Raumer tells us that while in Halle, Arnim pursued preferably the study of science (physics); when in Göttingen, he turned to belles lettres because his lady love there complained that his studies in physics and chemistry polluted the atmosphere with unpleasant odors. Therefore he discarded these studies, bought himself new clothes and fine perfumes and wrote *Hollins Liebeleben*. Friedrich von Raumer, *Lebenserinnerungen und Briefwechsel* (Leipzig, 1861), pp. 29, 43.

[45] Arnim-Brentano, p. 104.

the appearance of the *Wunderhorn,* 1806, saw also Arnim's venture into a second "science" period with the publication of a short article in the *Annalen der Physik.*[46] In 1807 he wrote another brief article for the same periodical,[47] and the three following years bring his best criticism and interpretations of natural philosophy. In 1808 two important books on natural philosophy appeared, *Ansichten von der Nachtseite der Naturwissenschaften* by the Dresden philosopher, Gotthilf Heinrich von Schubert, and *Theorie der Geisterkunde, in einer Natur-, Vernunft- und Bibelmäßigen Beantwortung der Frage: Was von Ahnungen, Gesichten und Geistererscheinungen geglaubt und nicht geglaubt werden müsse,* by Heinrich Jung-Stilling. Both books stirred Arnim's imagination. That of Schubert, he recommended highly. With regard to Jung-Stilling's, he wrote to Clemens, October 22, 1809, "What a magnificent, ponderous, and at the same time very human book it was, like a Greek mythology."[48] Without being invited, Arnim wrote at once a review of this "magnificent" work for the *Heidelbergische Jahrbücher.* In 1808 also Arnim met in Heidelberg Zacharias Werner who introduced him to his mystical *Naturlehre* and *System der Liebe.* The next year, while living in Berlin with Pistor, who was then engaged in making instruments for physics laboratories,[49] Arnim fell a victim to the political restlessness of those years and to discouragement over his own none-too-successful literary endeavors and resolved to go back to science as an academic profession. First, he thought of taking his doctor's degree at Heidelberg, but when the Berlin University was founded he hoped for a career at this institution.[50] However, this plan did not materialize. In 1810 appeared the last important publication of the unhappy physicist J. W. Ritter, *Fragmente aus dem Nachlasse eines jungen Physikers,* which Arnim immediately reviewed for the *Heidelbergische Jahrbücher.*[51]

These are but the general data of Arnim's second "science" period. It is marked by an entirely different attitude towards

[46] *Annalen,* XXII, p. 331, essay on "Steinregen".
[47] *Ibid.,* XXVI, pp. 479-80; "Eine Berichtigung, die Haarröhrchen betreffend."
[48] Arnim-Brentano, p. 261.
[49] *Ibid.,* p. 280.
[50] Cf. NHeidelbJbb., XI, 227, Anm. 2; 221, 231 235, 253.
[51] HeidelbJbb., Abt. I, Bd. II (1810), pp. 116-125.

science than that of a decade earlier when, under the spell of his teacher Ludwig Gilbert, he was working for the promotion of "true" science. Now he approached science under the influence of natural philosophy, and as a mystical romanticist, adopted an all-embracing monistic view of the universe. This *höhere Weltorganisation,* the unity behind all matter, was to be searched for intuitively, as Schelling's "World Soul" had taught him. This changed attitude appears in his review of Jung-Stilling's *Theorie der Geisterkunde:*

In our opinion, modern German physics cannot deny the existence of the spiritual world and is forced to adopt the idea of animal magnetism and a higher organization of the world, because physics notices and recognizes that from lower organisms, described by purely physical laws, higher beings evolve. The mechanistic view in physics is destroyed with Kant.[52]

Arnim's reviews of Ritter's *Fragmente* and Jung-Stilling's *Theorie der Geisterkunde* are extremely interesting as documents of a Romanticist's spiritual and scientific attitude towards the world and his own period, and they deserve to be discussed here at greater length. While both reviews were intended for the *Heidelbergische Jahrbücher,* only one, that of Ritter's *Fragmente,* was accepted for the philosophical section of this periodical.[53] August Böckh, representing the anti-Romantic clique of editors, rejected as too fantastic the review of Jung-Stilling's book, but it was finally published in F. W. Gubitz' *Gesellschafter* in 1817.[54] Here, indeed, the editor passed it on to the printer rather unwillingly.

Ritter had died in poverty in 1810, deserted by most of his former admirers. Arnim had throughout his life an appreciation and an understanding of Ritter's tragic personality. This sentiment is frankly expressed in his review of Ritter's *Fragmente*[55] and in his brief note on Ritter's death.[56] In the latter Arnim

[52] *Unbekannte Aufsätze,* pp. 22-23.
[53] August Böckh's letter to Arnim, April 2, 1810; cf. NHeidelbJbb., 1902, pp. 250-3.
[54] *Ges.,* 1817. pp. 385-6, 389-91, 394-5.
[55] HeidelbJbb., Abt. I, Bd. II, pp. 116-125; Arnim was especially interested in books of a biographical nature and preferred to review them: "Auf Biographien, besonders auf Selbstbiographien, bin ich auf steter Jagd." Arnim-Bettina, p. 374.
[56] This note was held up by the censor and never published during Arnim's life

objected to the false stories about Ritter and the unfair criticism directed against his intellectual associate:

During his life he found little encouragement and recognition among us, such as would have promoted his efforts and assured us of the fame of possessing such a man. His achievements were recognized abroad, where an effort was made to free him from oppressive poverty when it was too late. To a foreign country he bequeathed all of his writings, of which he had published only a small part in his remarkable *Fragmente eines jungen Physikers*.

More light on this human angle of Arnim's interest in Ritter is given by his review of Ritter's *Fragmente*. Although the review considers mainly Ritter's personality, it also touches upon his scholarly endowment. Here Arnim looks at him as a conservative man would, and in a tactful but critical tone deplores the direction that Ritter's life had taken, yet he praises his great talents.[57] Contemporaries were attracted, he declares, by Ritter's talents, but repelled from any sympathy with his scientific efforts by his disputatious nature. A friendly relationship with him was not possible on account of his biting, satirical attitude. He had all the self-confidence and air of superiority of a self-educated person. At Jena he showed that he could practice economy and maintain himself on a modest scale by his writings, and he understood how to exploit the fame that came to him. He drew around him those who were inclined to loose living and incapable of understanding him, as well as certain people of culture who in Jena at that time gave themselves over to a kind of frivolous life and whom Ritter formed to his taste. It was not without justification that Ritter complained of the type of culture he encountered in the educated circle at Jena. The flashy, superficial impressions of art which he received there stirred up the wish to do something extraordinary and to make himself conspicuous. This led to the premature

---

time, because he accused the government of negligence. It appeared first in "Gesammelte kleine Bemerkungen zu Dichtern und Schriftstellern des 18. und 19. Jahrhunderts" by R. Steig, *Euphorion*, Ergänzungsheft, XV (1923), 70-1.

[57] Arnim and Brentano must have tried to become more intimate with Ritter. In the spring of 1802 Brentano was for a short time in frequent correspondence with Ritter. Cf. Brentano's letter to Arnim, May, 1802; Arnim-Brentano, p. 34; Brentano's letter to Arnim, September, 1802; *ibid.*, p. 45: "Ritter, der mir viel schreibt . . . " later, in a disappointed vein: "Ritter hat mir keine Zeile mehr geschrieben. . . ."

announcement of discoveries, which in some cases were not realized, a behavior which was quite contrary to his nature. The alternation of dissipation and extreme want cut short fruitful efforts on Ritter's part and drove him to over-exertion. This was the cause of much slipshod work. It broke down his health and prevented proper scientific observations. At times he could do nothing at all; at times, supported by stimulants, he would write half a volume in a few nights. This, as Arnim sagely remarks, caused a different type of exhaustion from that which followed on the natural, prodigious exertions of a Luther or a Newton. In Ritter's *Fragmente* Arnim notes a religious attitude that lacks respect for the body which was made in God's image; and he accuses Ritter of making useless experiments to the damage of his own body, such as exposing his eyes to the sun. For his part, Arnim is convinced that experiments harmful to the investigator's life, by which young scientists of his day sought to prove their courage, have never led to important results.[58]

The beginning of Arnim's review ostensibly showed Ritter's attitude, but actually Arnim's attitude toward science in relation to the problems of the nation and the universe. The hopes and aspirations of the romanticists reflect here the restlessness of political life during these years. Like Ritter, Arnim questioned whether now (1810) it was still necessary to urge German youth to closer unity and collaboration in science, since political events had welded the nation and hence also the different branches and schools in science into one united front. German science was just as youthful and strong as the German nation, and was already showing signs of even greater vigor in comparison with science in other countries. Arnim alluded here to France, and he expressed the belief that with the birth of a new political world over there, Germany was proceeding to a new unification of knowledge and science which would fuse the peculiar and separate elements of all disciplines and the efforts of single scholars into a unified whole. Encouraged by the apostle (here Arnim referred to Ritter), the German nation has put all prophesies and all faith into science and art. Every German feels the urge to learn and to invent. Politics is only a hateful distraction, for a secret voice seems to

[58] Arnim's review of Ritter's *Fragmente*, p. 120, cf. note 51, above.

whisper that while the affairs of politics and the world are now the task of other nations, it is the German's destiny to show his love for the fatherland in devotion to science and art. From such whole-hearted devotion patriotic and political devotion will spring when called for.[59]

Finally Arnim discusses Ritter's religious beliefs and comes to the conclusion that they were the outgrowth of his conception of natural philosophy. Both Ritter and Arnim were deeply religious: "Uns bleibt Glaube, Liebe, Hoffnung . . . aber die Liebe ist die größte unter ihnen," Ritter quotes in his fragments. Arnim found that Ritter's autobiography was written in this spirit:

> We feel that his religion is not the product of inheritance and education, but rather the outgrowth of his innermost conviction and deep feeling, as in many contemporaries, who pondered much and forgot religion only to become deeply religious again when speculating on God and religion.[60]

In this connection he evaluated Ritter's contributions to science and natural philosophy. The conclusion is brief but enthusiastic:

> Part Ten, on animal magnetism, is perhaps the finest thing that has so far been written on the subject and serves well to characterize the soul of the author, whose beautiful words in this connection are not based on novel experiences, but on well-known phenomena. The reader should compare him here with Gotthilf Heinrich von Schubert's book *Über die Ansichten von der Nachtseite der Natur*. How he loves to organize the universe and bring it closer to us, with how much sagacity he uses philosophy without losing himself in it! . . . Never before has the new organic physics been proclaimed so brilliantly.[61]

To this extent then, Arnim defended Ritter's life and work in public. However, in his confidential letters to Bettina he strikes a more critical note. Speaking of the *Fragmente* in a letter of September 29, 1809, when he had just heard of the book, but had not yet read it, he voices the opinion that it must be highly entertaining and scandalous, provided it is a truthful account.[62] Later, in a letter of February 26, 1810, he regrets that Ritter's life fell short of the hopes and expectations of others; nevertheless, he thinks that one could say many good things about the book if a

---

[59] *Ibid.*, pp. 116-18.
[60] *Ibid.*, p. 123.
[61] *Ibid.*, pp. 123-4.
[62] Arnim-Bettina, p. 335.

group of Ritter's intimate friends could be gotten together.[63] However, romantic natural philosophy did not reach its mystical climax in the *Fragmente*.

The intermingling of science, philosophy, and religious mysticism is still more characteristic of Jung-Stilling's *Theorie der Geisterkunde*. Here the mystical author not only records his personal observations on magnetism, but correlates them with spiritualism and the conjuration of spirits. All is based on feeling and belief, not on experimental proofs. His view of nature and science was completely transcendental. He meditated on the supernatural, on presentiments and visions in a deeply mystical, religious way. This was particularly congenial with Arnim's thinking and feeling, for he found in Jung-Stilling's writings as well as in his philosophy of life a confirmation of his own attitude toward science, art, and life. Jung-Stilling's *Theorie der Geisterkunde* and *Heimweh* revealed "the author's matured faith in the world beyond, which is reflected in this visible universe,"[64] and the author is, in Arnim's opinion, the "honorable champion of a living faith" who with quiet confidence brings about a closer unity of kindred spirits. With this personal high esteem for the man and author it is comprehensible when Arnim in his capacity as reviewer either omits or shows kindly tolerance for many weak points in Jung-Stilling's *Theorie der Geisterkunde,* on which the enlightened critics of the *Jenaer Allgemeine Literatur-Zeitung* concentrated their attacks.[65] Arnim, with his scientific background, cannot help mentioning that many of the author's theories are antiquated; that hypotheses which should explain add only to the confusion of the difficult subject; that the manner in which the author employs concepts of time and space is questionable; that his emphatic opposition to mechanistic philosophy is uncalled-for and just as unnecessary as his discussion of the Copernican system. Yet, as Arnim goes on to show, all these are only minor issues within the brilliant major theory expounded by Jung-Stilling: "The wrestling human soul grows strong with the aid of miracles" (*Des*

---

[63] *Ibid.*, p. 384; compare also Bettina's remarks on Ritter, Arnim-Bettina, p. 373.
[64] *Unbekannte Aufsätze*, p. 18.
[65] Cf. *Jenaer Allgemeine Literatur-Zeitung*, 1808, pp. 809, 817.

Menschen Geist ringt sich am Wunderbaren stark). Thus deep insight and great wisdom make the *Theorie der Geisterkunde* the book of books among all that have been written about spirits and spiritualism. Arnim calls attention to the human ability for presentiment and vision which Jung-Stilling has demonstrated in the ordinary walks of life. Without this gift not even the humblest true verse is made, and it reveals itself in science and poetry in its best, purest, and holiest aspects. However, we can grasp the miraculous ether which pervades everything and surrounds us only if our faculties are sufficient. Dante possessed such spiritual greatness and thus became a believing, visionary poet, uniting the theological system of his age with his own world and with the knowledge of his time through the medium of art.

The review is the last milestone on Arnim's long, exploratory path through the field of science. It shows clearly the transformation which he had undergone. He had started with a materialistic approach and had finally come to realize how helpless and hopeless human reasoning is when it tries to lift the veil of the Beyond. Not reasoning power, but the soul and spiritual insight have the ultimate word in science. However, a spiritual approach is impossible without faith, the belief in a higher organization of the universe. Like Jung-Stilling, Arnim rejected all secrecy, hypocrisy, and coercion in matters of faith, as well as the "brutality which regards any faith as weakness and illness."

> Man is in need of the grace of God and must receive it humbly. . . . All our knowledge does not yet enable us to impart to a blind man the powers of his missing fifth sense by means of the other four senses he possesses, how much less can reason ferret out what is needed and meant for the heart. No eye has seen nor ear heard that which comes into the heart and is its future.[66]

This was Arnim's final answer respecting the problems confronting him in science: he saw only one way out, faith and trust in a higher being. It is no mere coincidence that at the time when he reviewed Ritter's *Fragmente* and Jung-Stilling's *Theorie der Geisterkunde* he was working on his own *Halle und Jerusalem*. He used this fantastic play as the vehicle to give artistic expression to his visions and his mystical religious philosophy of life. Was

---

[66] *Unbekannte Aufsätze*, p. 18.

Halle und Jerusalem intended to be the *Divine Comedy* of the Nineteenth Century?

Arnim's desertion of science was often deplored by his intimate friends. Josef von Görres expresses this feeling in his brilliant eulogy of Arnim, written in 1831 for the *Literaturblatt zum Morgenblatt* (Nr. 27-30):

> I often told him how much I regretted that he had abandoned this field, for I have always been under the impression that exclusive occupation with poetry has a disadvantageous and weakening effect; however, he never seemed to show any inclination to return to this neglected interest.[67]

Tieck voiced his regret still more forcefully, saying it was a pity Arnim had, to his own disadvantage, deserted a promising career in physics for literature, since he lacked poetic talent. He claimed that Arnim had stolen everything worth while from Schiller and himself.[68]

While still in the first flush of enthusiasm for natural science young Arnim came into contact with some of the leading figures in German literature. Soon production in this field came to take the place of his interest in scientific research. His early work and his critical attitude toward literature bear definite signs of the influence of three well-known men of letters of his time: Goethe, Tieck, and Brentano. The youthful Arnim had personal contact with all three of them, and they were to play an important rôle in his future, as is apparent in his "plan of life." Even as a young student Arnim became Tieck's faithful disciple in the matter of folk poetry. They differed only as to the proper methods of propagating the poetry of the people. While Tieck tried to interest the educated classes in "folkbooks" (*Volksbücher*), Arnim suggested taking the reverse path by appealing to the masses, for he believed that educated people, captivated by the refined form and conventional ideas of French poetry, would never appreciate fully the charm of popular poetry. He shared with his generation the admiration for Goethe, and considered it one of his tasks to make Goethe popular with the masses. In fact, it was his ultimate goal

---

[67] Cf. Josef Görres, *Ausgewählte Werke und Briefe*, hrsg. von Wilhelm Schellberg, 1911, I, 433.

[68] Reinhold Steig, *Brentano und die Gebrüder Grimm*, pp. 34, 63.

that Goethe's works should become as beloved as the old chapbooks. The close ties of friendship which existed between Arnim and Brentano are well known. They were cemented through their joint editing of *Des Knaben Wunderhorn*. It must be emphasized, however, that the *Wunderhorn* represents only the realization of a small fraction of their early idealistic plans for the revival of popular poetry.

Of the three poets, Goethe, Tieck, and Brentano, Tieck was Arnim's earliest acquaintance. They met in the Reichardt house in Halle as early as July, 1799, and Arnim then accompanied Tieck on a trip to Leipsic.[69] Two years later the first long stop-over of his "grand tour" was in Dresden, where he saw Tieck daily for three weeks. It is not possible to give instances of Tieck's early influence on him. But Arnim must have appreciated highly the association with the author of the *Volksmärchen für die Deutschen,* for he wrote to Clemens Brentano from Dresden on November 7, 1801, that it was a joy to him to be with Tieck, and that in his company he could always shake off the dust from his wings and return happily and courageously to the innermost springs of his soul.[70] At that time Tieck had already written his *William Lovell* (1795-6), his *Volksmärchen* (1797), the *Sternbald* (1798), and *Genoveva* (1799).

Arnim always kept himself well informed about the progress of Tieck's writings. He expressed his admiration for the elder poet in his letters to Clemens and in his own first literary attempts. He praised Tieck's "splendid poems," particularly the *Romanzen* in the *Muselalmanach 1802*.[71] In *Lovell* he saw a wealth of poetic innovations, a heavenly seed on the old, dry field of Richardson's influence.[72] Among Tieck's *Volksmärchen* Arnim must have liked best *Die schöne Magelone,* for Maria in Arnim's first novel, *Hollins Liebeleben,* is obviously elated when Hollin questions her about Tieck's story and passes the book over to him "with an indescribably joyous glance."[73] The epistolary form of Arnim's first novel reminds one of Tieck's *Lovell,* where we also find a

---

[69] Arnim-Brentano, p. 8. [70] Arnim-Brentano, pp. 25-6.
[71] *Ibid.*, pp. 26, 51; Arnim's letter of December, 1801.
[72] *Ibid.*, p. 41; Arnim's letter of summer, 1802.
[73] *Hollins Liebeleben,* hrsg. von J. Minor, p. 45.

correspondence which is carried on between several persons.

Both Brentano and Arnim had great hopes that Tieck might play an important rôle in German literature, especially in the drama. Brentano tried in vain to secure for him a position as theatrical manager at Frankfort, and Arnim wished that Tieck might move to Marburg, "in order to lecture there on the very timely subject of literature." "Literature," he adds, "has been used long enough merely as an introduction of materia medica."[74] The continuous travels of the next years loosened Arnim's relationship to Tieck. Furthermore, the latter did not encourage the two rambling idealists, Arnim and Brentano, in their poetic enthusiasm, as they had probably expected.[75] Still, for several years to come, Arnim looked up to him as the superb, shining German minstrel,[76] and Brentano lost no time in informing Tieck of his friend's high esteem, associating himself with it unreservedly. In January, 1802, he writes to the object of their enthusiasm:

> Arnim, whom you know and surely love, writes me his first letter from Regensburg, telling how delighted he is to know you and your work. I am certain that perhaps Arnim is the only German who reads your books as you would wish them to be read. If there are any who want to do or sacrifice something for you, they are Arnim and myself; he for the cheerfulness of your muse, I for its melancholy.[77]

With Goethe young Arnim was not so intimate as with Tieck.[78] He approached Goethe as a young apprentice, filled with deep reverence for the master, not like the older Romanticists, with a set program representing a literary school. In youthful enthusiasm he built a shrine for Goethe in his soul, and he felt himself called upon to bring Goethe's message to the whole world. Because of his scientific training, it is not surprising that he was at first

---

[74] Arnim-Brentano, p. 28. [75] *Ibid.*, pp. 43, 53; Holtei, III, 337.
[76] *Ibid.*, p. 23.
[77] Brentano's letter to Tieck, January 11, 1802.
[78] The relationship between Arnim and Goethe has never been sufficiently treated. Herman Grimm and Reinhold Steig intended to devote one of the volumes of *A. v. Arnim und die ihm nahe standen* to Arnim's relationship with Goethe as a man and poet. To a limited extent this subject is touched upon in the second volume *Arnim und Bettina*. More material is in the letters of the Weimar Goethe-Ausgabe, Vol. XIV; *Schriften der Goethe Ges.; Jahrb. Freies deutsches Hochstift; Bettinas Briefwechsel mit Goethe*, hrsg. von R. Steig; and Felix Scholz, *Clemens Brentano und Goethe*, Leipzig, 1927. Cf. Ch. VI, below, where the critical attitude of Arnim to Goethe is treated in detail.

interested in Goethe as a naturalist. As a young student he wrote long essays on Goethe's *Farbenlehre*.[79] Again in later life his interest in this side of Goethe's genius was renewed. He valued it more than Goethe's literary work, which he criticized as pretentious and full of dogmatic expressions.[80] When Goethe visited Göttingen in 1801, Arnim, together with other students, arranged a welcome for him, and he then received an invitation from Goethe to visit him.[81] Soon afterwards he set out on his "grand tour," which prevented closer personal contact with Goethe at this time, although Goethe's spirit and Goethe's works accompanied him on this trip. The landscape and places he saw reminded him of Goethe's former journeys or the descriptions of scenery in Goethe's works. While travelling along the Rhine, he began to understand and appreciate fully the beauty of Goethe's *Hermann und Dorothea*.[82] Riding through the Italian campagna, he and his brother sang Goethe's famous "Kennst Du das Land, wo die Citronen blüh'n," set to music by Reichardt.[83] During his trip Arnim also read and studied Goethe's *Wilhelm Meister*, the apprenticeship novel which proved to be so important for the problems of his own life.[84] He also read Goethe's most recently published works, the comedy *Was wir bringen* and the tragedy *Die natürliche Tochter*. The latter had on him, in his own words, "a very pure and tragic effect."[85]

Arnim's first literary attempt, *Hollins Liebeleben*, shows plainly traces of Goethe's influence, for his novel might be classified as a miniature *Werther*, put into new and peculiar garments. Arnim was aware of this poetic dependency and acknowledged freely in a letter to Clemens that this form of imitation was wrong and unworthy and might suppress the best of his own creative genius: "The demonical Werther and my misdirected admiration of Goethe's forms seduced me then to omit the best of *Hollin*," he declared, November 8, 1802, "in *Ariel* I shall create unhampered."[86]

[79] Cf. K. E. Henrici, *Auktions-Katalog, Nr. 149*, 1929, No. 5, p. 2.
[80] Bettina-Goethe, p. 238.
[81] Goethe's *Tagebücher*, June 8 and 21, 1801.
[82] Arnim-Brentano, p. 35.
[83] *Ibid.*, p. 42.   [84] *Ibid.*, p. 54.   [85] *Ibid.*, p. 71.
[86] *Ibid.*, pp. 51, 52; and Kummermann's remarks in *Halle und Jerusalem*, p. 251,

It must be emphasized at this point that the Heidelberg Romanticists would never have come into such sympathetic contact with Goethe during the years immediately following if Goethe had not abandoned, around 1800, his classical approach to literature in favor of popular poetry and returned to a more genuinely German lyric style. Goethe's poems published in the *Taschenbuch auf das Jahr 1804*, which were modeled after the style of folksongs, now became the pattern for the romanticists. It was this Goethe whom Arnim approached after returning to Germany, in the hope of benefit to his fatherland and to his own poetic efforts.

This enthusiasm for Goethe and Tieck Arnim shared with Brentano,[87] whom he met in the summer of 1801 in Göttingen. The two students soon became intimate friends. Bretano read his *Godwi* to Arnim, who had come to Göttingen to continue his studies in natural sciences, though his interest in literature was now gaining more and more the upper hand. The first plans for *Hollins Liebeleben* can be traced back to these student days in Göttingen. The end of the summer semester parted the two friends, and Arnim started on his "grand tour." During the next three years they met only once, when Arnim spent a week with Brentano's family in Frankfort, and then took a trip down the Rhine in Clemens' company, the journey so admirably described in Bettina's *Frühlingskranz*. The long and frequent letters exchanged between the two friends during the next two years reveal,

---

ought to be interpreted as Arnim's own opinions, not those of Brentano. Schönemann took them to be solely Brentano's (cf. p. 110): "Hieran erkenne ich mein eigenes jugendliches Treiben und Fühlen—ich habe auch so übertriebne Zeit gehabt, wo ich mit Werther liebetrunken schwärmte, nun bin ich weiter kommen. Es scheint mir nun un-Werther, die Liebe zu der Sünde, zu dem Altertume, die Verstocktheit gegen christliche Gesinnung, ein ewiges Verklären aller Nichtigkeit; so fühle ich, daß eine Kunst in unserer Zeit unmöglich sei; ich ließ mein Studium der Dichter und wendete mich hin zur göttlichen Natur, die ewig allein lebt. So weit bin ich gekommen."

[87] Arnim's criticism of Brentano's writings are found in letters to Brentano, Bettina, and others. It was a very understanding, friendly, yet frank criticism. In January, 1809, Arnim wanted to review all of Brentano's writings in the *Heidelbergische Jahrbücher,* but the editor Böckh preferred only a review of Brentano's latest book *Der Goldfaden*. Arnim complied, sending this review to Zimmer, but it was never printed. Instead an announcement by Wilhelm Grimm appeared (cf. NHeidelbJbb., 1902, pp. 199, 204). A brief review of Brentano's *Victoria und ihre Geschwister* by Arnim appeared in the *Gesellschafter* of the year 1817. Cf. reprint in *Unbekannte Aufsätze,* p. 82.

as one might expect, their thoughts and ideas on current literary problems and discuss also their own poetic creations. In these we find Arnim's views of the works of Brentano which appeared during this period, the second part of *Godwi* (1801), *Die lustigen Musikanten* (1802), and *Ponce de Leon* (1803).

Any discussion of Arnim's first criticism of Brentano's writings must take into consideration their intimate friendship and Arnim's youthful literary dependency on Brentano. In spite of this, frankness and honesty prevail to an astonishing degree. Arnim had himself participated in the second part of *Godwi*, and had written the "Rede auf dem Schützenfest zu G. vom Freunde A. gehalten," which, however, was not finally incorporated into the novel. Arnim did not regret the omission, writing Clemens that the book had become too serious for it.[88] Almost an entire year elapsed before he returned to a discussion of *Godwi*. In the meantime Brentano assumed the rôle of a severe critic of Arnim's productions. He felt obliged to judge Arnim's verse as superficial and slovenly[89] and explained his own fundamental principles as a literary critic: "I criticize only in order to do for myself what I request from others, namely to become just and severe toward myself."[90] Arnim, in youthful self-confidence, turned a deaf ear to criticism, declaring that "a thinking poet is a fool."[91] Soon, however, Brentano's frank strictures invited similar remarks from Arnim, who took up again the subject of *Godwi*. While praising highly Brentano's portrayal of "a young poet in the making," he nevertheless criticized details of the plot. It seemed to him that it was not well to have the young poet die. While he was in a fainting spell among the grief-stricken people, a happy piece of news should have come to bring about his recovery. It is all right for Diderot to have "Religieuse" turn out in the end to be nothing but a joke, an imaginary character, but to declare that of a serious and fascinating work, as Brentano does at the end of *Godwi*, is to destroy the effect intentionally, for the young poet in *Godwi* and Godwi himself have aroused the reader's interest more than the one who writes about them.[92] Arnim regretted that

---

[88] Arnim-Brentano, p. 25.   [89] *Ibid.*, p. 50, with reference to *Hollin*.
[90] *Idem.*   [91] *Ibid.*, p. 52.   [92] *Ibid.*, p. 53.

Brentano had not carried through the plan outlined in his preface to the second part of *Godwi,* instead of having one of the chief characters, the young poet, fail and die right at the beginning of his career. He recalled in this connection the principle set forth in *Wilhelm Meister* to the effect that the reader is more vitally interested in a hero who strives for and reaches a high goal than in one who fails.[93]

Arnim also criticized Brentano's *Die lustigen Musikanten* because of the vagueness of its plot and the inadequate treatment of the wealth of material. The scenes are too brief and too few and could have stood more elaboration and detail. Just as in the case of *Godwi,* Arnim was impressed by the seriousness of this *Singspiel.* He writes to Brentano; "They are not merry; on the other hand, it is one of the most thoroughly touching pieces that I know."[94] For *Ponce de Leon* on the contrary, Arnim had nothing but praise and admiration. Here he saw again in Brentano the great talented artist in whose footsteps he would have liked to follow. At that time he wrote to the author that he wished he could write something comparable to this perfect comedy, so full of suspense from beginning to end, and like a balloon finally disappearing in the bright sunlight.[95] He thought that Brentano had observed excellently the fundamentals of comedy-writing; and in this connection defined the nature of comedy: "It is to fuse with us completely; not to have the effect of medicine, like tragedies and farces, but to nourish us like food and drink, and cause us to grow, love, and become active."[96]

These lines were written on September 20, 1804. In December of the same year, Brentano, longing to see again his "song-brother," arrived in Berlin. A new era now began for both. The first plans for the *Wunderhorn* were made in those Berlin days. A year later, this work, which was to assure them of immortality in literary history, was given to the world.

[93] *Ibid.,* p. 54 (cf. Brentano's own interpretation, p. 58).
[94] *Ibid.,* p. 93.   [95] *Ibid.,* p. 113.   [96] *Ibid.,* p. 112.

IV
THE CRITIC AND THE HEIDELBERG CIRCLE

The great collection of folksongs, so important as a fountain of inspiration to the lyrical poetry of Germany in the following century, does not belong to our discussion. Suffice it to say that the year in Heidelberg which brought the first volume of the *Wunderhorn* into being was a golden period in the life of both young men. For Arnim it shines the more brilliantly because it was followed by the distressing events of 1806 and 1807, the military collapse of Prussia which swept him into the remote Northeast and finally awakened him fully to national consciousness. The maturing of this sentiment in its effect on his critical work will be examined in a later chapter. For the moment he was still under the ban of the *Wunderhorn;* and as soon as the way was clear for his return to the South, he set forth again for the university town on the Neckar.

When he rejoined the Heidelberg circle in January, 1808, it was his intention to take again an active part in reviving and propagating old German literature and art. He looked forward to a period of fruitful endeavor, as carefree and happy as that in the spring of 1805, when in a short time the first volume of the *Wunderhorn* was given to the world. But those joyful days were not to return. The experience of the war of 1806-7 had changed much in Germany. General uneasiness prevailed about the future of German culture. August Wilhelm Schlegel wrote at the time that the need of the hour was a direct, wide-awake, energetic and above all, patriotic poetry, not poetry of a dreamy sort.[1] Arnim himself had grown more mature and serious-minded. His views on art and life had taken on more definite shape, and were colored to a greater degree by patriotic feeling. This tendency found its chief expression in the efforts he made to perpetuate old German literature. His name had now penetrated literary circles and his opinions were respected by friends and enemies alike.

[1] Schlegel's letter to Fouqué, March 1806; Böcking, VIII, 144.

THE HEIDELBERG CIRCLE

Heidelberg and its cultural life had also experienced a change. The university, recently restored to its former prominence, had attracted many friends, but also not a few enemies of the "Wunderhornists." To the former belonged Görres and the Grimm brothers. Görres had arrived in Heidelberg in the fall of 1806. He was soon well-known as an inspiring lecturer and much admired for his versatile knowledge. Brentano and he became close friends and Arnim soon completed the trio. Brentano had already gained the interest and support of the Grimm brothers for the Heidelberg movement. In 1807 he wrote to Arnim that the Grimms were his "beloved, Old-German, intimate friends, . . . they know far more of everything than Tieck . . . you will grow very fond of these fine people, who are quietly at work preparing to publish later on a history of German poetry."[2] The future enemies of the Wunderhorn pair also had become well established in Heidelberg. Foremost among them were Johann Heinrich Voss, who had accepted a chair at the University of Heidelberg as early as 1805, and his son, Heinrich Voss, who was appointed professor there in February 1807.

In addition to working on the continuation of the *Wunderhorn*, Arnim hoped to devote himself largely to his much cherished journalistic pursuits, which he regarded as a very useful task for German cultural life and as a means of expression for his own ideas. As early as 1802 he bemoaned the fact that a people with as much reverence and love of art as the Germans were served by literary periodicals of extremely poor standing,[3] and in 1804 he regarded a journalistic career to reform this lamentable situation as his supreme calling.[4] Many years later, Görres, recalling the days in Heidelberg when they started out on their literary mission, characterized the situation as follows:

> The journals and newspapers, superficial, trivial, and uninspired beyond belief, compete in their base attitude. . . . The past, as it lived on through its poetic manifestations, seemed to Arnim, and with right, the most potent force to revive in some manner the stagnant present. And

[2] Arnim-Grimm, p. 4.
[3] Arnim-Brentano, p. 68: "Kein Volk habe so viel schlechte kritische Blätter wie das deutsche, und doch herrsche bei ihm stets die Ehrfurcht vor der Kunst."
[4] Arnim-Brentano, p. 106.

the poetry of the people just as it had never failed in its duty to earlier centuries, seemed also to offer its services here in order to bring the people into its own.[5]

Arnim hoped to obtain the co-operation of Brentano and the Grimm brothers, with whom these journalistic plans had been discussed in Cassel in November, 1807.[6] When the war of 1806-7 ended, he thought that the time had now come to start a new literary periodical to serve their purposes. In 1808 this ardent wish for a "periodical of the old style" (*Zeitung alter Art*)[7] was fulfilled when the *Zeitung für Einsiedler* appeared. Both Arnim and Brentano set forth on various occasions[8] the principles, the general make-up, and the aims which were to guide the editors. The *Zeitung für Einsiedler* was to take the form of an imaginary literary paper of the Middle Ages; it should become an attractive collection of an artistic character, making accessible to the public valuable contributions to art and literature from the past. Contemporary art and intellectualism were to be strictly excluded. In that manner Arnim hoped to create a periodical that should tower far above the superficial, wordy publications of his time. He realized that with these ideals he had thrown down the glove to the philistine public, but he hoped that the youth of his country would rally to his support. One question still to be solved was, how to make the new periodical palatable to the reading public. A keen sense of humor, comical announcements, a play on the curiosity of the public were to aid here. The paper should, in Arnim's words, become a "storehouse of merriment" (*eine Fundgrube von Lustigkeit*)[9], but the editors should not lose sight of the chief purpose of the paper, which was after all a very serious one, namely, to educate people in art and to bring them to an understanding of true cultural values. As Arnim wrote to Bettina, behind a comical mask for attracting people a serious face was

---

[5] Görres in a memorial sketch after Arnim's death; Menzel's Literaturblatt, 1831, No. 27-30, pp. 104-117.

[6] Brentano's letters to Zimmer, Nov. 1807.

[7] Arnim-Brentano, p. 238.

[8] *Ibid.*, "Ankündigung der allgemeinsten Zeitung. Zeitung für Einsiedler," Heidelb-Jbb., 1808, pp. 33-4 (Int. Bl. 4); also pp. 75-7 (Int. Bl. 9); Brentano's letter to Zimmer, November, 1807.

[9] Arnim-Bettina, p. 90.

to be hidden.[10] Likewise, in "advertising" the new paper he requested his readers to take serious account of everything it contained, even if it was presented in a frivolous manner. Only then would they grasp the true meaning.[11]

Similarly the editors emphasized that they intended to depart from the customary type of literary criticism. In the first place, they considered criticism very often superfluous. A work of art or literature can speak for itself, is self-explanatory, and should not need commentaries. Keeping this premise in mind, we can understand that Arnim's purpose, to "acquaint the reader with the remote and forgotten," was the next logical step in this "new" criticism.[12] In a letter to Tieck, Arnim admitted that criticism was not superfluous in connection with literary fragments or writings which might be difficult to understand because of a change in language or other peculiarities. He was also willing to let criticism of contemporary writings stand if it was in a spicy, humorous vein.[13]

Arnim's attitude toward criticism is expressed at various places in his *Zeitung für Einsiedler*. The introductory poem "Der freie Dichtergarten" contains several stanzas entitled "Kritik." The youthful poet's lyric effusion is here compared to the nightingale, bursting forth into song, in its rapture undisturbed by the cuckoo's call. The cuckoo, i. e., the critic, is questioned by children. Even the hawk—tricky criticism—is disarmed by the fresh beauty of the song and cannot harm the carefree nightingale:

> Fort kann der Falk sie tragen,
> Doch sieh den Falk
> Er hört ihr zu betroffen,
> Der lose Schalk,
> Und hält den Schnabel offen.[14]

In the "Rundgesang gegen Unterdrücker des Werdenden in der Literatur," the future poets are to flee away from the dark present

---

[10] *Ibid.*, p. 90.
[11] *Tröst Einsamkeit*, 4. Compare also Arnim's letter to Tieck: "So leicht meine Zeitung aussieht, ich wünsche viel Ernsthaftes damit und fühle mich rein von leerer Sonderbarkeit und parteiischer Begrenztheit." March 31, 1808, Holtei, I, 14.
[12] Arnim's letter to Goethe, April 1, 1808, *Schriften der Goethe-Ges.*, XIV, 126.
[13] Arnim's letter to Tieck, March 31, 1808; Holtei, I, 14.
[14] *Tröst Einsamkeit*, p. 22.

to the divine old songs and faith of the past, like a lark ascending the skies:

> Alter Glanz ist nun verflogen,
> Gestern ist ein leeres Wort,
> Scham hat unsre Wang' umzogen,
> Doch der neue Tag scheint dort.
> Unerschöpflich ist die Jugend,
> Jeder Tag ein Schöpfungstag,
> Wer mit froher reiner Tugend
> Fördert was sein Volk vermag.[15]

In the "Geschichte des Herrn Sonett" Arnim carries out his principle that criticism should be put into pleasing, humorous garments. Various contemporary literary quarrels are touched upon here, but his satire is chiefly pointed towards the older Voss, who reminds him of the philistine Wagner, and he introduces into his poems lines from the Wagner scene in Goethe's *Faust* with telling effect. The spirit of Faust admonishes the noisy fool (Voss?) for his pompous wordiness:

> Es trägt Verstand und rechter Sinn
> Mit wenig Kunst sich selber vor;
> Und wenns euch Ernst ist was zu sagen,
> Ists nötig Worten nachzujagen?
> Ja eure Reden, die so blendend sind,
> In denen ihr der Menschheit Schnitzel kräuselt,
> Sind unerquicklich wie der Nebelwind.[16]

Thus far we have seen that for Arnim the chief purpose of criticism was to open to his readers the literature of the past. Criticism in its ordinary sense he considered superfluous, or desirable only if it clarified the meaning of an otherwise obscure piece of literature. Furthermore, criticism, particularly criticism of contemporaries, should be put into a pleasing, humorous frame. He also suggests that criticism should not be poisoned by cheap publicity, that it should rather, like a true educative force, be brought into play as within an intimate circle, or even more confidentially, just as between two persons, the critic acting as the encouraging teacher. As a fine example of such positive criticism

---

[15] *Ibid.*, p. 314.
[16] *Tröst Einsamkeit*, p. 383; *Faust*, Part I, lines 197-203.

he published in the *Zeitung für Einsiedler* selections from letters of Schiller to a young poetess ("Auszüge aus Briefen Schillers an eine junge Dichterin").[17] In these letters, Schiller, with fine psychological insight, first called attention to the young writer's talent, whenever it revealed itself, thus encouraging her. He criticized only by making suggestions for minor changes, whenever she might feel herself in the right mood for it. This discussion illustrates the kind of literary criticism which Arnim put into practice in the *Zeitung für Einsiedler*. The periodical was therefore of necessity different from any other of its time. Virtually all its pages are pregnant with implied criticism of literary tendencies of the period. The periodical is thus a monument to literary criticism as Arnim conceived it.

The *Zeitung für Einsiedler* was published only for a period of five months, Goethe's good wishes to the editors notwithstanding. Apparently it did not appeal even to the chosen group of readers on whose interest Arnim had counted. For this failure, a bitter experience for Arnim, he blamed solely the reading public, to whom he addressed a sort of valedictory after publication of the *Zeitung* had ceased.[18] Taking off the "Einsiedler's" mask, he now declares very frankly his disappointment with the body of German readers. He has lost all confidence in it and intends in the near future to write of the origin and decay of the reading public. Apparently, he declares, the masses cannot appreciate real literature unaided; they must always have an authority for their guidance, they are incapable of enjoying anything genuine and feel only the urge of the times to pass judgment and criticise destructively. Thus they have remained blind to the purpose of his journal, which did not publish daily news and historical events. It had sought rather to reveal the dignity of the common national culture, to bring about a return "to a more remote, forgotten art of word and picture, to undertake a search for the national element and that which has been forgotten in every kind of popular enjoyment, in folklore, for all that which once affected our Germany so deeply, . . . but above all, [it sought] the awakening and

[17] *Tröst Einsamkeit*, pp. 196-9.
[18] *Tröst Einsamkeit*, "An das geehrte Publikum," p. 6.

revitalizing of the naive poetic and religious spirit of which our times are still capable."[19]

The failure of his periodical was a very bitter experience for Arnim. However, he was only twenty-seven years old, and still a novice in the literary field. Many possibilities were open to him, and his most important writings were yet to appear. Even in Heidelberg, he felt that he need not abandon his journalistic activities. Now he could throw all his efforts into the much better-managed *Heidelbergische Jahrbücher*. This prospect mitigated the disappointment over his experience with the *Zeitung für Einsiedler;* and he resolved to avail himself of this excellent opportunity, hoping that his Heidelberger collaborators and friends would do the same. Thus they would be able to make the *Jahrbücher* a mouthpiece for their literary ideas. His numerous reviews in this periodical during the years 1809 and 1810 show how fully these expectations were realized.

The young Heidelberg romanticists began their collaboration with the *Heidelbergische Jahrbücher* under the most favorable circumstances. They were in sympathy with the spirit of the periodical, and Friederich Creuzer, in charge of its philosophic-historical devision, approved and encouraged their endeavors. Creuzer, a classical philologist, shared in general Arnim's historical outlook, and the two were strongly attached to each other. They first met in March, 1808. Creuzer made a very scholarly and pleasant impression on Arnim, who characterized him as a very spirited man, possessing a soul susceptible to impressions.[20]

The spirit and ideas expressed in the announcement of the *Jahrbücher* and in Creuzer's first essay[21] were much like those of Arnim's *Zeitung für Einsiedler,* which had come into the world almost simultaneously. It was Creuzer's idea that a new national and productive spirit should prevail in the publication, a spirit not found in contemporary periodicals. The critical attitude to be adopted was laid down in the "eighteen rules" of the announcement, which contain the following declarations: "The age warns

[19] HeidelbJbb., 1808 (int. Bl. 8), pp. 75-7; "Anzeige des Inhalts des April und Maiheftes der Einsiedlerzeitung."
[20] Arnim-Bettina, p. 105.
[21] HeidelbJbb. 1808, I, Abt. 5, pp. 3-24: "Philologie und Mythologie, in ihrem Stufengang und gegenseitigen Verhalten."

of the degradation of literary criticism for the sake of profit and literary partisanship and dictatorship. Scholarly genius prohibits such a debasement."[22] Reviews were to set forth whether an author's writings contained anything worth while; anything novel, genuine, and creative, and therefore adapted for the enrichment of knowledge. The reviewer should not squander undue praise; his judgment should be fearless and firm.

While Arnim devoted himself to the investigation of German history and ancient culture in their relation to art, Creuzer envisaged this relationship as a problem of classical philology:

> How have the philologists administered the religious inheritance of the peoples entrusted to them? Have they appreciated its worth, and through its virtues sought to increase the worth of their own knowledge? Particularly, have they established it on a documentary basis and transmitted it to mankind, to whom it belongs, in its original and pure state?[23]

Creuzer also wanted to "acquaint the public with the remote and forgotten," voicing the trend of the historical school, and sharing in particular the point of view of the Grimm brothers, who were his highly esteemed collaborators on the *Jahrbücher*. It is not surprising, therefore, that Creuzer entrusted his young Heidelberg friends, Görres and Arnim, whose ideas were so much akin to his own, with reviews of outstanding works that were making a sensation and stimulating scholarly quarrels. Curiously enough, the third of the trio, Brentano, never wrote for the *Jahrbücher*, ignoring repeated invitations to do so.[24]

In 1808, because he was still very much occupied with his own periodical, Arnim contributed to the *Jahrbücher* mainly a few notices.[25] These referred to his *Zeitung für Einsiedler* and the *Wunderhorn*, and to the "Alte Bühne," which he planned at this time but never brought into being. His only extensive review was of F. H. Jacobi's *Über gelehrte Gesellschaften*. Here Arnim takes Rottmanner's criticism of Jacobi's work as his starting

---

[22] NHeidelbJbb., XI (1902), 182-4; R. Steig, "Zeugnisse zur Pflege deutscher Literatur in den *Heidelbergischen Jahrbüchern*."

[23] HeidelbJbb., I, Abt. 5, 1808, p. 4.

[24] NHeidelbJbb., XI (1902), 207; Creuzer's letter to Jacob Grimm, April 10, 1809.

[25] A more detailed discussion of Arnim's contributions to the *Heidelbergische Jahrbücher* appears below; cf. pp. 42 ff., 89 ff., 92 ff., 100 ff., 123.

point.[26] In writing this article Arnim welcomes the opportunity to speak for a united Germany in opposition to the narrow, local patriotism of Jacobi.[27] In his work, Jacobi, a North German philosopher then resident in Munich, had ridiculed Bavaria's low state of civilization and had found fault with the institutions of the Middle Ages, such as feudalism and the religious hierarchy. Patriotic students at Landshut, among them Rottmanner, criticized strongly these ideas. Arnim supported the students, applauded their patriotism, and reproached Jacobi for his narrow outlook. Jacobi, as president of the Munich Academy, Arnim pointed out, seemed to be interested only in general humanistic principles and a program of enlightenment.

In 1809 and 1810 Arnim contributed more important reviews, chiefly on topics assigned by Creuzer. However, his first article, the criticism of Jacobi, had stirred the indignation of Voss and others, and they contrived that in the future Arnim's contributions were to appear anonymously.[28] They could not oust him altogether because of Creuzer's intervention. In the summer of 1808 the "Einsiedler" group had reached the zenith of its literary career in Heidelberg. Thereafter they had to give way to the elder Voss and his circle, whose maturity, literary prestige, and academic influence finally brought victory in this literary quarrel. Görres left Heidelberg at the end of the summer semester,[29] Brentano almost at the same time,[30] and Arnim went back to Berlin in November.

Arnim, who still contributed frequently to the *Jahrbücher* during the two years following, remained in close contact and correspondence with Creuzer. His letters reveal his attachment to Heidelberg and to Creuzer, and his vital interest in the maintenance of the original program of the *Jahrbücher*. However, only three months after his departure from Heidelberg, he had come

---

[26] HeidelbJbb., I (1808), pp. 362-372; Arnim reviewed the following three publications: F. H. Jacobi, *Über gelehrte Gesellschaften*, München 1807; Rottmanner, "Kritik der Abhandlung F. H. Jacobis über gelehrte Gesellschaften," Landshut; Aman, "Nachschrift über Etwas, was Fr. Heinrich Jacobi gesagt hat," 1808.

[27] In this connection the *Zeitung für Einsiedler* published an abstract of Jean Paul's *Friedenspredigt* and Viller's *Überblick der Universitäten*.

[28] NHeidelbJbb., XI (1902), 194; Creuzer's letter to Arnim, December 18, 1808.

[29] *Schriften der Goethe-Ges.*, XIV, 132.

[30] Arnim-Brentano, pp. 254-5.

to realize that his efforts were in vain, and in sadness he wrote to Creuzer:

> I was not mistaken in my premonition that you would be the only one in Heidelberg to continue to think of me. Not a word has come from Zimmer, and perhaps you also are leaving soon. . . . Then Voss will rule Heidelberg. I am sorry, for I am still much attached to the faithful mountain and the airy castle.[31]

In April 1809, to Arnim's deep regret, the management of the philosophic-historical division of the *Jahrbücher* passed into the hands of Böckh and Wilken, Creuzer having accepted a call to the university of Leyden. Arnim felt keenly that Heidelberg was now deserted by all his friends and mourned the severance of all ties. He was afraid that the *Jahrbücher* might soon become nothing more than an expensive edition of the *Göttinger Anzeigen,* unless the new editors showed discretion and determination.[32] Everyone in favor of the romantic trend in the *Jahrbücher* suspected the new management. "I feel sorry for the *Jahrbücher*," Arnim wrote to Creuzer, "because of the hopes others and I cherished, to see preserved in them freedom and impartiality of judgment."[33] In a letter to Görres, Creuzer complained: "It is going to be something very fine when these three people[34] undertake to arbitrate on theology, philosophy, literature, and art."[35]

These suspicions were indeed justified. The entry of the new editorial board signified a departure from the "Einsiedler" group. This became still more marked when Wilken's influence assumed greater proportions and Böckh gradually withdrew. In 1810 Wilken's and Thibaut's proposal to exclude Arnim was defeated by Böckh.[36] Nevertheless, the result was that for more than a year Arnim was not invited to contribute reviews. It is not surprising, therefore, that the young Heidelbergers were very indignant and expressed their disgust in strong language. They were justified in their attitude, for, indeed, literature and art fared badly in the hands of the new editors, and Arnim could well complain that important works like Goethe's *Wahlverwandtschaften* and

---

[31] NHeidelbJbb., XI (1902), 198-9; Arnim's letter to Creuzer, Jan. 25, 1809.
[32] NHeidelbJbb., XI (1902), 208; Arnim's letter to Cruezer, April 22, 1809.
[33] *Ibid.* [34] Wilken, Böckh, and Thibaut.
[35] *Görres-Briefe,* hrsg. von M. Görres and Fr. Binder, 1858-74, II, 161-2.
[36] NHeidelbJbb., XI (1900), 146; Görres' letter to Arnim.

the writings of Jean Paul were not even mentioned in the *Jahrbücher*. Nevertheless, the standard of the *Jahrbücher* was still higher than that of other contemporary periodicals.

Arnim's connection with the *Jahrbücher* was re-established in November, 1811, when he visited Heidelberg on a trip to Strassburg and Frankfort. He was asked again to collaborate, and contributed two minor reviews in 1812 and 1813.[37]

In the meantime his literary pursuits and possibilities had gravitated from Heidelberg to Berlin. The depressing years of 1807-8, when social and intellectual life in Berlin stagnated, were followed by a period of forceful and brilliant activities. At Christmas, 1809, the royal couple again took up residence in their capital. The newly founded university had enticed several old acquaintances of Arnim's to come to Berlin, among them Savigny. Other important persons, like Heinrich von Kleist, Fichte, and Adam Müller, were now also there. They all found themselves united in the "Patrioten- und Kriegspartei" and in the "Christlich-deutsche Tischgesellschaft," where Arnim presided. Their united efforts were bent toward one goal: a spiritual and cultural renaissance of Germany and liberation from Napoleon's yoke.

However, the day of national uprising, so longed for by Arnim, was not to dawn for several years. The intermediate period, which witnessed the final break-up of the Heidelberg circle and the preparation for the resurgence of Prussia, provided ample leisure and the necessary stimulus for the execution of ideas and plans of long standing. Hand in hand with this went a greater clarification of the literary theories of the younger Romanticists. All the writings of this intermediate period, whether Arnim's or Brentano's, the Grimm brothers' or Görres', must be interpreted as the outgrowth or continuation of the literary movement that started with the *Wunderhorn* and the *Einsiedlerzeitung*. The five young men kept in close touch with each other during those years. After September, 1809 Brentano resided in Berlin in the same lodgings with Arnim, almost without interruption for two years.[38] Wilhelm

---

[37] Arnim-Brentano, p. 292. The two reviews were of *Gottfried August Bürgers Ehestandsgeschichte*, HeidelbJbb., 1812, Abt. 2, pp. 1199-1200, and Bornemann's *Plattdeutsche Gedichte, ibid.,* Abt. I, pp. 305-9.

[38] Arnim-Brentano, p. 286

Grimm came at this time for a visit. Without doubt the reunion of the trio meant a revival of discussions of their literary and philological plans. The question of a fourth volume of the *Wunderhorn* was debated. Von der Hagen joined in the discussion of the *Nibelungenlied*. An active search began for old books. After Wilhelm Grimm had left Berlin the exchange of ideas was continued in a correspondence of great literary interest.

A brief examination of the writings and plays which were planned for the near future by these five members of the former Heidelberg circle is instructive. It was indeed a time of great literary activity. Arnim had compiled from old sources the stories of his *Wintergarten,* published in 1809. His novel *Armut, Reichtum, Schuld und Busse der Gräfin Dolores* followed in 1810. The same year he completed the drama *Halle und Jerusalem.* In 1811 four short stories were published, and in 1813 the first volume of the *Schaubühne.* Brentano was working on the *Romanzen vom Rosenkranz,* on a collection of fairy tales, and on *Die Gründung Prags.* He was constantly on the look-out for rare old books, so that Arnim gave him the nickname "sleuthhound for godly books" (*Gottesbücherspürhund*).[39] He contemplated a philological study on the folksong, and Wilhelm Grimm wanted to entrust him with the writing of a modern version of the *Nibelungenlied.*[40] Now it was that the Grimm brothers joined the ranks of nationally known writers with the publication of Jacob's *Über den altdeutschen Meistergesang* and Wilhelm's *Altdänische Heldenlieder, Balladen und Märchen.* Between 1812 and 1815 they brought out the *Kinder- und Hausmärchen,* and three years later, 1816-1818, their *Deutsche Sagen* appeared. Görres' activities and interests were more akin to those of the Grimm brothers than to those of any other member of the Heidelberg circle during these years. No

[39] Arnim-Bettina, p. 342.
[40] Arnim agreed with Wilhelm Grimm that the *Nibelungenlied* either had to receive a new version which would enable it to drive its own roots from new sap, or that it should be handed down from generation to generation in its dry, unrelieved antiquity. In a letter to Tieck, December 3, 1807, Arnim voiced his regret that Tieck's version of the *Nibelungen* had not yet been published, for "I do not like Hagen's, with its baroque dialect, its boresome annotations, and the omission of all other tales which you had so cleverly interwoven." Karl von Holtei, *Briefe an L. Tieck,* I, 10-13. Cf. also the report on the discussion of the *Nibelungenlied* in Hagen's presence at Arnim's home on Nov. 12, 1809; Arnim-Grimm, pp. 26, 29.

wonder that Görres carried on a very active correspondence with the Grimms. In Görres' *Die teutschen Volksbücher* and *Mythengeschichte der asiatischen Welt* the Heidelberg circle found much stimulating material for discussion.

This long list of novel and serious writings from the pens of the Heidelberg circle—all having folklore as their subject matter and all appearing within a decade—invited eager interest and much discussion among the reading public, and most of all, among the members of the romantic circle itself. There was dire need of profound discussion, for it must not be overlooked that these young men and their subject matter had risen to sudden prominence. Popular poetry (*Volksdichtung*) as a genre, its origin and characteristics, its value and purpose for literature, philology, and history, and especially as a national treasure, all this had to be clarified. Such questions as the following provoked discussion: Should a folksong be handed down to posterity in its original form, or was it permissible to subject it to alterations, additions, or subtractions, retaining the ancient spirit? Should the *Nibelungenlied* or the *Edda* be published in their original form, merely with a commentary, or should they, for a better understanding, be modernized or only be translated into modern High German? This again entailed a discussion of the rank and rights of the modern poet in comparison to those of the poet of the people (*Volksdichter*), and finally the very fundamental question of distinction between "popular" or "natural poetry" and "art poetry" (*Volks- oder Naturdichtung und Kunstdichtung*).

Already while collaborating on the *Wunderhorn* Arnim and Brentano had taken different points of view with regard to rendering the folksong. In 1805 Brentano objected that Arnim had introduced changes into some folksongs. Later, in 1808, after publishing the third volume of the *Wunderhorn*, Arnim tried to justify his stand in a letter to Clemens. Arnim is for new creations which preserve the old form and old spirit, yet adapt themselves to modern taste and understanding, so that they have a universal appeal to the public.[41] In support he cites Macpherson's *Ossian* and Goethe, who had stated that he liked the most extreme combinations of the ancient and the modern, "for only in these

---

[41] Arnim-Brentano, pp. 225, 229.

THE HEIDELBERG CIRCLE

has the vitality of antiquity stood the test."[42] Arnim also called attention to the uncertainties as to what and how much single poets had contributed to the *Iliad,* and referred to the use of ancient sources by Shakespeare, Plato, and Schelling.[43] He believed that a poem can be put into a different context without changing its content or characteristics, as a painter can change his grouping by means of different light effects.[44]

Arnim and Brentano cherished the hope that collections similar to the *Wunderhorn* would soon be started by their friends, and that the same program for reviving interest in folklore, by a simple editing rather than by learned discussion, would guide them. Görres had published *Die teutschen Volksbücher* in 1807, much to Arnim's chagrin, for it was a book about chapbooks rather than a new chapbook. He expressed his vexation to Brentano and Tieck in two similar letters, characterizing the book as superfluous, superficial, aesthetically wordy; superfluous, because it was not evident for whom the literary portion had been written; superficial because while treating one collection, it generalized about all of them, betraying, "with one word, the whole modern arrogance born out of a lack of talent and imagination." "It would have been better if he had followed our plan and reprinted fully and whole-heartedly from the best sources for the people, giving his own opinion only in a condensed form."[45] Arnim had the same criticism for Büsching and Hagen's collection of folksongs, which he found permeated with a "faulty critical spirit, holding life in its clutches like death, usurping beauty as well as ugliness with the same fervor."[46]

The literary-theoretical controversy was opened on a broad basis in the correspondence between Arnim and the Grimm brothers, conditioned by the fundamentally different outlook of the two parties. This became even more pronounced in the following years. The Grimms had a scientific approach to art, literature, and history, while in Arnim the poetic element dominated. Thus Arnim wanted to interpret to his contemporaries the past in an

[42] *Ibid.,* pp. 234-6. Like Goethe, Görres was a keen sponsor of new creations and combinations in old folksongs.
[43] *Ibid.* [44] *Ibid.*
[45] Arnim-Brentano, p. 221; Arnim's letter to Tieck, Dec. 3, 1807. Cf. Karl von Holtei, *Briefe an L. Tieck,* I, 12. [46] Arnim-Brentano, p. 220.

attractive poetic manner, while the Grimms, as philologians, had a scholarly, objective attitude.

The immediate cause of the debate was Jacob Grimm's essay, "Gedanken: wie sich die Sagen zur Poesie und Geschichte verhalten," published in Arnim's *Zeitung für Einsiedler*.[47] Here Jacob maintained that there is a clear-cut distinction between the "poetry of nature" and the "poetry of art," more specifically, epic poetry versus dramatic poetry, poetry of the uneducated versus poetry of the intelligentsia. "The former," Grimm contended, "is transmitted without any effort, like a sound carried from afar, so faithful, pure, and innocent are the heroic deeds and legends recorded, constituting a common sacred treasure." But the "poetry of art" expresses only individual feeling, opinion, and experience. "Just as these two forms of poetry are of fundamental, intrinsic difference, they are also of necessity separated by time and can never appear simultaneously."[48]

In a commentary, added to this essay of Jacob Grimm, Arnim demands historical proof, for in his opinion both types of poetry are current at present. In a letter to Jacob he elaborated this idea, adding that he could demonstrate both types even in the worst poetry, and a third element which disturbed and obliterated the distinction between *Natur- und Kunstpoesie*.[49] It is obvious that Arnim could not share Grimm's point of view, for it would have meant that not a single one of Arnim's own creations could anywhere near reach the standard nor compare in intrinsic value with what was in Grimm's opinion the superior "poetry of nature." Not even Goethe's works could qualify under this definition. Furthermore, Arnim as a philosopher and scientist had learned that art and nature, reflection and intuition, experience and revelation, fact and faith, must exist simultaneously and in all periods of the history of mankind. In his student days at Halle and Göttingen these questions had been much discussed. Schelling also had occupied himself with "national poetry," "popular poetry," "poetry of nature" in contrast with the "Poetry of Art."[50]

[47] *Zeitung für Einsiedler*, pp. 199-204.
[48] *Ibid.*, p. 200.   [49] Arnim-Grimm, p. 14.
[50] Arnim and the Heidelberger used Herder's "National-," "Volks-," and "Naturpoesie" interchangeably, preferring "Naturpoesie" as the all-inclusive term. A

With the publication of Arnim's *Gräfin Dolores* and *Halle und Jerusalem* in 1810 the divergent opinion of the Grimms' became still more apparent. Wilhelm did not quite share his brother's severe criticism of Arnim's recent literary creations, but both had now learned to esteem and honor to a still higher degree all national poetry, sagas and legends, because they were convinced that only in this type of literature artistic perfection was attained. "National poetry (*Nationaldichtung*) is written by God himself; no patching and mending is apparent as in human productions."[51] Hence they considered it their duty to protest emphatically against any alterations in the sagas. Jacob's chief objection to *Gräfin Dolores* and *Halle und Jerusalem* was that Arnim had offended against these principles. He had made superficial and pretentious use of historic material in *Halle und Jerusalem*. His novel was untrue, and its plot incredible.[52]

This conclusion grew also out of the knowledge of the Grimms' that Arnim had little interest in historical facts, and hence did not study carefully historical documents. The culprit made no attempt to clear himself of this charge, but admitted that he read the "Nibelungen" for the sake of poetry and not to collect data about its origin or its author.[53] His interest in the Minnedichtung and the Meistergesang, on which Jacob was working at that time, followed the same lines. Here he judged also from the poetic point of view, admiring the art of word-play in the Minnedichtung, criticizing the boresome and often clumsy composition of the Meistergesang. He disagreed with Jacob's thesis that Minne-

definition, as far as possible according to Herder's usage, may not be amiss. "Naturpoesie" are the saga and epic; the emphasis lies on the aesthetic and beautiful, and it is characterized by innocence and unconsciousness, pure objectivity, and infinite contemplation of its subject matter (cf. *Herders Werke*, hrsg. von Suphan, I, 399; VI, 27). "Volkspoesie" is the saga; the emphasis lies on the psychological and emotional; it is characterized by a penetration and a recording of the event, disregarding often place and time, and it lives on even if the nation in question has changed its boundary lines and affiliations (IV, 10, 12, 35, 45). "Nationalpoesie" emphasizes the national historical event, preferably the heroic. It takes account of place and time and obviously is recorded for, and adapted to, a definite audience (IV, 34). Cf. also Ernst Lichtenstein, "Die Idee der Naturpoesie bei den Brüdern Grimm und ihr Verhältnis zu Herder," *Dt. Vierteljahresschr. f. Lit. Wiss. u. Geistesgesch.*, VI (1928), 513-47; also Elisabeth Blochmann, "Die deutsche Volksdichtungsbewegung in Sturm und Drang und Romantik", *ibid.*, I (1923), 419-52.

[51] Arnim-Grimm, p. 89.   [52] *Ibid.*, pp. 72, 99.   [53] *Ibid.*, p. 76.

dichtung was predominantly "natural poetry" (*Naturpoesie*), while Meistergesang was "art poetry" (*Kunstpoesie*). In this controversy it was his belief that:

neither the one nor the other form of poetry can exist by itself unalloyed. Both always coexist in the creations of an individual, even though one or the other may predominate for a time. If in Minne poetry the impulse of nature, in the Mastersong a consciousness of art predominates, then it would be indeed interesting to note the occurrence and the details for the sake of history.[54]

Almost simultaneously with Jacob's *Über deutschen Meistergesang* Görres published his *Die Mythengeschichte der asiatischen Welt,* in those days a book of far-reaching importance for the formulation of literary-historical conceptions. Naturally the Grimm brothers rejoiced at the advent of such a book, for it confirmed their belief that there is *unity* in the fundamental mystical thoughts of all people, and that all myth has come into this world by divine revelation. The spirit of poetry, the divine, is the same in all peoples; the myth is the first sound uttered by this divine spirit when it begins to break the fetters of nature, and this first sound is poetry. Thus all myth was originally poetry, and all poetry was originally mythical.

Arnim discussed Jacob Grimm's and Görres' books in the same letter, addressed to the former. Again he emphasizes that the natural impulse (*Naturtrieb*) and art-consciousness (*Kunstbewußtsein*) coexist, a fact which, he declares, has been overlooked by Görres.[55] Jacob Grimm had gone so far as to attribute not only the origin of religion, of myth, poetry, and language to divine revelation, but also all forms of language and poetry, such as alliteration and rhyme. He believed that he could prove his contention by the fact that identical myths and poems are found in all languages. This could be possible only by transmission from a single source, namely, divine revelation, otherwise the same poems would have been invented and imagined by different individuals in different languages. In other words, Jacob gave no credit to the individual poet, something which Arnim considers a grievous injustice to the greatest individuals of all times.[56] In this connection Arnim points out that his own enthusiasm for

[54] Arnim-Grimm, p. 109. [55] Arnim-Grimm, p. 109. [56] *Ibid.*, p. 109.

popular poetry (*Naturpoesie*) is based upon the fact that it is good poetry which has stood the test of time, and not because it is, as Grimm seems to believe, poetry of a different nature and art than the one practised at present. This does not mean that Arnim denied outright the divine origin and successive development of myths. He agreed with Görres that all myth was derived from India and from there brought to other countries; nevertheless he criticized Görres' book as one-sided because it emphasizes too much this one aspect, popular poetry (*Naturpoesie*).[57]

The exchange of ideas between Arnim and Jacob Grimm had thus led to still more detailed and complicated distinctions. Unsurmountable obstacles now existed in the way of a common agreement as to *Natur- und Kunstpoesie*.

Wilhelm Grimm tried to mediate in this controversy between his brother and Arnim. He himself leaned more towards Arnim's point of view. With regard to Görres' *Die Mythengeschichte der asiatischen Welt*, Wilhelm rejected Jacob's single source of all myth: the divine revelation, and postulated a double one: the inner source, the *one* spirit of which all human beings partake;[58] and the external source, transmission of poetry by means of communication between nations. Wilhelm then summarized his conception of *Natur- und Kunstpoesie*, agreeing with Arnim that in "natural and national poetry" the element of reason, conscious artistic reflection, is present, citing the *Nibelungenlied* and Homer, which his brother Jacob classified as "natural poetry." On the other hand, Wilhelm saw in Goethe's "Fischer" and "König in Thule" folksongs, equaling the best in the *Wunderhorn* collection.[59]

Before starting on his extensive trip with Bettina to her native city of Frankfort, in August, 1811, Arnim desired to clarify his position in this dispute about *Natur- und Kunstpoesie*. From his final letters his ideas may be summarized as follows: Poetry is nourished by eternal springs, flowing at all times, even in those when no verses are made, and perhaps more purely in them. "At the moment, however, when inspiration creates an outer form and

[57] *Ibid.*, pp. 109, 125.
[58] Corresponding to Jacob's "divine revelation," the *only* source of *Naturpoesie*.
[59] Arnim-Grimm, p. 124.

tries to communicate its inner joy, it becomes a vehicle of observation, and is no longer entirely true to the unconscious spring by which it is nourished."[60] Therefore *absolute* natural poetry (*Naturpoesie*) does not exist; there exists only a difference of greater or less degree in the development of both, "natural" and "art poetry" (*Natur- und Kunstpoesie*).[61]

Arnim admitted that there is a difference between the ancient poets of the people (*Volksdichter*) and those of modern times. Nevertheless, it is not a question of talent and inspiration, but rather of environment. In former ages a people lived more simply and primitively; there was none of the complexity of the modern world in the national life; hence thought and social life were more uniform. Anyone with poetic inspiration could embrace the whole, and therefore was a poet of the people, and the creations of several popular poets (*Volksdichter*) could easily form a poetic unit. However, in modern times individual talent is restricted to a narrower field. But whoever understands and embraces three elements: the history, life, and love of a people, will have a universal appeal even today.[62] Thus Arnim ranks the modern poets with these of antiquity, and rejects Jacob's glorification of the latter, the *Volksdichter*. By reason of his national, philosophical outlook Arnim could not very well agree with Jacob Grimm. Unless he was to despair of the possibility of a spiritual renaissance in his fatherland, he had to have faith that the glorious past was not a closed chapter, never to be reopened, but that a continuous spiritual stream was flowing and effective still today.

Jacob Grimm had approached the problem historically. Popular poetry (*Volkspoesie*) was a thing of the past and could not be repeated. Herder, Goethe, A. W. Schlegel had an aesthetic approach. They regarded *Volkspoesie* as the expression of a noble but primitive civilization. Arnim, whose attitude was somewhat comparable to that of Tieck or Fouqué, believed with ardent expectation that the present complex civilization could yet be permeated with the noble spirit of *Volkspoesie* of past ages, and that this would replace the scholarly poetry of the intelligentsia. All poetical endeavors should be directed towards the attainment of this lofty aim. Not only in Germany, but also abroad Arnim

[60] Arnim-Grimm, p. 142.   [61] *Ibid.*, p. 134.   [62] Arnim-Grimm, pp. 134-5.

observed that the golden days of the poetry of the people had withered and that a poetry of the intelligentsia was predominating. The fate of *Volkspoesie* in France he pictured as follows: As late as the Fifteenth Century *Volkspoesie* still existed in France; thereafter it was confined to Paris and finally to the so-called noble society of Paris. When this society ceased to exist, *Volkspoesie* also vanished and now exists only in historical documents.[63] In another place he wrote:

> In this turmoil of novel things, in this supposed rapid establishment of paradise on earth, also in France all folksongs were extinguished even before the Revolution. Perhaps the disappearance of folksongs hastened the coming of this state of social turmoil. Even now the French are poorly endowed with them—what could bind them to that treasure, which ought to be of lasting value to them as a people? In England, too, the singing bards and minstrel songs have become rare; in Italy the national folksong gives place to the opera, to please people of little depth; even in Spain folksongs are said to be lost and nothing important has been substituted.[64]

The poetry of the intelligentsia has also a universal appeal: not to the people, the masses, but rather to the higher social classes of all nations. It rises above the horizon of the common people. The language used in this literature is merely something accidental. The poet of the intelligentsia, enamored of strange material and novel forms of expression, cannot but produce works that are foreign to his people.[65]

The interest and research in folklore by the Heidelberg circle naturally included also the fairy tale. However, while it did not take long to bring about a revival of interest in the folksong and saga and the collection and study of these forms, interest in the fairy tale remained dormant for a while. Nevertheless, the Grimm brothers had been busily gathering material since 1808, and began the publication of the *Kinder- und Hausmärchen* by the end of 1812. On the other hand, Brentano's *Märchen* appeared very slowly and sporadically, some not until after his death.[66] Never-

---

[63] From Arnim's unpublished note-book.
[64] DNL, CXLVI, I, p. 51; Arnim's essay "Von Volksliedern."
[65] *Unbekannte Aufsätze*, p. 79.
[66] Cf. DNL, CXLVI, I, p. CXLVIII-CLI, also H. Hamann in *Die literarischen Vorlagen der Kinder- und Hausmärchen und ihre Bearbeitung durch die Brüder Grimm* ("Palaestra," XLVII).

theless, Brentano with the publication of the fragment *Die Rose* in 1800 had been the first worker in this field among the Heidelberg Romanticists. Five years later Arnim's summons to start collecting sagas and fairy tales, instead of only folksongs, was the first signal for renewed effort in this direction.[67] The same year Brentano wrote Arnim that he was adapting Italian fairy tales for German children,[68] and that he wanted to publish a collection at Zimmer's press in Heidelberg in 1809.[69] During his stay in Berlin from 1809 till 1811, encouraged by Savigny and Schinkel, and later on his estate at Bukowan in Czechoslovakia, Clemens continued his work on fairy tales.[70] However, before they actually appeared, they were discussed and criticized in the circle of friends, who were already acquainted with Clemens Brentano's tales or had heard of them. One was especially anxious to compare them with Grimm's *Kinder- und Hausmärchen*.

We have ample proof that Arnim took great interest in the collection of fairy tales by the Grimms.[71] Here difference of opinion and old disputes made their appearance again. Are fairy tales "natural poetry" (*Naturpoesie*), or must they be assigned to the field of "art poetry" (*Kunstpoesie*)? Is it permissible for modern poets to make alterations? To what extent is it possible to regard the fairy tale as the expression of a pure and noble naiveté? In Arnim's opinion fairy tales are not fixed, but in constant flux. The purpose of the fairy tale is to occupy the child's mind and to stimulate the imaginative talent.[72] Children when they relate fairy tales are apt to omit incidents or add new ones. Here again Jacob Grimm had a different point of view. He insisted that fairy tales have been told with truth and honesty, so that they must be regarded as *Naturpoesie*, admitting, however, that a mathematical truth is impossible, even in the "truest, sincerest tale."[73] The purpose of the fairy tale is not to stimulate the child's imagination

---

[67] Arnim-Brentano, p. 151; "Aufruf von Dezember 17, 1805."
[68] *Ibid.*, p. 156.
[69] Brentano's letter to Zimmer, Dec. 12, 1809.
[70] Arnim's letter to Jean Paul, Jan. 1, 1811.
[71] Arnim-Grimm, pp. 213-273; e.g., *Die Kinder- und Hausmärchen*.
[72] *Ibid.*, p. 223.
[73] Cf. also Arnim's and Jacob Grimm's different views on translations. Jacob would publish the *Edda* only in the original version, with a detailed commentary. Arnim suggested a translation of the *Edda*, not a simple, literal one, but a more

to new inventions and self-occupation. Children do not invent, though they may forget beautiful incidents. Variations found in fairy tales are comparable to the dialects of a language.[74]

Arnim's "Anmerkungen zum Märchenbuch"[75] is a critical analysis of the Grimms' *Kinder- und Hausmärchen*. In the first place Arnim did not wish that children should themselves read the fairy tales, but held that adults should select from them for telling children. He would have liked to see this advice printed on the front page ("Für Ältere zum Wiedererzählen nach eigener Auswahl"). He made this suggestion for the simple reason that the different styles in fairy tales of this collection make them difficult for children to understand. A fairy tale in which one child kills another is entirely unsuitable for children. He wanted the *Geschichte vom Fischer und syner Fru* omitted from the collection, because especially this tale is not suitable for children. *Machandelbom* he considered also a little too cruel for a children's collection, and the story of *Frau Füchsin* perhaps unmoral and at least dubious.

Arnim's suggestions did not at first meet with Wilhelm's and Jacob's approval. While Wilhelm was ready to omit *Frau Füchsin*, Jacob refused, for he maintained that to the pure in heart everything is pure, and that they will not read another meaning into the story. For the same reason both brothers scorned Arnim's suggestion that the title page indicate that adults were to read the book and then select for children. There cannot be, and perhaps ought not to be, any book for children which they can fully grasp. If ideas and words are sometimes over their heads, so much the better, for they will sink in and bear fruit in later time. "This," Jacob declared, "was comparable to reading to children from the Bible, where they also might not understand the meaning of 'God' or 'devil'." Yet it is good for them to hear these passages, as the Grimm brothers knew from their own childhood experiences.[76]

It must be noted, however, that in later editions of the *Kinder-*

---

poetic rendering than the original (*poetische Erhöhung*). "Religious sincerity", he said, "lies at the bottom of all literal translations, but playful enjoyment alters old pieces of poetry." Cf. Arnim-Grimm. pp. 131, 137, 143.

[74] Arnim-Grimm, p. 255.
[75] *Ibid.*, p. 262.
[76] Arnim-Grimm, pp. 266-7.

und Hausmärchen all of Arnim's suggestions found due consideration.

While the Grimm brothers were publishing their Märchen, Brentano was also busy with the fairy tale, and his work was included in this discussion. A definite judgment of Brentano's fairy tales was not yet possible because of incomplete knowledge, due to fragmentary publication. Very apparent and much discussed, however, was the different approach of Brentano, his leaning to the poetic side. Arnim and his family had spent the summer with Brentano in Teplitz, where Brentano had given them an intimate acquaintance with his work. Arnim was thus in a position to give detailed reports to the Grimms. The fairy tales were "decorated with several new additions,"[77] as Arnim wrote to the brothers, adding, however, that Brentano's chief interest at the moment was in the drama, namely in his dramatic poem *Aloys und Imelde,* and in the mythical legends about the founding of Prague. In spite of the great hopes Brentano cherished for his drama *Libussa* (*Die Gründung Prags*), which centered around the founding of Prague, Arnim wrote less optimistically to the Grimm brothers: "*Libussa,* excelling in language and details, lacks unity of action and character, as may happen so easily with mythical stories. There are beautiful single passages, interesting situations, so that I regret extremely that he did not carry out his original plan to write an opera."[78]

In November, 1814, Brentano announced to Arnim that his *Libussa* was finished, completely rhymed and revised four times.[79] Even for the author Arnim had little encouragement, criticizing especially the superabundance of poetical words and untimely declamation.[80] He voiced a similar criticism in his later correspondence with Wilhelm Grimm, being unable to understand how such beautiful tragic material could be spoiled. Brentano was, he declared, in dire need that somebody should devise a plot for him.[81] The reaction of the Grimm brothers was characteristic. Wilhelm, polite and understanding, pointed out that excessive revising and polishing deprived Brentano's works of all vivacity and natural charm. Jacob referred again to the fallacy of adapt-

[77] *Ibid.,* p. 211. [78] *Ibid.,* pp. 210-11. [79] Arnim-Brentano, p. 306.
[80] *Ibid.,* p. 306. [81] Arnim-Grimm, p. 320.

ing and rearranging myths and fairy tales. He reproached Clemens and all modern poets for their attempts to imitate *Naturpoesie;* a veritable weakness, he contended, probably never to be recognized by Clemens in his erroneous desire to create something better.[82]

Arnim felt hurt by Jacob's vigorous criticism, not only of Brentano, but of modern poets. He felt that with equal right he could criticize the tiresome and often mechanical old poets. He took great pains to explain to Jacob the poetic elements in Brentano's poetry, especially in his fairy tales. "These are *new* fairy tales, which his innermost soul urged him to write. One can criticize only Brentano's vain coquetry which prompted him to display his skill in words."[83] Arnim saw the fundamental difference between the Grimm brothers' fairy tale collection and that of Brentano in the fact that the latter did not meet the immediate needs of children but rather had to be adapted for them by adults. It was a collection that would stimulate the imagination of adults, who could fashion it into a constant source of fascinating enjoyment for children.[84]

Some years later, in the *Gesellschafter* of 1818, Arnim reviewed F. V. V. Schmidt's free translation of Italian fairy tales, which had been published in 1817 under the title *Die Märchen des Straparola*. To suit the taste of the German reading public Schmidt had omitted many questionable jokes and episodes from the original, a procedure which, as Arnim informs us, was justified and by no means cast any reflection on Italian morality. It was rather a difference in taste, which has to be considered in transmitting the literature from one nation to another. Like the Grimm brothers, Schmidt had equipped his translation with valuable notes.[85]

The fertile discussion with the Grimms, an attempt to clarify questions so vital to the Heidelberg romanticists, was interrupted by the war of 1813-14. The struggle, with its far-reaching consequences, and the new political constellation in Europe brought new issues, particularly to Arnim, Görres, and Brentano. During

---

[82] Arnim-Grimm, pp. 219-20.
[83] *Ibid.*, p. 223. Cf. the inconsistency of Arnim's opinion, *ibid.*, p. 263.
[84] *Ibid.*, p. 223.
[85] *Ges.*, 1818, p. 44; F. V. V. Schmidt, *Die Märchen des Straparola.*

the war years the friends did not meet and their meagre correspondence was concerned chiefly with political events. Then in September, 1814, after having been absent from Berlin for more than three years, Brentano returned to the Prussian capital. It seemed as if the stimulating influences and friendships he found in Berlin would bring the dawn of a new era of activity for him. Berlin society had attempted to revive and to cultivate again literary interests. Soon friendly bonds united Brentano with E. Th. A. Hoffmann, who had made Berlin his permanent residence in September, 1814, and with Karl Friedrich Schinkel, the great architect. Had Clemens also found the stimulation and assistance of his friend Arnim as in former years, he might have regained the inner peace of mind and the joy necessary for new and creative work. But as early as the spring of 1814 Arnim left Berlin again and for reasons of economy, settled on his family estate, Wiepersdorf, then almost a day's ride from Berlin. Furthermore, the shift in his literary interests and his constant financial worries prevented a renewal of the old ties of close association. For these reasons the two friends did not return to the brotherly intimacy of literary effort of former days.

Only one field attracted their mutual interest during the remaining years of Brentano's residence at the Prussian capital, from the autumn of 1814 to the autumn of 1818: the Berlin stage. Both wished now to realize their long-cherished plan of winning the stage for romantic plays. Earlier, both had attempted to gain entrance to the theater for their dramatic productions: Brentano unsuccessfully in Vienna, and Arnim, together with Kleist, in Berlin in 1810, also in vain. Now both, Arnim in the capacity of stage producer and Brentano as playwright, were eager to bring before the public their impressions of the stage of the day and their views of the necessary stage reforms. These ideas were set forth in a satirical and belligerent manner in the "Briefe über das neue Theater." These were fictitious letters which began to appear in the *Wünschelrute*,[86] in 1818. They were soon discontinued, for

---

[86] The *Wünschelrute*, hrsg. von H. Straube und J. P. von Hornthal, was a short-lived publication which was supposed to be the mouthpiece of the so-called "Poetische Schustergilde in Göttingen" (from January until June 1818). The "Briefe über das neue Theater" were published from March 19 to April 27, 1818.

the reason that Arnim's contemporaries were at a loss to understand the mixture of satire and seriousness which marked their style. From Arnim's letter to the publisher which accompanied the manuscript it is apparent that it was the intention of Arnim and Brentano to write an evolutionary history of dramatic production, setting forth the obstacles that had beset its path and their ideas for its future development. Arnim was to write in the capacity of a modern stage producer. As the spokesman for the stage producers, he soon discovered that these unfortunates had much reason for lamentation.[87] The two friends never tried to revive their project as a co-operative enterprise, but Arnim returned to the subject[88] a decade later in the "Sammlungen zur Theatergeschichte."

In this connection it is of interest to examine Arnim's attitude towards the later literary work of his close friend and colleague. Of all of his notes on Brentano's writings, only one deserves mention, an announcement of *Victoria und ihre Geschwister* in Gubitz's *Gesellschafter* of the year 1817.[89] Arnim classified it as a gay pageant, interspersed with serious commentaries, originally planned for the comic stage and now adapted for the reading public. He considered the commentaries, the Schoolmaster's serious remarks, especially valuable. These refer to the political situation of the time and contain a grave warning to the victorious nations not to be overjoyful and conceited.

The spheres of interest of the former friends now drew further and further apart. This separation reached a crisis when Brentano turned as a penitent to find refuge in the bosom of the Catholic Church, a step that was hastened by his unhappy love for the pious Luise Hensel. With the year 1817, news of the change in

[87] Arnim's letter to the publishers of the *Wünschelrute*, Prenzlau, February 23, 1918. Cf. *Literarische Mitteilungen, Festschrift zum zehnjähringen Bestehen der Litteraturarchiv-Gesellschaft* in Berlin (Berlin, 1901, Litteraturarchiv-Gesellschaft), pp. 76-8.
[88] "Sammlungen zur Theatergeschichte" in *Monatliche Beiträge zur Geschichte dramatischer Kunst und Literatur*, hrsg. von Karl von Holtei. II (1828), 1-42. Two other projects of the friends from an earlier time were a biographical collection by Bettina, Clemens, and Arnim, and a collection of war letters. Cf. Arnim-Bettina, pp. 333, 355.
[89] *Victoria und ihre Geschwister mit fliegenden Fahnen und brennender Lunte. Ein klingendes Spiel von Clemens Brentano*, Berlin, 1913. Ges. (Berlin 1817), p. 644.

Brentano began to be disturbing to the friends, for it seemed that his restless spirit was seeking refuge in Catholic mysticism. In recalling the happy days they had spent in Heidelberg, Arnim wrote to Jacob Grimm March 30, 1917:

> A very pleasant time I had there, living with Clemens, and writing the first part of the *Wunderhorn.* His wife Mereau was still alive. At times he suffered from rheumatism or was in a bad humor, but he was more religious then than now, when he crosses himself, goes to confession, and acts like a converted sinner.[90]

In the fall of 1818 Brentano took a further step toward severing his relations with Arnim and to Berlin by his departure for Dülmen, where the "tired pilgrim" tried to find peace in the presence of the stigmatized nun, Anna Katherine Emmerich. When Arnim saw Clemens again during the latter's brief visit in Berlin in January 1819, Brentano impressed him as a Catholic fanatic. Nevertheless, he expressed to Görres his satisfaction that Clemens had at last found a path and an aim in life.[91]

In later years, in the correspondence between Arnim and the Grimm brothers, Brentano's life and work were still discussed occasionally. Arnim expressed enthusiasm for what he called Brentano's "beautiful fragment 'Der arme Heinrich,' " by which he probably meant "Der arme Johannes," and referred to *Aus der Chronika eines fahrenden Schülers.*[92] Finally, the year 1828 brought an end to the friendship. Arnim's letters to Wilhelm Grimm during the summer of that year, when Arnim was visiting Brentano in Frankfort, contain many interesting remarks. In these letters we hear a note of chagrin and disappointment that two of his best friends, Brentano and Görres, were now wasting their energies on behalf of the Catholic clergy. Political trends and confessional zeal had taken them into another camp. As South Germans, ardent Catholics, and Romanticists, they embraced whole-heartedly the ultramontane program, which Arnim, a stout Protestant and a North German, could not accept. Arnim blamed the *Zeitgeist* for their desertion. They were victims, he thought,

---

[90] Arnim-Grimm, p. 372.
[91] Arnim's letter to Görres, February 4, 1918.
[92] Arnim-Grimm, p. 369.

of the "bad times." In this sense he wrote to Wilhelm, February 29, 1828:

I can hardly tell you how desperate I am sometimes when I come to think how two men of such great talent as Clemens and Görres have been thrown off their path by this rubbish about faith, this malady of distorted views. I should not have objected, had they gone like hermits into the desert, or mounted the pulpit like Werner; but they are under some inhibition, full of complexes which they do not understand. In the last analysis, they have just gotten stuck in the mud of the time.[93]

While thus in the spring of 1828 Arnim only expresses regret at their going astray, half a year later, after visiting them in southern Germany, he condemns them more severely. His pan-German sentiments were deeply hurt. It was his conviction that such people were very dangerous to the nation because of their very inactivity and their negative attitude, and their contempt of the world.[94] Thus the beautiful friendship, born out of youthful idealism for the fatherland, had received its death blow at the hand of petty local politics and party spirit.

In later years Arnim paid little attention to Görres' literary-historical writings. He did review his *Altdeutsche Volk- und Meisterlieder* in the *Gesellschafter* in 1817. Here again he emphasizes the author's historical approach, the same method which had been employed by the Grimm brothers. Görres' work was an extensive collection of folksongs, containing valuable contributions similar to those in the *Wunderhorn,* together with a brilliant historical essay. Görres' interest centered on the historical aspect of poetry, whereas in the *Wunderhorn,* as Arnim points out, he himself had emphasized the artistic side of the folksong and interpreted its "soul" by means of selection and alterations in accord with the spirit of his own time.[95]

Among all his friends the Grimm brothers remained closest to him in later years. Arnim esteemed deeply their personal qualities, especially their kindness and modesty. However, the more they concentrated on literary-historical scholasticism, the less was Arnim able to follow them. This became apparent on the publication of the first volume of Jacob's *Deutsche Grammatik* in the

---

[93] Arnim-Grimm, p. 576. [94] *Ibid.,* p. 582.
[95] *Unbekannte Aufsätze,* pp. 83-5.

spring of 1819. The poet Arnim had little interest in this book. He refers to it only humorously. On the whole, he seems to have considered the teaching of German grammar as superfluous, except in districts where dialects prevailed. In case it was to be taught, he advocated that a German grammar be added to a book on Latin grammar.[96] Again, in 1818, he reviews briefly the second part of the Grimms' *Deutsche Sagen,* published in that year.[97] Once more the old dispute as to how far legends (*Sagen*) were *Natur-* or *Kunstpoesie* is revived, and the critic believes that he has now the opportunity to define and clarify the point definitely. The most difficult problem is to determine what oral material successive generations have added to the nucleus of the original saga, which originated under simple conditions. Simplicity of life and culture distinguishes for Arnim the original element of a saga from the creations of the modern poetic spirit. Nevertheless, whatever is "good" in the poetry of all times has been written "out of inner necessity" by poets who "could think thus and not otherwise." This living treasure of poetry is eternal and will remain eternal.

Among the writings of the last years of his life, the essay on Jacob Grimm's *Deutsche Rechtsaltertümer*[98] is noteworthy as a formulation of Arnim's attitude toward an important creation of the German spirit through past ages. This work was very much to Arnim's taste, and was in his opinion entitled to a prominent place among the various collections of folklore. He had waited impatiently for the publication of the book, and on its appearance he hastened to express his appreciation and delight to Wilhelm Grimm:

This book I like best among all of his [Jacob's] writings because here he has created something highly important out of almost nothing, that is, he has collected something from sources hitherto unavailable, from manuscripts never used for such a purpose. You will understand, how pleased I am, for I have never liked the scholarly criticism of old poems, nor the grammatical discussions of language.[99]

It had been Arnim's intention to write an extended review of the

---

[96] Arnim-Grimm, p. 435.
[97] *Ges.,* p. 532; cf. *Unbekannte Aufsätze,* pp. 89-90.
[98] *Ges.,* pp. 156-8; cf. Arnim-Grimm, pp. 596-602.
[99] Arnim-Grimm, p. 581.

Deutsche Rechtsaltertümer, but he did not feel equal to the task, nor did he think that any contemporary scholar could qualify for writing critically on this monumental piece of work. As Arnim pointed out in his essay, Jacob's book did not deal merely with interesting linguistic forms, nor was it only a collection of ancient legal documents and customs, but rather something more organic and unified, revealing the ancient civilization, the free and noble system of old Germanic law. The "Weistümer" were not legal decisions dictated by reason, but rather a voice of the people in its own popular, poetic, rich, and sensuous language, which was at times phrased in the ancient alliterative form. Hence they were essentially, from the cultural point of view, on a par with the folksongs. As a champion of Germanic law, Arnim pointed out how easily these old laws had been accepted by the German people after they were reintroduced from French and English translations into German territory, e.g., into the kingdom of Westphalia in the "code Napoleon". He challenged two of Jacob Grimm's contentions. The first was the statement that in the province of Brandenburg, mostly inhabited by people of Slavic origin, no old Germanic laws were found. On the contrary, Arnim claimed to find many traces of these ancient laws in Brandenburg, and he concluded, therefore, that this province must have been inhabited by Germanic tribes before the advent of the Slavs. Secondly, he protested against Grimm's criticism of present-day conditions in his introduction. Here Grimm remarks that "the serfdom and slavery of the past were in many ways easier and more attractive than the oppressed existence of our peasants and factory workers."[100] As an aristocrat and landowner, Arnim must naturally have a different opinion on this issue; and he points out that since the overthrow of Napoleon land had been confiscated and allotted by the state for the purpose of creating an independent peasantry.[101] The extensive notes which conclude Arnim's essay on Grimm's work reveal his wide knowledge of folklore and legal subjects.

Less than a year after Arnim wrote this review he passed away. In his last letter to him Wilhelm Grimm urged Arnim to be more

---

[100] Jacob Grimm, *Deutsche Rechtsaltertümer* (1828), p. XII.
[101] Arnim-Grimm, p. 599.

active as a critic, a calling for which he was so well equipped and which was so well suited to his talents.[102] After his death Wilhelm Grimm published Arnim's collected works. By means of this edition and the deeply appreciative introduction that opened it, he set up a lasting monument to their friendship.

[102] *Ibid.*, p. 615.

V
OLDER ROMANTIC CONTEMPORARIES

The most significant literary acquaintances which Arnim made on his grand tour of 1801-4 were Friedrich Schlegel and his circle in Paris. When speaking critically of Friedrich Schlegel and August Wilhelm Schlegel Arnim preferred to make no important distinctions between the brothers, for he found their literary tastes and judgments to be similar, even though they differed widely in their writings. He would have preferred that they should have published their voluminous writings jointly, as they had done with the "Charakteristiken," instead of separately. In that manner, he thought, their work would have been of greater value for posterity.[1] Even though Arnim had not much in common with the Schlegels, as regards character and personality,—he thought them too arrogant and propagandistic,—he nevertheless esteemed them very highly as men of letters. In his writings he mentioned them often together with Goethe and Tieck.[2]

Prior to his meeting with Arnim, Brentano had known Friedrich Schlegel in Jena, and he told Arnim much about him. In their reserved attitude toward Schlegel, both Arnim and Brentano were influenced by Tieck. They wanted to prevent the cold current of Schlegel's criticism from chilling their own work. Arnim was always reminded of translations when thinking of Schlegel.[3] It was in agreement with Arnim's and Brentano's nature to choose the modest, quiet paths in art, following Tieck's example, instead of the "Programm-Romantik" of the Schlegel brothers, whose aggressive nature, "like an accursed trumpeting," disturbed the serenity of all artistic endeavor.[4] In his letters to Clemens from

---

[1] *August Wilhelm Schlegels poetische Werke*, reviewed by Arnim in the HeidelbJbb. (1811), pp. 1188 ff.
[2] Arnim-Brentano, pp. 247, 357.   [3] *Ibid.*, p. 58.
[4] *Ibid.*, p. 96; Clemens' letter to Arnim, August, 1803. In spite of this antagonism, Arnim's writings show traces of Schlegel's influence, e.g., in "Heymars Dichterschule," the use of paintings and stories in teaching. In *Halle und Jerusalem* Schönemann points out certain similarities to Schlegel's *Lucinde*. Cf. Schönemann, *op. cit.*, pp. 113-14, 145.

Switzerland during the summer of 1802, Arnim condemned Friedrich Schlegel's criticism of Jacobi's *Woldemar*,[5] and said that he intended to use the polemic activity of the Schlegels satirically as "one of the best episodes" in his *Ariel*.[6]

Arnim knew that he was going to live in the same boarding house with Friedrich Schlegel in Paris. Nevertheless, as he wrote to Clemens from Geneva on November 8, 1802, he had not the slightest intention of seeking Schlegel's association and friendship, much less of writing for his periodical *Europa*. With youthful zeal he wanted rather to challenge and to scold him, and to call him to his face a "Casso senza pensieri."[7] However, a few months later, in February, 1803, after he has met Schlegel, he changes his opinion very decidedly and writes to Brentano that Friedrich really would be a good fellow if financial adversities had not developed envy and affectation in his character. He finds him and his wife modest. Schlegel was at that time lecturing on the history of modern philosophy and literature in a manner which Arnim considered quite boring.[8] Most likely Arnim was also very much attracted by Schlegel's romantic-religious conception of art, which was opposed to the inadequate and hazy imitation of the ancients which was in vogue at this time.

Of all the members of the Paris circle, Arnim was perhaps the one whom Schlegel liked best. Apparently he appreciated very much his "Erzählungen von Schauspielen" written for the *Europa*, for he asked him for a similar article on the London stage.[9] In later years Schlegel also asked Arnim for contributions to his various periodicals and almanacs.[10] Arnim did not comply with these requests; on the other hand, Friedrich accepted readily Arnim's invitation and wrote for the *Einsiedlerzeitung* in spite of his hostile attitude toward the *Wunderhorn*.[11] Schlegel did not approve of the "Wunderhorn spirit"; to him it was an "unclean spirit," and he therefore held aloof from the rest of the "worthy

[5] Arnim-Brentano, p. 41. [6] *Ibid.*, p. 54. [7] *Ibid.*, p. 54.
[8] *Ibid.*, p. 67.
[9] Joseph Körner, *Briefe von und an Friedrich und Dorothea Schlegel*, 1926, p. 528.
[10] Especially to the *Poetisches Taschenbuch von 1806*. Schlegel also asked Arnim for a review of this almanach in the *Elegante Zeitung*, or in another equally suitable place. Cf. Arnim-Brentano, p. 163, and Schlegel's letter to Arnim, January 3, 1806.
[11] Josef Körner, *Schlegel-Briefe*, p. 505.

society in Heidelberg."[12] Nevertheless, he was polite enough not to attack Arnim in public.

In 1810 Arnim wrote a rather unfavorable review of *Friedrich Schlegels Gedichte*[13] for the *Heidelbergische Jahrbücher*. The review was characterized best by Schlegel himself in a letter to Friedrich Wilken, editor of the *Jahrbücher:* "Your periodical contained a well-meaning notice of my poem, by Arnim I think; only it had more in it about the *Athenaeum* than about my poems."[14] It is true that Arnim was apt to judge the writings of the Schlegel brothers only in the light of the *Athenaeum* and the literary-critical activities of the Jena group. In this review of Friedrich's poems he emphasized that a poet is not independent of his age and group, hence must be judged accordingly.[15] The attacks of the Schlegel brothers on current literary trends had met with Arnim's approval, and he gives expression to this in the review. He thought that valuable work had been accomplished by this drive against the tedious array of mediocre writers. What he objected to was, that the new trends were presented by the Schlegels in their characteristic bombastic manner.[16] In the review Arnim also expressed the opinion that the attacks of the Jena group would have reached their goal sooner had they been preceded by productive work; and he pointed to the example of Goethe, who had first shown the way to something better by his works, and then tried to bring about improvement by means of criticism. What the Schlegels expressed had been felt for a long time by all the better writers, who had kept silence only from a false reserve. In this connection Arnim referred to certain critical expressions in Heinse's correspondence:

> For a long time the better class of writers had been disgusted with the useless shifting about of philosophical formulas and analysis, the mushy sentiment and syllable-counting, especially the ambitious manner of

---

[12] Schlegel to Boisserée in Heidelberg, February 16, 1811.
[13] HeidelbJbb., I (1810), pp. 145-153. The "Gedichte" were published (Julius Hitzig, Berlin, 1809) as the first volume of Schlegel's *Sämtliche Werke*. The volume contains the two longer works, *Alarkos* and *Roland,* in addition to such poems as "Andacht," "Der alte Pilger," "Spessart," "Frankenberg," "Windesrauschen," "Geistes Licht," "Eulenspiegels Rat."
[14] Josef Körner, *Schlegel-Briefe*, p. 131, March 13, 1811.
[15] HeidelbJbb., I (1810), p. 148.
[16] *Ibid.*, p. 147.

laying down narrow rules in judging works of art, a task which every one felt called on to undertake. It is easy enough now to give an opinion as to how the editors of the *Athenaeum* should have gone about their undertaking, but it was only at that moment that one could judge how much ridicule was necessary in order to blow up the old fortress of firmly established usage. Who could then stop to think of the few simple households that might see their activities endangered, I mean the few writers who were no longer finding a market and yet were writing only for the market.

He adds that it was remarkable that in those fateful days in Europe when the *Athenaeum* appeared in the only region which still enjoyed peace, the attention of every one could have been so riveted on literature. Thus it was that writers like those of the *Athenaeum* concentrated their zeal for reform almost entirely on literature, to the exclusion of every other form of life.[17] Arnim recognized clearly, however, the importance and far-reaching effects of the new conception of art originating in Jena, in contrast to many who felt that the efforts of the group had been useless: "What was then limited to that small town, belongs now to the whole world. Schlegel's ideas have become the subject of many university lectures, particularly those of his former enemies."[18]

Turning now to discuss Schlegel's poems, Arnim criticizes chiefly those of the youthful period. These he finds defective in meter, something which to him betrays a lack of practice. He also notes in them a detachment from reality, or at least, a reflection of the inner rather than the outer world:

> The range of these poems shows in general rather a tendency to seize the vital aspects of what he has read, to develop ideas, than to present what has been a matter of genuine experience. I do not deny that many things were based on experience, but it was certainly experience in a different form. It is due to this, that when a factual experience quite permeates the inner realization, as in the case of people who wear glasses, there results no broad observation, but a strangely profound and penetrating look. It is not until later on the Rhine that we find more universal sympathy, a fellow-feeling, an interest in popular life in general.[19]

Finally Arnim discussed in detail the tragedy *Alarkos* and the epic *Roland*. Brentano had written to Arnim as early as Septem-

[17] *Ibid.*, p. 147. [18] *Ibid.*, p. 148. [19] *Ibid.*, p. 148.

ber, 1802, how much he disliked *Alarkos,* calling it the worst tragedy he knew, a tragedy, which because of its artificiality bordered on the comic.[20] The chief fault Arnim finds is the neglect of fundamental stage principles: "One notices that the author's staging and construction of the plot is faulty, and that he has not mastered language, style, nor subject matter. Consequently he has not been able to avoid many things that hinder a general understanding. These may not cause difficulty in reading the work, but certainly do on the stage."[21] He also finds fault with the *Roland.*[22] He considers Schlegel's version of this epic so inadequate and artificial in comparison to the *Chanson de Roland* that it would probably never attain the universal appeal of a folk-epic. Certainly, he declares, the artificiality could have been avoided had the author taken the *Nibelungenlied* as an example rather than seeking his patterns in the Spanish romances. Since Schlegel has so often praised the dignity of the Old Germans and their literature, he should have put his theories into practice.[23] Finally he comes to the general conclusion that the poems reveal Schlegel as a divided personality. His reason and his ideas attracted him to Goethe's perfected form of poetry, but his true nature was romantic, of that enthusiastic originality which transcends all form, reminding one of Jean Paul.[24]

Schlegel's reaction to Arnim's review consisted of a severe criticism of Arnim's *Halle und Jerusalem* in a letter to Friedrich Wilken, March 13, 1811. Here he declared that the work did not even approach the standard that would make it worthy of being treated in a review.[25]

The following years witnessed a gradual estrangement between the two men. During the years of national revolt against Napoleon Schlegel again approached Arnim, for he wanted to make contact with men of Arnim's type who were seriously concerned with the German language and learning. On February 17, 1813, he wrote to Arnim, "recalling earlier friendship," asking for contributions to the *Deutsches Museum.*[26] In view of this cordial approach, it is

---

[20] Arnim-Brentano, p. 45.   [21] HeidelbJbb., I (1810), p. 151.
[22] *Roland. Ein Heldengedicht in Romanzen nach Turpins Chronik.*
[23] HeidelbJbb., I, p. 152.   [24] *Ibid.,* p. 153.
[25] Josef Körner, *Schlegel-Briefe,* p. 131.   [26] *Ibid.,* p. 179.

surprising to note that Friedrich wrote to Tieck only three months later: "I am very fond of Fouqué. To be sure, my enjoyment of him may possibly be much greater as a result of my disgust for Arnim and all the other freaks (*Fratzen*)."[27] Arnim did not answer Schlegel's request till six months later, in August, 1813, when Brentano was visiting Vienna, where Schlegel was then living. Through his friend Arnim sent an essay, a patriotic poem, and a copy of his *Schaubühne* for the *Deutsches Museum*. Schlegel could not use any of them since he was preparing to discontinue publication of the *Museum,* which came to an end the following year.[28] This was the last of their literary contacts.

Not so close, and less important, were Arnim's relations with August Wilhelm Schlegel. They met first in 1808 in Heidelberg, where Schlegel was in attendance on Mme. de Staël. Schlegel pictures Arnim in Heidelberg as follows: "a talented young man; however, not without an admixture of vanity and foolishness; nevertheless, one has to esteem his knowledge of old German books and his love for them."[29] Like his brother, August Wilhelm promised contributions to the *Zeitung für Einsiedler*. A brief correspondence ensued, in which Schlegel encouraged Arnim to begin researches in the history of the literature of the Sixteenth Century. Arnim rejected this suggestion because he did not consider the historical evaluation of literature so important as the revival and popular presentation of old Germanic literature and works of art: "One work of art is better than the whole history of literature. . . . Germany's chief passion now is skill in talk and chatter rather than action and achievement along any line."[30]

In the form of a review in the *Heidelbergische Jahrbücher* of the poetical works of A. W. Schlegel, Arnim published in 1811[31] an

[27] Holtei, III, 337; May 12, 1813.

[28] Arnim-Brentano, p. 317; Arnim-Grimm, p. 185. Arnim intended, in collaboration with Wilhelm Grimm, to write a review for the *Heidelbergische Jahrbücher* of Friedrich's *Deutsches Museum*, which would have turned out, most likely, not very complimentary for Schlegel. Cf. NHeidelbJbb., XI (1902), 132-3.

[29] Arnim-Bettina, p. 169; Schlegel's letter to Carl von Hardenberg, August 4, 1808.

[30] Arnim to Schlegel, September 26, 1808.

[31] HeidelbJbb., Abt. 4 (1811), pp. 1185-1195; Arnim's review of *August Wilhelm Schlegels poetische Werke. Erster und zweiter Teil*. Heidelberg bey Mohr und Zimmer. Wilhelm Grimm and Görres agreed completely with this review. Görres thought at first that Wilhelm Grimm and not Arnim was its author. Cf. NHeidelbJbb.

interesting character study of the author and an appreciation of his literary achievements. Apparently Arnim thought very highly of this review, for he wrote to Brentano that he believed that he had expressed some truths in it.[32] Here he greets August Wilhelm, who had been travelling around in Germany and abroad since 1805, as the "returning German Poet . . . who can live only in his home. Foreign lands produce many plans, but little fulfillment . . . the contact with his people and with his language will awaken within him all that foreign lands put to sleep when it was on the way to realization."[33]

Nevertheless, in spite of his long absence from Germany, August Wilhelm was for Arnim at this time the central figure in the controversies and literary battles that had been going on in Germany for the past decade. As in his review of Friedrich Schlegel's *Gedichte,* he saw the brothers' endeavors in literary criticism in a favorable light, and expressed again his conviction that such a house-cleaning process as had been accomplished by the Schlegels was a necessity for a healthy development of German literature:

> The diseases, envy and arrogance, which brought about the political destruction of Germany; envy and debasement of every distinguished individual and of the German peoples in comparison with each other, and arrogance over against the grandeur of earlier history in order to magnify the present moment, these had shown themselves ever since the foundation of the *Allgemeine Deutsche Bibliothek,* especially in the critical journals of Germany. Perhaps Shakespeare and Calderon and Goethe would never have attained their universal recognition, perhaps our literature would have been hamstrung by criticism as French literature was after Racine, but for the fact that Schlegel united with the knowledge of the old forms of criticism that suited the masses, a feeling for all that had real greatness, and by giving clear expression to the contradiction of "to be" and "not to be," brought about a change in the weather and thereby cleared the atmosphere for genius.

Arnim recalled that Schlegel's reviews in the *Jenaer Literaturzeitung* had stood up against many an enemy of poetry. It was

---

(1902), 149-150. Arnim's suggestion that Schlegel should publish a third volume of poetic translations was accepted by Schlegel, who made arrangements with the publisher Zimmer. His sudden departure for Russia, however, interfered with this plan.

[32] Arnim-Brentano, p. 300.

[33] HeidelbJbb., Abt. 4 (1811), pp. 1185-1187; Arnim's review of *A. W. Schlegels poetische Werke.*

especially his dispute with the *Jenaer* that toppled over the authority of the critical journals and brought it to pass that the present-day reading public was able to criticize the critics, and enjoy wit when it appeared, yet at the same time recognize the lasting and vital creations of the soul.[34]

This review is important for our purpose, as it gives evidence that Arnim was stimulated to his own journalistic activities by the procedure and methods introduced by the Schlegels. The critical analysis in Schlegel's *Europa,* of the different periodicals concerned with reviews,[35] Arnim regarded as a masterly achievement in literary criticism.[36] Yet Arnim wonders whether August Wilhelm Schlegel had not given too much time in the different periods of his life to the thankless task of criticizing the work of others, thus depriving himself and the world of his own creations and of more of the translations for which he had shown such marvellous talent: "Perhaps," Arnim continues, "his 'Tristan' would have been completed by now, perhaps also his 'Shakespeare' and 'Calderon,' and all the untruth and vain glory which he discovered and chastized in literature would have disappeared without effort before such magnificence."[37]

Arnim draws a parallel between the Silesian literary schools of the Seventeenth Century and the activities and interests of the Schlegel brothers. Both groups had cultivated an interest in the ancient and the Romance literatures and had adapted their forms to German literature. He praises A. W. Schlegel especially for restoring the sonnet and the elegy to their rightful place. Arnim must have welcomed the opportunity to raise his voice again for the sonnet as a poetic form.[38] He regretted, to be sure, that it, or for that matter, any literary form had been abused so much. In his elegies, Arnim declares, Schlegel had also attained perfection

---

[34] *Ibid.,* p. 1186.

[35] As Arnim said, "Es gibt wenig so Herrliches als die in der *Europa* von Schlegel (II. Bd., Seite 18) aufgestellte Charakteristik der meisten rezensierenden Institute, ja es ist vielleicht die erste Ermunterung zum Rezensieren für die geworden, welche es ernstlich mit Kunst und Wissenschaft meinten."

[36] HeidelbJbb., Abt. 4 (1811), p. 1187; Arnim's review of *Schlegels poetische Werke.*

[37] *Ibid.,* p. 1186.

[38] The so-called *Sonnettenkrieg* is reflected in the *Zeitung für Einsiedler* of 1808; cf. Fr. Pfaff's introduction to *Arnim's Tröst Einsamkeit,* 1883.

of form, except that in the elegy "Rom," which Schlegel considered as one of his best, the contents did not correspond to the excellence of its outer form, for, as Arnim puts it, it was a "historic abstract in verse."[39]

The classical drama *Ion*, which had been staged once under Goethe's direction in Weimar, is severely criticized, chiefly because Schlegel had failed here to put into practice his own theoretical principles of drama. In Arnim's opinion, no contemporary playwright can ever attain perfection merely by imitating or utilizing the subject-matter of the classics. Hence Schlegel's *Ion* as well as Goethe's *Iphigenie* were failures in Arnim's eyes. Schlegel had himself come out in favor of Euripides in contrast with Racine's *Phèdre* and his own attempts in the classical styles with their mingling of ancient and modern elements. He had also, the reviewer reminds him, called Goethe's *Iphigenie* a weak reflection of antiquity. His *Ion* is therefore exposed to much unfavorable criticism if we compare it with the best of all Euripides' dramas: "We have a strong feeling that Goethe's *Iphigenie* and Schlegel's *Ion* belong, as concerns details, to the most finished achievements of dramatic poetry, but as a whole they are not to be compared with the ancient stage."[40]

While Arnim could not see the possibility that any laurels could be earned by intermingling the modern with the antique, he was in favor of translating the ancient dramas. He was aware, however, of certain inherent difficulties: no literal, word-for-word translation was wanted, but rather a free rendering based on a deep insight into the dramatic effects to be produced, so that the richness and power of the ancient drama might be experienced fully by the modern audience.[41]

When Schlegel's *Tristan* appeared, it brought special joy to Arnim, champion of old German literature as he was; and he expressed the hope that Schlegel's future literary productions might be of this nature.[42]

Arnim, then, looked upon the Schlegel brothers as militant prophets of a new epoch in art. On the other hand, there is little

---

[39] HeidelbJbb., Abt. 4 (1811), pp. 1190-1191; Arnim's review of *Schlegels poetische Werke*.
[40] *Ibid.*, pp. 1191-2.   [41] *Ibid.*, p. 1193.   [42] *Ibid.*, p. 1194.

mention in his writings of Novalis, the third member of the triad which had been so active in formulating the program of the *Athenaeum,* who is often referred to as the high priest of early Romanticism. Only during the first years of his literary career do we find in Arnim's letters a few remarks about Novalis and his *Heinrich von Ofterdingen*. These make it quite apparent that he lacked any deeper understanding of this one of his contemporaries. To Arnim the high priest of the new spirit in literature and art was Hölderlin rather than Novalis, and he regretted deeply that neither of these poets saw the national arising and the new political era in Germany.

It is, indeed, easy to understand that the youthful Prussian Junker, filled with a zest for life, was not attracted to the dreamy nature of Novalis, whose spirit was occupied more with the Beyond than with the earthly present. They were opposite poles, in spite of the great power of romantic imagination which both possessed. Where Arnim is simple and bright as daylight, Novalis is as pensive and as supernatural as the powers of night. A critical comparison of the outstanding novel of each, *Die Kronenwächter* and *Heinrich von Ofterdingen,* would be interesting and illuminating. Briefly a few points may be indicated. Both novels are a glorification of the historic past, written in the vein of romantic imagination and romantic natural philosophy; but while Novalis chose as background the Middle Ages, with its mysticism and universalism, Arnim chose the restless years of the Renaissance. Novalis' hero is a dreamer searching for the mystic "blue flower," while Berthold in Arnim's *Kronenwächter* is destined to accomplish great national and practical tasks. Arnim's commentary on *Heinrich von Ofterdingen* was sketchy and rather insignificant. After praising Tieck's *Lovell* highly he turned to *Heinrich von Ofterdingen:*

> In contrast, I must confess that I find Novalis' *Heinrich von Ofterdingen,* as a whole, thoroughly mediocre, although beautiful in many details. Is there any narrative episode in it as fine as one of a dozen in *Lovell?* The pedantic stupidity of the chatter of the peasantry through it all; most of all, the "Märchen," a bore if you can't spell it out, and insignificant if you do understand it! . . . The examination of the second volume of *Ofterdingen* left me in a queer frame of mind. I finished it

with the conviction that literature cannot be written in such a manner in the future. It exhausts itself with the conception of the plan.[43]

At times in Arnim's writings, especially in *Halle und Jerusalem*, one finds what may be interpreted as a satire on Novalis. Now it is the "neo-poetic Christians" that are ridiculed, now "nature mysticism" or the exaggerated, distorted, philosophical descriptions.[44] It is regrettable that in later years, when he had acquired more mature judgment, Arnim attempted no general evaluation of Novalis and his work. Yet it should be noted that in 1828, when writing about Hölderlin and seeking a poet with whom he could compare Hölderlin's impressive characteristics, his thoughts turned to Novalis.[45] This, after all, must lead to the conclusion that in his later years he had a better understanding and appreciation of Novalis as a poet than in his Heidelberg period.

Arnim was the first critic who noticed the kinship between Hölderlin and Novalis. The common characteristics of their poetry are great sincerity, a depth of ideas, and a melancholy, restless element, which is of the greatest tragic effect. Both had only a small group of admirers at first, and it was much later that their genius was generally recognized. Hölderlin was one of the few poets whom Arnim accepted without any reservation. He liked to turn to him in the most serious hours of his life and remained deeply interested in his literary aesthetics until his death. When his first youthful enthusiasm had subsided, he was often critical of Goethe and Tieck, but never of Hölderlin. Caroline von Günderode certainly expressed the true sentiment of the Heidelberg group when she wrote that they rated Goethe and Hölderlin as the first great masters of Romanticism.[46] Arnim regarded Hölderlin as a great German idealist who was devoted to the mission of his art with a deep sincerity. With the greatest sorrow and sympathy he followed Hölderlin's tragic life. As he saw it, a lack of recognition by contemporaries was the common lot of Hölderlin and himself.

[43] Arnim-Brentano, pp. 41, 136: "Die Durchsicht des zweiten Bandes von *Ofterdingen* ist mir sonderbar bekommen; er hat mich fester überzeugt, daß so überhaupt keine Dichtung weiter entstehen kann, sondern daß sie da mit der Entwerfung des Planes aufgebracht ist."
[44] Werke, XVI, *Halle und Jerusalem*, pp. 336, 308. Cf. Arnim-Grimm, p. 110.
[45] *Berliner Conversationsblatt;* "Ausflüge mit Hölderlin"; Nr. 33, 1828.
[46] G. Bianquis, *Caroline von Günderode* (Paris, 1910), p. 42.

The interest in Hölderlin finds its first expression in 1808 in the *Zeitung für Einsiedler,* which contained several specimens of Hölderlin's free verse.[47] In Arnim's "Briefe über das neue Theater" Hölderlin's *Hyperion* is given the same rating as the works of Shakespeare and Calderon.[48] How much *Hyperion* meant to Arnim personally, is apparent from a letter written in 1813, where he declares that beside his own work, *Hyperion* is the only poetic work that he still finds to his taste.[49] One can only regret that Arnim never carried out his intention of writing a book on literary aesthetics, which he had intended to base on *Hyperion.* About this plan he wrote to the Grimm brothers October 21, 1817: "Several years ago I intended to do a work on aesthetics, following Hölderlin's *Hyperion,* for by its very nature a system of literary aesthetics should depend on the elegy, and the most magnificent of all elegies would then be the occasion for it."[50] In the "Literary Notes" in the periodical *Der Gesellschafter* during the following year (1818) Arnim referred again to Hölderlin's art and tried to arouse interest in a collection of his works,[51] a task which he felt had been unduly neglected.[52]

On this occasion he also discussed the slow progress of poetic art during recent years. The essence and task of art is "to render a true picture of life, emphasizing moral values, i.e., to evoke an ethical enthusiasm."[53] One might take exception to this as a very limited definition of art, but Arnim mentioned that also Goethe, using the pastor in *Hermann und Dorothea* as his mouthpiece, emphasized the element of "ethical enthusiasm" (*sittliche Begeisterung*) in art.[54] Arnim did not give up hope that this "true" art would eventually come into its own and he consoled himself with Hölderlin's words, "O Seele! Seele! Schönheit der Welt! Du unzerstörbare, du entzündende mit deiner ewigen Jugend!"[55]

In a later publication "Ausflüge mit Hölderlin," written shortly

---

[47] *Zeitung für Einsiedler,* Nr. 10, May 4, 1808.
[48] *Wünschelrute* (Göttingen, 1818), Nr. 25-28.
[49] Arnim-Brentano, p. 316.   [50] Arnim-Grimm, p. 402.
[51] *Unbekannte Aufsätze,* p. 98.
[52] *Ibid.,* p. 98; in Arnim's own words: "Vollständig müßten sie gegeben werden, weil er nie ein leeres Wort geschrieben."
[53] *Ibid.,* p. 97: In Arnim's words, "Kunst ist ein treues Bild des Lebens, sie weiß die sittliche Begeisterung darzustellen, wie jede andere [Begeisterung]."
[54] *Ibid.,* p. 97.   [55] *Ibid.,* p. 97.

before his death,[56] Arnim paid the highest tribute to Hölderlin. Pigenot, one of the most discriminating critics of the great Swabian poet, refers to Arnim's "Ausflüge mit Hölderlin" as the best article on Hölderlin written in a long time.[57] Arnim's essay contains a forceful arraignment of the critical spirit in literature during the preceding decades and apparently includes ideas which he was going to elaborate in his proposed "Aesthetics." He expresses his delight that Hölderlin's name, that of "the greatest of all elegiac poets," has not appeared as yet in any aesthetics; hence it has not been misused, he adds ironically, in order "to praise his faults." How do critics become famous? asks Arnim: "By tearing to pieces the laurel wreaths of poets!" To avoid unjust criticism and misrepresentation by critics, he wished that the poets might rather give their own annotations or explanations; but he realized the difficulties, for a true artist creates unconsciously, follows the divine spark of his genius:

Authors, one might say, ought to call attention to their own views, to the real value of their efforts, but the modesty which prevents them from uncovering the roots of their work is so natural. They fear that these cannot find again the soil from which they sprang, the unconscious and the unknown. Yet especially in the case of Hölderlin we must regret that he attained to no explanation of this kind, still less to an autobiography, because his art is too serious to be confused by an effort of that kind; especially because his life for the world and for his own talents came to such an early end.[58]

Of Hölderlin's poems Arnim discusses here only those of the poet's later years, e.g., "Die Nacht," "Die Herbstfeier," and "Die Wanderung." He points out the novel and effective way in which Hölderlin utilized a simple vocabulary. Of Hölderlin's "Patmos-Hymne"[59] our critic gives a poor evaluation. He considers it Hölderlin's most peculiar poem, bearing marks that foreshadow his mental unbalancing. In conclusion he wonders how other poets would have treated the Patmos material. The only

---

[56] *Berliner Conversationsblatt,* "Ausflüge mit Hölderlin," Nr. 31-34 (1828).
[57] *Hölderlins Sämtliche Werke,* hrsg. von. Hellingrath, II, 545.
[58] *Berliner Conversationsblatt,* "Ausflüge mit Hölderlin," Nr. 33, 1828.
[59] The "Patmos-Hymne" was first published in 1808 in *Seckendorfs Musenalmanach.* "Ohne Kenntnis dieses Druckes, von A. v. Arnim im *Berliner Conversationsblatt,* vom 18 Februar 1828, in ganz entstellter Form veröffentlicht." Cf. Hölderlins *Werke,* hrsg. von N. von Hellingrath, IV, 353.

other competent one, he thought, would have been Novalis: "None other occurs to me who could have taken hold of this theme, except perhaps Lavater. However the sublime inspirations which he had were drowned in words. But neither Lavater, nor Klopstock nor any other contemporary of Hölderlin can be regarded as the spark of his flame."

Arnim himself valued this essay on Hölderlin highest among all of his articles and reviews,[60] and in this he certainly was justified. With increasing age and a better understanding of literary values he was becoming a critic with deep insight into the nature of the poet and his creations.

While Hölderlin was the greatest poetic genius among the early Romantiscists, the greatest dramatist of this group was Zacharias Werner. Today in literary history Werner appears chiefly as the inventor of the fate-tragedy; to his contemporaries he was the greatest dramatist after Schiller, indeed, some even set him above Schiller. Arnim met Werner first in Heidelberg in 1808.[61] In speaking of this meeting in a letter to Bettina he refers to him as a "theater-poet, who is an up-right but happy-go-lucky fellow."[62] In December of the same year Arnim and Werner met again, this time in Goethe's house.[63] What appealed most to Arnim in Werner's plays was the revelation of the dramatist's deep inner religious life, reminding Arnim of Jung-Stilling in its mysticism. However, Arnim refused to take seriously the so-called "love-system" which Werner expounded to him at length at their Heidelberg meeting. "All the time," he writes Bettina, "I vacillated between a terrible outburst of laughter and deep sadness, as he talked about himself again and assured me that he writes solely for the purpose of expounding his system."[64]

Werner's "love-system" was to be regarded as the key to an understanding of his dramas. Two years after their first meeting Arnim wrote for the *Heidelbergische Jahrbücher* a review of Werner's *Attila*.[65] Here he tries to do justice to this peculiar feature

---

[60] Böhmer's letter to Jacob Grimm, Oct. 23, 1839.
[61] Arnim-Bettina, p. 175.
[62] *Ibid.*, p. 176; Arnim's letter of July 12, 1808.
[63] Bettina-Goethe, p. 322.
[64] Arnim-Bettina, p. 176; Arnim's letter of July 12, 1808.
[65] HeidelbJbb., I, 1810, pp. 8-15, 145-153.

of the playwright's creation by calling attention to this hidden "system" running through all of his plays, like *Die Söhne des Tals, Das Kreuz an der Ostsee, Luther,* and *Attila.* The review is not limited to a discussion of this tragedy, but is much wider in scope, in fact it is a general appreciation of the romantic playwright, with many interesting comparisons to Schiller. According to Arnim, Werner's "love-system" is based on the belief that the transcendental world manifests itself to our senses and becomes comprehensible to the individual through the medium of love. It is love also which forms the ties in human institutions, in society and the state.[66] Arnim points out that Werner's "love-system" is rooted in the Biblical statement, "God is love, and whosoever lives in love, lives in God." This would explain the abundance of religious and ecclesiastical motives in all of Werner's plays, which he uses chiefly for the presentation of "an eternal community of goodness."[67]

As most of the titles suggest, Werner took the subject-matter of his plays from history. Arnim, who associated poetry and all forms of literary expression so closely with history, in this review of *Attila* dwells at length on the question of historical truth in literature. Whenever history forms the background of a work of literature, he demands a detailed, faithful picture of a single historical event. His ideas coincide here, as a whole, with those of Herder, who in his *Ideen zur Geschichte der Menschheit* discusses the literary treatment of history with great seriousness and understanding.[68] Literature, Arnim declares, has to be a faithful presentation of history, otherwise it is a false and arbitrary allegory.

From this historical angle Arnim goes on to discuss each of Werner's dramas. *Die Söhne des Tals* is in his opinion the most accomplished one of these, revealing greater historical truth than all of Werner's later plays. Here Werner never deviated from historical facts, he only added what history forgot to relate, or con-

[66] *Ibid.*, pp. 9-10: "Es drückt sich aus in einer gleichartigen, sinnlichen Einwirkung einer übersinnlichen Welt, die sich dem Einzelnen in der Liebe versinnlicht, Staaten und heilige Gesellschaften in Staaten zusammenhält."
[67] *Ibid.*, p. 12.
[68] *Ibid.*, p. 13: "Mit tiefem Ernst und mit möglichster Treue gegen die Geschichte hat Herder in seinen *Ideen zur Geschichte der Menschheit* dasselbe allgemein durchzuführen versucht, aber ohne ein enges Anschließen an das Einzelne, schließt sich das Herz nicht auf."

densed in accordance with the requirements of dramatic art, as Shakespeare did in his historical dramas. Arnim does not venture to pass judgment on *Das Kreuz an der Ostsee,* since only the first part had been published, but he has the more to say on Werner's *Luther* and on *Attila. Luther* is entirely unhistorical. Wherever Luther's own words are rendered by the author, they leave one with a strange impression. In Arnim's opinion this "allegorical" play, as he called it, might well serve as a prologue to a truly historical drama on Luther. After seeing it performed on the Berlin stage, he writes to Brentano: "There is no trace, with the exception of a few expressions and anecdotes, of what you and I would expect from a Luther drama. Otherwise it is a peculiar product characteristic of Werner's art, betraying his singular imitative sense."[69] *Attila* shows the same defect in its lack of fidelity to history, but this play appears more authentic, because historical reports on Attila are scanty. Arnim mentions three historical sources: the report by the historian Jordanes, the *Nibelungenlied,* and a chap book from Venice entitled *Attila, flagelum dei,* which is little known. All three sources give different accounts of Attila's death. Werner in his *Attila* follows none of these accounts, but gives his own version of the death of the great Hun, something which does not serve to improve artistically the historical picture. In comparing *Attila* with Schiller's *Jungfrau von Orleans,* Arnim points out that Schiller commits the same *faux pas.* But Schiller knows far better than Werner how to unite artistically single historical events which have been torn away from their context into a great symbolic picture, as e.g., in the *Braut von Messina.* With Werner such symbolism leads only to meagre, empty scenes. In *Attila* as well as in *Die Jungfrau von Orleans* prophecies and visions occur too frequently to be effective. Actors will find it impossible to perform such scenes with continued natural beauty and art. The prophecies and visions will impress the audience the same way as letter-writing in novels, when these epistles appear just at the crucial moment to conclude the story. Arnim thinks that *Attila* was the outgrowth of the author's own imagination, his personal life and experiences rather than the

---

[60] Arnim-Brentano, p. 182.

product of an inspiration by historical prototypes. The play was boldly constructed and well reasoned out, and improves as the action progresses.[70]

In concluding the *Attila* review, Arnim hints again, as he had done at other times, at the unsatisfactory stage of Iffland. It had overlooked this interesting drama, he declares, because actors and managers were too lazy, and each stage manager had his own favored playwrights. If the stage manager happens to be an actor himself, even the worst playwrights are favored, since usually they are lenient in permitting alterations and arbitrary interpretations.

About Werner's best known fate-tragedy *Der vierundzwanzigste Februar* Arnim wrote only briefly to Brentano on September 14, 1811, after seeing the performance on the Weimar stage. "It is a sort of centaur," he reports, "beautifully mystical but gruesome in the beginning. But the conclusion is an ordinary creature which ruins everything."[71]

During the same year, 1811, Werner turned from Protestantism to become an ardent Catholic priest. He documented his conversion in his *Die Weihe der Unkraft*, which Arnim reviewed briefly in 1814[72] in the *Preussische Correspondent*. Naturally Arnim, a convinced Protestant, felt obliged to denounce this "horrible confession."[73] He can no longer take Werner seriously, and he ridicules his religious belief. Once he had been wrapped up in his "system of love." This he had now supplanted by a "system of mastership, fraternity, and discipleship (*Jüngerschaft*)." Arnim thinks that Werner's new confession as set forth in this work is full of errors, and that the author is least of all justified in seeking to teach and convert others with a few generalized and sententious phrases, for he is the one who is misled and ill advised.[74] Thus, Arnim's relation to Zacharias Werner ended on a disharmonious note.

[70] HeidelbJbb., I (1810), 151-2.
[71] Arnim-Brentano, p. 288.
[72] *Der Preussische Correspondent*, Berlin, 1814, No. 11, pp. 3-4.
[73] *Ibid.*, p. 3.
[74] *Ibid.*, p. 4; "Die ungerechteste Unkraft in dem Büchlein scheint es zu sein, daß der Unberatenste Rat geben will, und daß dieser Unkräftige die Lumpereien seines eigenen Lebens mit Kaisern und Königen und einigen allgemeinen Sentenzen durchgeknetet ganz Deutschland auf die Haustafel setzen will."

Strange as it may seem, in view of his idealism and sincerity of character, it is nevertheless true that most of Arnim's friendships and literary connections came to an early end. Among his many acquaintances of the Heidelberg period, it was with Wilhelm Grimm alone that Arnim retained a friendly intimacy until his death. His idealistic but very stubborn personality was a barrier to the cultivation of lasting personal connections, and this was also true of his relation with the older romanticists. Even the great admiration of the youthful Arnim for Ludwig Tieck and his devotion to this author gave way in later years to a complete disregard of this most congenial member of the older romantic school. As early as October 23, 1812, he commented sourly on Tieck's *Phantasus* in a letter to Brentano. "Is not the introduction a bad example of how a man who once wrote so enjoyably can degenerate in his writings to a mere play with words?"[75] Throughout his life Arnim maintained his definite idealistic views, reminding one in this respect of Herder. As we shall see in the next chapter the firm belief in the righteousness of his *Weltanschauung* was also reflected in Arnim's contacts with Goethe.

[75] Arnim-Brentano, p. 306.

VI
CLASSICISM

The great contrast between the so-called popular German ideology and the ancient Greek philosophy of life and art became a tragic issue in Hölderlin's career. The same problem confronted also A. W. Schlegel and Friedrich Schlegel. Arnim never experienced this antithesis, for he never felt himself attracted to ancient patterns in literature. He did not even go so far as Tieck, who in his drama *Niobe* had chosen one theme from the world of antiquity. In general, Arnim's opinion and appreciation of classic antiquity and its rôle in German culture had its roots in the teachings of Herder and Tieck and was largely molded by these authors. The former had said, "We want to learn to appreciate them (the Greeks), without becoming Greeks ourselves";[1] and the latter had objected to viewing Greek art as the *only* art.[2] Both had emphasized that the Greeks were an organically unified people and as such had given noble expression to their national spirit and their native characteristics. It would, they felt, be altogether illogical to attempt to build up a German national culture solely on imitation of the Greeks. Instead of devoting a great deal of time and energy to research into antiquity and to spreading a knowledge of its thoughts and ideals, it would be more appropriate to direct these efforts into more productive channels, namely toward acquiring a familiarity with the history and culture of the fatherland.

In his autobiographical references in "Wunder über Wunder," written in 1826,[3] Arnim described himself as having been a romantic child living in an imaginary magic world. His school-days were spoiled by severe requirements of memorizing and scanning Horatian verse and studying the artificial meters of the then fashionable Roman school-poets, thus blurring all impulses to

---
[1] *Herders Werke,* hrsg. von Suphan, XIV, 105.
[2] Tieck, *Kritische Schriften,* II, 251.
[3] *Landhausleben,* Werke, I, pp. XVII-XXI. Also in "Von Volksliedern," cf. DNL. CXLVI, 1, 62.

natural expression. After such a training in childhood, he felt like a "trained horse, clicking automatically the time of the meter." He became a severe critic of the curriculum in the German schools. There was too much Latin and too little teaching of German history and culture, or none at all. His early years at the university were devoted to the study of natural science, and he lived at this time under the influence of Schelling and Ritter. It was as a natural scientist that he found his way to literature and art. Unlike the Schlegel brothers, Lessing and Goethe, he had never delved into the world of Hellenic thought and beauty; never had he felt, like Goethe, a deep longing for the serene clarity of Rome. His soul longed rather for the severity and mysticism of the northern landscape.

It was Arnim's opinion that language and art had a great natural rhythm of their own, which must be felt by the soul and in which one must live. Greek declamation may be imitated, but for a German it can never become his own through personal experience. Arnim's brief youthful discussion "Über deutsches Silbenmaß und griechische Deklamation" (1805) voiced this conviction.[4] Here he states quite naïvely that he has written poetry without knowing the least thing about rhyme and meter, and yet has never failed to achieve good poetry! He declares that he attaches no value to the teaching of prosody. Just as one is far from being a philosopher if one has merely mastered logic, no matter how completely, one cannot become a poet if one is merely an expert in prosody. One must keep in mind that the syllables are only constituent parts of the original language (*Ursprache*). Whosoever uses this *Ursprache* without artificialities is a poet.[5]

Manifestly Arnim was not the man to ponder on these problems. It was rather a matter of instinct and of feeling with him when he rejected the suggestion that classic antiquity alone was

[4] *Berlinische Musikalische Zeitung*, 1805, No. 32. Although published in 1805, this essay was conceived and written earlier, on his grand tour in Switzerland in 1802.

[5] *Ibid:* "Ich habe früher gereimt, als ich das mindeste vom Silbenmaß wußte und fast nie gefehlt; was ich davon weiß, entdeckte ich wie eine neue Ansicht in der Schweiz auf den einsamen Wanderungen; ich las nachher mancherlei, und es schienen mir alle diese prosodischen Versuche wie die Logik, wenn man in ihr das gesamte der Philosophie zu erkennen glaubt. Silben sind Worte der Ursprache . . . schwierig wird sie nicht dem, der darin lebt, sondern dem, der sie lernt und lehrt."

true art and should therefore be studied and made to penetrate German civilization, so that it might give to the Germans an art based on the classics. His references to these questions and remarks concerning them are not definite or precise, but are rather garbed in symbolical phraseology, as in the essay, "A Humorous Hodge-Podge on the Imitation of the Saint," (1808)[6] or in his poem "Dreams."[7] In the former he introduces a young man, shabbily elegant in appearance, who seeks to enlighten the mystical, monkish fools (the Romanticists) on paganism. He declares: "I am a pagan of the ancient Greek race and want to look at everything plastically." The audience demands why, then, is he dressed like other people; as a true pagan he should appear staging a tragic exhibition on a wheelbarrow, and collecting money for it. The young elegant takes this seriously and offers to donate the proceeds for the building of a central pagan temple for Germany, with casts of the gods. To be sure of genuine models, he is ready to take a trip to Italy: "I must tread classic soil. I have consecrated myself entirely to the pagan world." Arnim voices then his disdain for the imitative attitude of the German classicists through the comment of a wise old man: "Can you not feel and form your gods from your innermost soul; must you still put them together from broken fragments? . . . Art is a basilisk that destroys itself when it sees its reflection in the mirror."[8]

Similarly in his short story "Metamorphosen der Gesellschaft," published in 1826, Arnim declares that one does not become a true artist by selling oneself to paganism. True art in its quest for beauty emanates spontaneously from the genius, revealing his personality and emotions. But true art also bears the stamp of the time and the nation. Greek art is great art because it fulfills completely these requirements, and did not imitate. The Germans in their eagerness to imitate will never discover the beautiful. At present Richardson and Sir Walter Scott are widely read and

[6] *Tröst Einsamkeit*, pp. 60, 98, 260, 317, 324, 338.
[7] In *Der Wintergarten:* Werke, V, 192-198. First published in 1809.
[8] *Tröst Einsamkeit*, p. 319. The "Elegant" says: "Haben wir nur erst die obern Götter in guten Gypsabgüssen beisammen, die untern wollen wir dann schon kriegen, ich will mich selbst der Reise nach Italian unterziehen, nach den Korkmodellen läßt sich doch schwer bauen, ich muß den klassischen Boden betreten, ich habe mich ganz dem Heidenthum gewidmet."

praised in England in spite of their defects and weaknesses, because they "described successfully some features of the English national character."⁹

The concluding chapter of the "Humorous Hodge-Podge," "Der entfesselte Prometheus," brings a discussion, again symbolical in character, between the "Herzbruder," a young poet, and the Schoolmaster, a stubborn classicist and an undiscriminating critic. The latter is finally converted and has to admit that his belief in classicism and the world of Greek models as patterns for poetic form is entirely wrong. Neither Prometheus nor Hercules is a messiah, according to Arnim, speaking through the Schoolmaster. The one is dissolved and "flows away like lava, the other flies away in smoke."¹⁰ However, from their ashes new gods arise; and the Schoolmaster is filled with new hope, for now he recognizes and supports whole-heartedly the true German poet, namely the "Hermit" (*Einsiedler*). Of course, Arnim and his circle are the "Hermits" who now bring to life again the only true poetry, the poetry of the people (*Volkspoesie*). Other poets and critics, as the converted schoolmaster rightly interprets from the warning hieroglyph in the temple of Sais, may be compared to a flock of foolish birds which swallow the same piece of undigestible food, i.e., classicism. This hieroglyph, it should be noted, was pinned to the invitation to the festival of the *Einsiedler* as a warning to all the "foolish birds" to stay away.¹¹

The only other significant formulation of Arnim's attitude towards classicism is found in his poem "Träume," written in 1811. The writings of Winkelmann "der ein Landsmann von mir, mich dem Lande entzog," as Arnim puts it, had enticed him to dream of ancient Greece. Arnim relates then how once, when war and death had robbed him of friends and happiness, he longed for Greece, with its abundance of marble from which the creative artist fashions his work. But Greece and all its marble hold nothing but

---

⁹ Werke, XVIII, pp. 11-12. "Metamorphosen der Gesellschaft": "Mag Richardson die Wahrheit durch übermäßige Reflektion unwahrscheinlich machen, mag Scott die abenteuerlichsten Gewächse und Bewerke, Staatsaktionen und Hof-Carrikaturen in unwahrscheinlicher Verwicklung aufstellen, die wohl bekannten schottischen Gesichter, die großartige Geschichte der britischen Völker bringen alles zur Wahrheit der Furcht und Hoffnung, erwecken in uns dieselbe Teilnahme. . . ."

¹⁰ *Tröst Einsamkeit*, p. 347; "Der entfesselte Prometheus."

¹¹ *Ibid.*, pp. 347-8 (August 30, 1808).

CLASSICISM

illusions, and he turns away to dig in the sand of his native Brandenburg:

> Ach und wie tief ich grabe im Sande von Brandenburgs Erde,
> Immer nur find' ich den Sand und er ist mir so lieb,
> Ja ich beiße mich ein in diesen viel lockeren Boden,
> Schaff ich kein Leben darin, so begrab ich mich selbst.[12]

The main theme of this poem is the contrast between the Greeks and the barbarians in the worship of their gods. Barbarians of Taurus, visiting the Greek market, do not admire the perfect statues of the gods on the market place, but are attracted and deeply stirred by primitive childish models. The Taurian sees clearly that the Greeks, like Narcissus, honor only their own image, not the mystical and unfathomable, which reveals itself only to the innocent and unsophisticated:

> Toren, Ihr wollet verehren
> Euer menschliches Sein, diesen vergänglichen Glanz,
> . . . .
> Nur was die Kinder gemacht, ist rein in Unschuld geworden,
> Ach ich ehr, als Gott, weil ich den Sinn nicht versteh.[13]

The discussion which follows between Phidias and the barbarian shows a widely different conception of the gods. The Greek emphasizes beauty, strength, and physical enjoyment, all of which the barbarian condemns, for strength itself entails only greater servitude to the gods. The Greek puts himself almost on an equal footing with the gods. Reason and clarity predominate in his art and religion. Phidias says:

> Du schändest Götter, verachtest Du Armer Dich selber.
> Willst Du die Stimme des Gott's, horche der eigenen Brust.
> Wisse, das Beste an Dir, es sind die Herkulischen Muskeln.
> Daß von dem Göttlichen Stamm Dir ein Zeichen auch blieb.[14]

The god of the barbarian, on the other hand, is an awe-inspiring divinity. His splendor is set off by a dusky background and mystical symbols and he demands servitude or death from his trembling worshipers.[15] In the end, Greek and barbarian speak different languages; one does not understand the other; just as at home (in Prussia) masters and servants do not understand each other, due

---

[12] Werke, V, 192-3.   [13] Ibid., p. 196.   [14] Ibid., p. 196.
[15] Ibid., p. 197. The barbarian god Radegast is described as follows:

to the faulty and imperfect system of education. The final note, as so often in Arnim's writings, is an optimistic one. He believed that he could interpret with prophetic insight the history of art. From his dreams he awakens to "nordic work"; a peasant enters and shows him "Victoria."[16]

As set forth in a previous chapter, Arnim takes a similar position in a review of *August Wilhelm Schlegels Poetische Werke*, written in 1811 for the *Heidelbergische Jahrbücher*.[17] To mix the modern with the antique is utterly wrong, he holds. It is unnatural for a German writer to utilize classical subject-matter and to imitate its form, language, and style. The result will never be a great art like that of the ancient originals. Thus Goethe's *Iphigenie* and Schlegel's *Ion* can never endure comparison with their ancient prototype. If, however, modern poets prefer antique subject-matter, then they should follow Shakespeare's example and interpret ancient times in the modern spirit. Furthermore, translations are valuable, in so far as they are not simply literal and incomprehensible, but serve to enhance the artistic value of the original version.

It may be emphasized here that Arnim never spoke of classicism and romanticism as opposite literary tendencies, nor did he at any time take sides against the classicists. As is quite clear in his review of A. W. Schlegel's works, he felt no animosity towards classical literature and art as such. He was concerned only that Greek and Roman cultural achievements be assigned to their proper place in the frame of German culture. He was quite categorical in his statement that one can learn much from the ancient Greeks in contrast to the Roman poets, which were studied to exhaustion in German schools.[18] Nevertheless, the Greek poets should not be imitated literally by German poets, and at no time should Greek principles of art enslave German culture. In a foot-

---

    Gräßlich blickt er uns an in nächtlicher Lampen Erleuchtung,
    Wenn wir geblendet am Tag treten in's heilige Haus,
    Zeichen zaubrischer Art umziehen die blutigen Wände,
    Golden scheint sein Gesicht, Purpur sein flatternd Gewand,
    Wen er verlanget zur Speise, den töten die harrenden Priester,
    Immer verlanget er den, der sich von Arbeit befreit.

[16] Werke, V, p. 197.   [17] HeidelbJbb. II (1811), 1185-95.
[18] Werke, I, p. XIX.

note in the *Zeitung für Einsiedler* he emphasized that he subscribed to none of the so-called literary schools or movements of his age. In 1808, then, he believed that both classicism and romanticism were coming to an end, and that the literature which would survive would be a unit, with genuinely German characteristics of inner strength and vitality. His periodical was to serve for the purging of romanticism and classicism and for a discussion of their striking peculiarities.[19] In an unpublished entry in his notebook he declares that the fact that so much attention was paid to antiquity is to be interpreted as a sign that the Germans felt the need of an ancient art. If one would revive primitive and ancient German art rather than Greek and Roman antiquity, one would have a basis for the discussion of later and contemporary German art.[20] It is to be noted that when he thus acted as the champion of a new, vital literature, Arnim believed himself in complete agreement with Goethe, whose fundamental concepts also stressed the importance of a full-blooded literature, and for whom it was of minor consideration whether such a literature was plastic or romantic. He found that in *Dichtung und Wahrheit* Goethe had preserved a feeling for the harmony and unity of the past and present.[21]

While Arnim emphasized little the difference between romanticism and classicism, he did stress heavily the difference between a vital national literature and the current literature of rationalistic tone, with its philistine interpretation of ancient Greece. In his opinion, the latter tendency was exemplified supremely by Johann Heinrich Voss, a rationalist and a pedantic admirer of Greece, without feeling for, nor faith in, an original, vital German literature, such as was sponsored by Arnim and Brentano. Voss, they declared, was a "petrified spirit" (*versteinerter Geist*),[22] whose chilly breath killed whatever was original and perfect, youthful

[19] *Tröst Einsamkeit*, p. 71, footnote: "Der blinde Streit zwischen sogenannten Romantikern und sogenannten Klassikern endet sich; was übrig bleibt, das lebt, unsre Blätter werden sich mit beiden und für beide beschäftigen; man lernt das Eigentümliche beider Stämme wie in einzelnen Individuen erkennen, achten, und sich gegenseitig erläutern, und in seiner Entwicklung erkennen."
[20] From Arnim's unpublished notebook; cf. Carl Henrici, Katalog 149, p. 5.
[21] "Von Volksliedern", cf. DNL, CXLVI, 85.
[22] Arnim-Brentano, p. 247, Brentano's letter to Arnim, March 15, 1808.

and courageous in art. Their antagonism was well founded. Very soon Arnim had to give way to Voss and abandon his literary endeavors in Heidelberg.

For Arnim the contemporary problem of classicism in Germany crystallized itself in and revolved around Goethe as the central figure. Neither Arnim nor the other Romanticists comprehended and appreciated the greatness of Schiller.

On his way home from Heidelberg in December 1805, Arnim visited Goethe for the first time.[23] The attitude of the Weimar master toward the various literary movements was rather indefinite. Just at that time he was neglecting his Greek classical interests and turning more toward the primitive poetry of nature and the people. He fully appreciated therefore a romantic publication like the *Wunderhorn*. Arnim was full of admiration for him as a poet of the people, the author of popular ballads like "Der König in Thule"; and he overlooked the "Greek" and the "pagan" in Goethe. In this spirit he had dedicated the *Wunderhorn* to him with great enthusiasm. Goethe gave Arnim a most cordial reception, invited him to dinner at his house, and travelled with him to Jena. He was much impressed both by the enthusiastic young poet and the handsome, accomplished aristocrat, and in return for the affection and admiration of the younger man, the master continued for a few years to extend to him a fatherly interest. On his return to Berlin Arnim received from him an album-sheet with the motto: "Consiliis hominum pax non reperatur in orbe,"[24] a gift which made a deep impression on Goethe's young admirer. One can find the echo of these words repeatedly in Arnim's later works: peace is not regained by human action but rather by a new spiritual attitude. Goethe's affection for Arnim was an exceptional one. Brentano wrote enviously: "You have hardly started on your poetic calling when you meet the master, who stretches out a friendly, consoling hand. Goethe has befriended you; no other youth has ever been so fortunate."[25]

After returning to his native Brandenburg Arnim cultivated the

---

[23] Arnim stayed in Weimar from Dec. 15 till Dec. 18, 1805. Cf. Goethe's *Tagebuch*.

[24] In answer to Goethe Arnim began his letter by translating these words as follows: "Nicht durch Menschen wird der Frieden wiedergewonnen." *Schriften der Goethe Ges.*, XIV, 97.

[25] Arnim-Brentano, p. 157.

acquaintance with Goethe in a lively correspondence. Three long letters of the year 1806 show his devotion.[26] Here he writes interestingly of social life and mutual acquaintances in Berlin, and tells of his own life and travels in Brandenburg. In the first of the letters he expresses his gratitude to Goethe for the favorable review of the *Wunderhorn*,[27] which makes him believe that the master will grant further support and approval if he, Arnim, continues his literary endeavors along the same lines. He hopes that in the future he can count on Goethe as an ally in the struggle against barren scholasticism and philistinism: "I feel," he writes, "that my undertaking is justified since it has met clear-cut approval and disapproval; since it has found support in your kindness, and malice and hatred from the *Freimütigen*."[28] In still more glowing words he speaks to Brentano of his trust in Goethe: "I admire his determination to champion always the right cause, and if he has thus recognized our literary endeavors as worth while, he will do everything for us, will assist us and take an interest in our future path."[29]

In his controversy with Brentano about their treatment of the folksongs he wrote to Clemens that Goethe preferred the intermingling of old and new elements, for only in this way does the vitality of the old songs become apparent.[30] Goethe answered Arnim's letters very cordially. He writes how much it pleases him to become acquainted with the great city of Berlin through Arnim's descriptions. Again he speaks of the pleasure of cultivating new friendships: "It is fine to become better acquainted. Your full letters, perhaps mysterious to others, always put me into the mood in which you are and convey an enjoyable picture of interesting surroundings. . . . Do please continue to think of us, to write, and to send me something occasionally."[31]

The war of 1806-7 between Prussia and France made it more difficult for Arnim to keep in contact with Goethe. As soon as Middle and Southern Germany were accessible again, he retraced

[26] *Schriften der Goethe Ges.*, XIV, 82 (Feb. 1806), 97 (May 1806), 117 (Sept. 1806).
[27] *Jenaer Allg. Literaturzeitung*, I (1806), Nr. 18-19.
[28] *Schriften der Goethe Ges.*, XIV, 94.
[29] Arnim-Brentano, p. 163.   [30] Arnim-Brentano, p. 235.
[31] *Vierteljahresschrift der Goethe-Ges.*, 1936, H. II, 137; also *Schriften der Goethe Ges.*, XIV, 95.

his steps to Weimar from Eastern Prussia, where as a Prussian nationalist he had been a refugee. From November 8 to 10 he and Brentano and Savigny were daily callers at the master's house.[32] After this brief sojourn Arnim went on to Heidelberg, where he hoped to resume his idealistic literary pursuits, counting on Goethe's support and definitely on his sponsorship for his *Zeitung für Einsiedler*. Already in his last letter of 1806 Arnim had informed Goethe of his intention to publish a "Tageblatt für das Volk,"[33] and in the same letter poured out his hopes and fears for his youthful literary endeavors. He complained that criticism and controversies tended to cripple youthful efforts, while the political situation was forcing young men into early maturity. The mob and the philistine make no distinction between the mature and the immature. They designate all youthful attempts and creations as mere vanity and tear them to pieces with mockery.[34]

The *Zeitung für Einsiedler* began to appear in April, 1808. On the first day Arnim wrote to Goethe: "Surveying as editor the periodical which I sent you, I feel how poor it is to be submitted to you. It may satisfy the masses, and in their interest, which lies nearest the hearts of us both, I take the liberty to ask you for contributions."[35] Arnim's veneration for Goethe found discreet expression at various places in the periodical itself. The literary content of the first two numbers consists solely of Arnim's poem "Der freie Dichtergarten". He closed the first number with the motto that Goethe had written in his album, "Consiliis hominum pax non reparatur in orbe," and opposite this quoted from the Bible, "And God spoke, 'Let there be light!' and there was light."[36] Did this not imply that to Arnim, Goethe had given hope and light for the future? Goethe indeed was his god! In the eighteenth number of May 31, in Arnim's "Lehrgedicht an die Jugend," the symbol of the sun stands for Goethe's name in the following significant passage:

> Fühle Trost in jungen Jahren
> An dem Gott in Menschenkleid,

---

[32] Arnim-Brentano, p. 226.
[34] *Ibid.*, 123.
[36] *Tröst Einsamkamkeit*, p. 20.
[33] *Schriften der Goethe Ges.*, XIV, 124.
[35] *Ibid.*, p. 125.

> Manche sich durch Schrift bewahren,
> Einer lebt in unserer Zeit:
> Will er mild den Arm dir reichen
> Drück ihn nicht wie andre Freund',
> Glück das paart sich nur in Gleichen,
> Gott ist mehr als Menschenfreund.
> Und erscheint als Gott dir ☉
> Auf der Menscheit höherm Thron,
> O so glaubt der Abendröte,
> Werd' nicht rot vor ihm mein Sohn;
> Rüstig dann mit tücht'gen Händen,
> Wirst du frisch zum eignen Werk, . . .[37]

Arnim's great expectations for his *Zeitung für Einsiedler* were never realized. Its failure may be attributed largely to the complete indifference of Goethe to Arnim's undertaking. The great master in Weimar did not comply with his requests nor further his ambitions, obviously because he did not wish to interfere in the struggle between the "Einsiedler group" and the conservative group, headed by the elder Voss. As early as April 1, 1808, in the letter to Goethe which announced the publication of the *Einsiedler-Zeitung,* Arnim mentioned the formation of these two antagonistic camps and added that Voss regarded the periodical as a mockery of his person and interests.[38] After the period of the *Xenien* Goethe was ever wary of literary polemics. Even though he had little sympathy for Voss, the situation in Heidelberg struck him as unpleasant, and he did not wish to take sides. Consequently Arnim pleaded in vain for contributions for his new periodical, and it was only through Bettina's mediation that Goethe sent through her in May, 1808, a few obliging, but not very encouraging phrases.[39] Not until November 14, 1808, did Arnim hear directly from him in answer to his long letter of September 29 preceding. Again Goethe had only polite remarks. He indicated that he disapproved of certain things which he would prefer to discuss personally with Arnim.[40] The *"Wunderliche Zeitung,"* as he called Arnim's undertaking, evidently did not catch his fancy

---

[37] *Ibid.,* p. 182.   [38] *Schriften der Goethe Ges.,* XIV, 126.
[39] *Bettina-Goethe,* pp. 66-7.
[40] *Vierteljahresschrift d. Goethe-Ges.* 1936, H. 2, pp. 139-40. This letter, only recently discovered and published, moderates somewhat the traditional idea of Goethe's indifference and aloofness.

as the *Wunderhorn* had done. Its content was too strange and was beyond his realm of interest. In view of this, Arnim's friendly reception in Goethe's house December 19 to 24, 1808, on his return from Heidelberg to Berlin, should not be overrated. Goethe's cordiality was not meant for the poet and editor of the *Zeitung für Einsiedler,* but rather for the attractive Prussian aristocrat and friend of the Goethe and Brentano families.[41]

The year 1809 finally brought the realization to Arnim that he had overestimated Goethe's interest in the old-German movement. Then another of his attempts to gain Goethe's support failed, when the latter left unanswered his entreaty to write a brief introduction to Wilhelm Grimm's translations of the old Danish heroic legends.[42] Arnim was very anxious for this introduction, which should reveal Goethe's attitude definitely, for as Arnim declared in a letter, "Goethe's ballads 'Thule,' 'Fischer' and 'Erlkönig' contain the gruesome elements of Nordic poetry, while, on the other hand, all his ambitions and tendencies lie in the gracefulness of Greek art and the enjoyment of a rounded life."[43] Later he formulates in a letter to Wilhelm Grimm a similar conception of the dual nature of Goethe's literary interests.[44] In the year follow-

[41] Arnim-Bettina, 249. Nothing has come down to posterity about this meeting or any literary or personal discussions which may have taken place between Goethe and Arnim except a passage in Arnim's letter to Bettina; "Den ersten Mittag empfing mich Goethe mit zwei Küssen, was ihn Gott segne mit zwei Küssen höherer Liebe; seine Lippen wie die Finger großer Musiker haben eine eigentümliche Rundung, Bildung und Beweglichkeit, so daß man schon darin sehen und fühlen kann, wie er die Sprache wunderbar erregen und verbinden kann. Über meine Zeitung (für Einsiedler) sagte er wiederholentlich soviel Schönes, ebenso die andern, was mir besonders herzstärkend war. Voß erkannte er ganz genau." "Die andern" refers to Zacharias Werner and Kügelgen, who were Goethe's guests at the time of Arnim's visit (Bettina-Goethe, pp. 94, 332). Similar descriptions based on the impression he had of Goethe, are found in Arnim's writings. Thus in *Halle und Jerusalem* (p. 178), when Arnim speaks of Germany's master whom he had seen in Lauchstädt: "Ganz befangen von dem ernsten Blick, dem festen Gang, dem freundlich schön Vollendeten der Lippen, an diesen Lippen ist der Meister aller Worte, aller Sprachen zu erkennen, so zierlich sind sie geschnitten, ein jeder Hauch von ihnen ist ein Flötenton, kein falscher Ton fliegt je von diesen Lippen in die Welt."

[42] *Schriften der Goethe Ges.,* XIV, 142. They are the *Altdänische Heldenlieder, Balladen und Märchen,* which were not published until 1811.

[43] Arnim-Bettina, p. 333.

[44] Arnim-Grimm, p. 41. "Daß Goethe nichts hinzugefügt, ist mir nicht allein wegen des Honorars, es ist mir der Sache selbst wegen unangenehm, er hätte bei der Gelegenheit sicher viel Treffliches über den Eindruck der nordischen Sagen, Götterlehren, so wie sie ihm erscheinen, gesagt; während er sich selbst nach seiner Bildung so ganz nach den Griechen gewendet, hat seine Natur ihn doch in mehreren

ing the collapse of the *Einsiedler-Zeitung,* it was only through Bettina that Arnim remained in contact with the master. She assured Goethe repeatedly in most affectionate words of Arnim's undiminished devotion to him.[45]

In 1809, while Arnim and his friends in Berlin were delving still more deeply into old Germanic literature and folklore, Goethe published his modern, most timely novel, *Die Wahlverwandtschaften.* Strange as it may seem, Arnim read this modern psychological novel with great interest. Its stimulating effect can be traced in his own novel on a similar theme, *Armut, Schuld und Buße der Gräfin Dolores.* Wilhelm von Humboldt testifies to the depth of Arnim's penetration into the ideas of Goethe's work. In a letter to its author he says that he could discuss the *Wahlverwandtschaften* better with Arnim than with anyone else.[46] Arnim wrote to Bettina that he had discussed *Die Wahlverwandtschaften* and argued about it a great deal, because some people sought to interpret the novel in favor of Napoleon. He adds that he wants to write a review of it for the *Heidelbergische Jahrbücher.* He did not write the review; but he gives an indirect criticism of the work in his *Gräfin Dolores* and makes incidental remarks concerning it in various letters.[47] From these it is apparent that he found the novel too long, a fault which he ascribed to Riemer's influence; but that he was deeply impressed by the truth and perfection of the descriptive elements and the philosophy which it contained. However, he admitted he could not visualize the characters, except the architect.

One might conclude, basing the deduction also on the ideas

---

seiner schönsten Gedichte, im Erlkönig, im König von Thule, wieder in jene Gesinnung und Gemütsfarbe zurückgeführt."
[45] Bettina-Goethe, p. 121. "Er hat Dich lieb ohne Rücksicht/ ohne Aber, ohne Außerdem, er hat Dich lieb mit ungeschwächter Liebe/ er darf keinen Sinn leiten/ sie gehen alle von selbst zu Dir, so wie meine auch/ darum sind wir beide höchst einig mit einander, und werden es ewig bleiben. Wenn ich wieder zu Dir komme/ so werde ich Dir manches von ihm erzählen/ wie ungemein groß edel diese Neigung zu Dir ist, die Du erschaffen hast in ihm, mit einer Kraft/ deren Du selbst nicht wissend bist. Oft hat er mir den Willen geäußert, mit mir in Deiner Nähe zu sein, er selbst weiß nicht/ daß er zwischen mir und Dir sowie ich zwischen Euch beiden keine Ruhe hab."
[46] Humboldt's letter to Goethe; February 10, 1810. *Goethes Briefwechsel mit den Gebrüdern von Humboldt,* hrsg. von F. Th. Bratranek (1876), p. 236.
[47] Arnim-Bettina, p. 383; *ibid.,* p. 350; Arnim-Grimm, p. 83, *Goethe Schr.* XIV, 144-155.

Arnim developed in *Gräfin Dolores,* that he did not approve of the moral issue involved in the *Wahlverwantschaften* since it was in conflict with his own strict principles respecting religion and marriage. Arnim did not have the ability to write psychological novels, to delve into the intricacies of emotion and the life of the soul. He wrote his novels to illustrate ethical principles, consciously rejecting the exhibition of the inner life; and he considered Goethe's *Wahlverwandtschaften* chiefly as an excellent picture of the life and problems of a certain class in contemporary society. "Let us thank God and His servant Goethe," he says in a contemporary letter to Bettina, "that again a chapter of this dying age is faithfully preserved for posterity."[48] He wrote to Goethe expressing his deep gratitude, a gratitude perhaps mingled with sadness because of the tragedy so clearly presented in the novel.[49] It was, as he knew, a tragedy personally experienced by many contemporaries.

In the letter to Bettina mentioned above, Arnim was more specific about the contemporary social problem involved.[50] Goethe had succeeded in an enviable manner, he thought, in portraying in the first volume the boredom of the leisure class, and had, with keen observation, selected its best possible representatives, namely types from the educated country gentry. Arnim was only too well acquainted with this group, and agreed heartily with Goethe's ideas. All of its members, he declares, suffer from a peculiar morbid melancholy. Because of caste tradition and education, they feel superior to the active, landowning class of farmers, and are segregated from them. Without definite aims in life, they cook away at their own domestic soup until nothing is left in the pot. Anything new that enters this circle and interrupts its state of mutual ennui is felt to be a disturbance. There are more divorces among them than among any other class.

Bettina, Arnim, and others sought in vain for any hint of national consciousness or any patriotic element whatever in

[48] Arnim-Bettina, p. 350, Arnim's letter to Bettina, November 5, 1809. *Gräfin Dolores,* Part II, p. 50.
[49] *Schriften der Goethe Ges.,* XIV, 114-5.
[50] Arnim-Bettina, p. 349.

Goethe's characters, motives which Arnim had introduced into his *Gräfin Dolores*. This is another instance of the wide difference in outlook between Goethe and Arnim. Divergence in national attitude and in ethical principles were to become more and more pronounced as time went by.

Goethe's coolness and unfriendly attitude toward Arnim and Bettina has been often attributed to a quarrel between their wives, in September, 1811. It had, however, an earlier and deeper cause which has been overlooked, viz., a fundamental difference in *Weltanschauung*. As early as 1808, when the *Zeitung für Einsiedler* appeared, Goethe had already lost interest in Arnim and in what the latter believed to be his poetic mission. The great man was not only annoyed by the quarrel between the Heidelberg group and Voss, but disliked heartily the chief literary interests of the former, which centered on the revival of old-German literature. In October, 1810, one year before the quarrel referred to, he had denounced vehemently this literary movement with its slogan, "back to the Middle Ages," as "the foolishness of the present day."[51]

Arnim was well aware of Goethe's lack of interest. He also felt keenly the injustice of Goethe's indifference to Kleist, whose friend Arnim had become in Berlin in 1810. Regretfully he wrote Bettina in 1809 that Goethe was lost to their cause, since "all his tendencies and ambitions lie in the gracefulness of Greek art and the enjoyment of a rounded life."[52] Yet Arnim could not have given up all hope of winning over the Weimar master, for at the time of his and Bettina's marriage, March, 1811, the young couple looked forward eagerly to making a surprise visit to Goethe's home on the later's birthday in the following August. Arnim announced their coming to Riemer, Goethe's secretary, expressing his hope for "good weather," meaning that Goethe might be in a good mood. He hinted that he feared the conspiracies of old Voss in Jena. As mentioned above, the visit of the young couple was cut short by the quarrel between Christiane and Bettina. After that Goethe's aloofness became still more apparent.

[51] Goethe's letter to Reinhard, Oct. 7, 1810.
[52] Arnim-Bettina, p. 332.

Preceding this quarrel Bettina does not seem to have had a clear perception of the difference in character and philosophy of life between Goethe and Arnim. When Arnim began to doubt as to whether he ought to follow in Goethe's footsteps as a poet, she tried to persuade him to do so: "Goethe lures you as a sunbeam lures the blossoms."[53] Goethe and Arnim were the two men of genius who had attracted her and whom she had come to adore. In them her restlessly striving personality and womanly vanity sought an object upon which they might expend themselves. To Arnim she writes, on November 21, 1809: "God desires that both of you should share the cup of my love, for never before has Goethe bestowed upon me such an abundance of kindness. . . . Thus Goethe loves both of us; let us press close to him that we may become quite like his children."[54]

Through the mediation of Riemer Arnim tried to mend the breach in their friendship caused by the quarrel of the women, but in vain. A second attempt in January, 1812, was also fruitless.[55] How earnestly he tried to cover up the unpleasant situation is apparent from a letter to Grimm on September 22, 1811, immediately after the sudden departure of the Arnims from Weimar. The quarrel between Christiane and Bettina is not mentioned. Arnim refers to Goethe's wife simply by remarking that her manners and behavior separate Goethe from all decent people.[56] It soon became apparent, however, that Goethe was no longer the idol of his disciple. Arnim's conception of Goethe as an outspoken, obstinate individualist interested only in the world of ancient Greece, became more intensified after the fateful visit. Goethe acted, he felt, as though he had to withdraw from the present, its events and ideas, and flee to the "Greek world of perfection." Arnim now reflected that it was ridiculous that he had told Goethe of his new ideas for literature, and he recalled that Goethe had then remarked in whimsical fashion, "Well, those are good jokes, but they do not concern me."[57] He had told Arnim repeatedly that he shunned all direct contact with the

---

[53] Arnim-Bettina, p. 271. [54] *Ibid.*, pp. 351-3.
[55] *Idem.*, Bettina-Goethe, pp. 222 and 228.
[56] Arnim-Grimm, pp. 146-7. [57] *Ibid.*

CLASSICISM

present world and avoided current literary discussions. He had never thought it worth while to comment on Wilhelm Grimm's translations from old Danish epics, and he was indifferent when Arnim praised the "nordische Romanzenmanier," which Goethe had previously derided as confused.

Goethe's impersonal attitude toward the urgent patriotic problems of devastated Germany brought Arnim to despair. He found the Weimar poet as much confused regarding German history as Johannes Müller. He noted in the same letter to Grimm that Goethe in revising his poem on Schiller had omitted all passages referring to the fatherland.[58] In all this he judged that Goethe certainly acted wrongly, but it was not his duty to call his attention to it.

At the time of the quarrel between the Goethes and the Arnims the first two volumes of *Dichtung und Wahrheit* had just been published. Arnim, a great lover of biographies, was keenly interested in the book. He held that critics should, because of the very nature of their profession, be very fond of autobiographies, for they represent a form of self-criticism and give a survey of uncompleted works.[59] It was quite natural that Arnim should have looked forward to the appearance of the work, since he knew Goethe personally and through Bettina and Clemens Brentano he had become familiar with the environment and circumstances of his youth in Frankfort. In fact, he had once intended to write a biography of Goethe. After reading the first two parts he wrote his impressions to Brentano and Grimm, praising the author's reticence. Nevertheless, he admitted that he had found the book a bit quaint. While Goethe had formerly wanted to embrace the whole universe, now, on reading the story of his life, it seems as if he wanted to withdraw and explore his own soul.[60]

The year 1812 brought no improvement in the relationship be-

[58] Arnim-Grimm, p. 147; letter of September 22, 1811.
[59] *Literatur-Blatt*, Nr. 66, August 16, 1822, p. 261.
[60] Arnim-Brentano, p. 289; Arnim-Grimm, p. 146. Note the interesting criticism of *Dichtung und Wahrheit*, Part I, by Jacob Grimm, who is also quite enchanted by the beauty of the book and praises in particular the first and last third. The middle is too drawn out, as are epics and history. This, however, makes them profound and more valuable. Arnim-Grimm, pp. 152-3.

tween the Goethe and Arnim families. In August of that year they stayed at the Spa in Teplitz at the same time, but ignored each other. Goethe, writing to his wife, says: "Take no notice of the Arnims, and I am glad that I have gotten rid of these crazy people."[61] Arnim's esteem for Germany's greatest poet, however, is still apparent. He continues to send him copies of his writings during the succeeding years: in 1814, *Die Befreiung Wesels;* in 1817, *Die Kronenwächter,* which he submits, "in well-founded loyalty."[62] This dedication seems justified when one considers that the *Kronenwächter* is a novel of apprenticeship like *Wilhelm Meister* and that Arnim to some extent was a disciple of Goethe's narrative art. In the *Kronenwächter* and still more in his later short stories he followed Goethe's example in the effort to create "reality" artistically. As early as 1809 Arnim was conscious of this principle of founding artistic creations on reality. In reviewing various novels by Ernst Wagner[63] and comparing them with Goethe's *Wilhelm Meister,* he wrote: "All poetry rests upon coarse, square reality and without this human feature, it would be superhuman, a light without form."

In the same review he called attention to the novel in general as a tool of poetic expression and as a unique literary means of national education. This, he thinks, had become particularly apparent with the publication of *Wilhelm Meister*. In the search for quick methods of education, legends and the Bible have been brushed aside in favor of practical arithmetic, writing, etc. The theater cannot offer a substitute for the older material, because it is interested merely in female stars and not in the production of good plays. Thus only the novel remains. But novels must be written like *Wilhelm Meister;* the interest of youth must be kept in mind. The manner of presentation is negligible, while action and power, as in history,[64] and the development of character are

---

[61] Bettina-Goethe, p. 230.
[62] *Schriften der Goethe Ges.,* XIV, 148, 152.
[63] HeidelbJbb. 1809, pp. 169, 179. Here Arnim reviewed the following by Wagner: *Willibalds Ansichten des Lebens, Die reisenden Maler, Reisen aus der Fremde in die Heimat.*
[64] HeidelbJbb., 1809, p. 170: "Wer käme darauf, in der Weltgeschichte sich durchaus etwas anders denken zu wollen, als es geschehen, und viel authentischer sind Romane."

to be emphasized. In Wagner's *Wilibalds Ansichten des Lebens* Arnim found evidence of an imitation of *Wilhelm Meister* in the description and development of the hero, the rich inner life and balance of power with which he is endowed. Certain incidents in Wagner's book, like the countess' visit in the garden, are almost identical with Philine's visit in *Wilhelm Meister*. But Wagner and other novelists still have to learn from Goethe in other respects: 1) to practice due restraint in descriptions of nature and of the effects of music; 2) to show moderation in dramatic effects; 3) not to neglect the secondary characters in favor of the hero; 4) to avoid excessive emotionalism. Concluding, Arnim raises the question whether Goethe's ending in *Wilhelm Meister*, with Jarno's plan to migrate to America, has the hidden significance that in devastated Germany poetry may not survive, but it may find new roots in other lands.

Another novel under the influence of *Wilhelm Meister*, yet opposing some of Goethe's ideas, was *Die Versuche und Hindernisse Karls*, which originated in the Berlin "Nordstern" circle in 1808, and was written jointly by Neumann, Varnhagen and Fouqué. Arnim's criticism of this novel will be discussed in a later chapter.[65] However, in reference to *Wilhelm Meister*, it needs to be considered briefly here. In defense of Goethe, Arnim stresses that the poetic element in *Wilhelm Meister* was not destroyed when the hero abandoned the theatrical career and turned to the practical side of life. The authors of *Die Versuche und Hindernisse Karls* had made this accusation. Arnim points out that one need not cease to be an artist or to be interested in art merely because he gives up his ambition to become a reformer of the stage. Wilhelm Meister had left stage reforms to some successor, for whom he had paved the way and who might be even more successful than he. He had, however, only turned from the theater to interest himself in other fields of art, painting and the plastic arts of the past and present. Arnim reads this interpretation into the novel from the description of the house, filled with art treasures, in which Wilhelm Meister was to reside after leaving the theatrical group, and from Goethe's continuation of the novel in the

[65] Chapter VII, p. 139.

Tübinger Taschenbuch. Goethe in this continuation has stated the truth of the actual relationship between medieval treasures of art and those of the present; according to Arnim Goethe has emphasized that this age has now realized that art treasures of ancient times must be collected, appreciated, and incorporated into the art of the present and no longer regarded solely with religious feelings.[66] That this interpretation of *Wilhelm Meister* was much more a reflection of Arnim's wishes and feelings than of Goethe's, became, of course, apparent in later years, when the other continuations of *Wilhelm Meister* were published. Then Arnim probably had less reason for rejoicing.

These are the two reviews (of Ernst Wagner's novels and the *Versuche und Hindernisse Karls,* by the Nordstern circle) in which Arnim applied comparisons to *Wilhelm Meister* in detail. They both date from a time when he still saw in Goethe the spiritual leader of the nation, and they preceded the quarrel between the Goethe and Arnim families in 1811. From a much later date comes an interesting literary study by Arnim, based on *Wilhelm Meister,* which he designated as "a Wilhelm Meister echo." He gave it the odd title "Wunder über Wunder, indische Mährchen," and published it in his collection *Landhausleben* (1826) as a "Wednesday story" by the dean of the theatrical school. "Wunder über Wunder" is not an echo of *Wilhelm Meisters Lehrjahre,* but of his *Wanderjahre,* as published in Goethe's first version in 1821.

In this story, which is prefaced by a prologue, Arnim creates a counterpart to Goethe's "Pedagogical Province" of the *Wanderjahre*. The prologue is of greater interest to the literary historian. This introduction was necessary, for one might otherwise have been tempted to interpret Arnim's pedagogical narrative as another of the many parodies written on Goethe's novel by his contemporaries. Arnim expresses most emphatically his disgust with these numerous commonplace, and not even humorous, parodies, which, he declares, have failed to grasp the true *Wilhelm Meister*. In order, then, to guard against a wrong interpretation of his own "echo of Wilhelm Meister," he finds it necessary to write

---

[66] HeidelbJbb. 1810, pp. 347-9; review of *Die Versuche und Hindernisse Karls.*

this prologue. Here he becomes superlative in praise of the *Wanderjahre,* the "bright star on the firmament," which none of the many imitations or "false Wilhelm Meisters" can even approach in splendor, for these are dull and empty and are written in an imitative style that has grasped few details of the masterly original. He compares the tremendous influence of Goethe to a mighty stream, of which his conscious or unconscious imitators are but tributaries. Some of them are misled by their own arrogance, e. g., those who write these commonplace parodies.[67] Goethe's mighty influence was evident not only in true or false imitations, it had also opened new paths in literature and art. Arnim admits his own great indebtedness to the master. The delightful account of the "Pedagogical Province" has stimulated him to write "Wunder über Wunder." Whoever has seen Goethe knows how creatively his influence affects those who approach him:

> I have observed how the very tone of his voice, his posture, and movements, yes, even his favorite expressions were unconsciously imitated by a visitor; and when I called on him, I had to discover to my surprise that I formed no exception.... He compels one to exactitude and to limitation in new forms without sacrificing freedom. Like no one else, he is receptive to impressions from the world and then casts them into more beautiful, more comprehensible and lasting forms.... In addition to Goethe's poems, one has to count the innumerable poems which he stimulated in others and which they call their own, but which really belong to no one.[68]

In the prologue Arnim also rejects the belief, so often read into the novel, that Goethe portrayed himself in the character of Wilhelm Meister; and he assures the reader from his own acquaintance with Goethe, that none of Wilhelm's outstanding traits correspond with Goethe's. Wilhelm is rather the author's spiritualized conception of a talented youth of the period ending with the French Revolution. Arnim characterizes Wilhelm as kind, but weak; as zealous, persuasive, whimsical, egotistical, but also altruistic; he has an inferiority complex, but also great self-confidence. Above all, he is possessed by an inner urge for knowledge and education, while the world and public life concern him little; in short, he is the ideal of his period, equipped with all the

[67] *Werke,* XIX, 263.   [68] *Ibid.,* pp. 263-267.

talents and good traits it admired and experiencing all the current temptations and vicissitudes. Nevertheless, no genuine talent drives him in a particular direction. If a whole nation were composed of people like Wilhelm, civilization might blossom but would soon be ripe for decay.[69] Thus the prologue expresses, indeed, admiration and love for the author of *Wilhelm Meister,* as well as gratitude to him.

In the story or study proper ("Wunder über Wunder") Arnim relates chiefly impressions from his own school days and sets forth the ideas growing out of these experiences, employing Goethe's "Province" as his frame and Wilhelm Meister as his mouthpiece. He scourges the conceit of contemporary educators and their so-called "education," "this peculiar, fashionable puppet."[70] Nevertheless, he is convinced that in the long run the indestructible spirit of youth will withstand the onslaught of these pseudo-pedagogues. In conclusion he sets forth his own ideas on education, applying Hölderlin's words: "You will never grasp why your pedagogical practices are useless; in the meantime the stars above follow their eternal course as ever."[71] Here, as frequently in later years, he turned to Hölderlin's wisdom.

The plot describes briefly the efforts of a pedagogue to create a better world by novel, unnatural methods of education in a school of stereotyped rules and regulations,[72] efforts which naturally failed. Only when Wilhelm Meister arrives on the scene and the pedagogue adopts enthusiastically his ideas of art and the theater as means of education, can excellent results be obtained. The pedagogue now transforms his school into a travelling theatrical school, which visits small, unspoiled towns and thereby accomplishes a twofold task: training the children to be great actors for the future and educating the adults who attend the excellent performances of masterpieces of literature and thereby satisfy the need of their souls to see a picture of human life and its vicissitudes[73] presented in a dignified, noble manner, unlike the circus-like contemporary theater, which emphasizes only external

---

[69] *Ibid.*, pp. 267-8.   [70] *Ibid.*, p. 313.   [71] *Ibid.*, p. 313.
[72] *Ibid.*, p. 271. The new educational plan was called "Schule der Gesetzmäßigkeit."
[73] *Ibid.*, XIX, 311-12: "Befriedigen im edlen Sinne das Bedürfnis, ein Bild der Menschheit im großen Wirken und im Gedränge aller Art geistiger Kräfte zu sehen."

effects. In this way the public may acquire a taste for beauty and real art, and the present deplorable and degenerate theater will vanish.

Just as Arnim was stimulated through Goethe's *Wilhelm Meister* to write the "echo," "Wunder über Wunder," he was also aroused by Goethe's monumental drama *Faust* to work up this material. He approached it, however, from a slightly different angle than Goethe. He called his version, a comedy, "Auch ein Faust." This work came to posterity as a fragment.[74] Arnim's undertaking was closely related to the studies on *Faust* which he had made in 1818, as an introduction to Wilhelm Müller's translation of Marlowe's *Doctor Faustus*. The translation and his introduction were sent to Goethe in March, 1818. In the accompanying letter Arnim touches on the question as to why Shakespeare, who had used so many old and historic themes, neglected Faustus. Was it because this drama was already too well-known and outgrown? Arnim believes that the old German popular play (*Volksschauspiel*) of Faust probably had its origin in Marlowe's *Faustus,* and that therefore Marlowe's drama does not strike one as foreign, even though it has a seriousness and grandeur lacking in the German Faust-play. Indeed it prepared the ground for Goethe's *Faust*.[75]

In his introduction Arnim makes a serious plea for more extensive studies and further poetic treatments of the theme. Not enough "Faustus" plays have been written as yet. He offers several rather far-fetched suggestions for possible treatments, such as the portrayal of Faust's fiendish urge to grasp the whole universe, including the infinite realm of the imagination and the soul, and to analyze it and tear it in pieces by scientific experiments; or the presentation of the tricks of criticism in their diabolical nature. Faust might be presented as a writer who sacrifices his soul and immortality to his work and is annihilated by it; or one might make use of the Faust story to show in general the disparity between intention and success, to demonstrate the

---

[74] This is an unpublished fragment of about ten pages. Many years earlier Brentano had mentioned to Arnim Tieck's idea of writing an "Anti-Faust," a comedy in which the devil is deceived by man. Arnim-Brentano, p. 97; Brentano's letter to Arnim, August 1803.

[75] *Schriften der Goethe Ges.*, XIV, 155.

questionable value of human merits and endeavors.[76]

Arnim knew, of course, only the first part of Goethe's *Faust*, as it appeared in 1808 with the publication of the twelve-volume edition of Goethe's works. Here he found already the full power of Goethe's all-embracing views and philosophy, for, as he says, Goethe has made here his own confession and also expressed the feelings and ideas of his age. In a masterly way Goethe has shown the struggles of Faust's soul and its fall, minimizing such superficialities as the pact with the devil and the devil's fetching away the soul, which was the chief scene of interest in the old popular play (*Volksschauspiel*).[77] Goethe has exposed the foibles and false beliefs of his age and driven home the danger of arrogant scientific speculation and experiment, by which the "scientist" or alchemist through delusions and occult practices thinks he can compel the powers of another world to interfere with natural events in our sphere.

Naturally, it was not Arnim's task in this introduction to discuss Goethe's *Faust*. He sought rather to show the relation of Marlowe's *Faustus* to Germany, and how it happened that the undeniably German subject matter found its way to England. It was not yet possible for Arnim to determine Marlowe's source, nor whether it reached the British Isles in the form of a story or a drama. He surmises that it most likely found its way through the mediation of the Netherlands, where one was engaged in active trade with England. The fact that the Grafschaft Emden and the Duke of Anhalt are mentioned by Marlowe might lead to this conclusion.[78] Arnim seems to have been well acquainted with the historic Faust legend, for his attempt in the introduction to trace the relationship between the old German story and Marlowe's *Faustus* is, on the whole, successful. After giving a biographical sketch of Marlowe, he points out that at the most Marlowe could have had access only to a German story, never to a drama. Even the best German historic dramas of those times were mere stories, since any dramatic development was impossible because of the

---

[76] Arnim's introduction to Wilhelm Müller's translation of Marlowe's *Dr. Faustus* (1818), p. XXIII.
[77] *Ibid.*, p. XXIV. [78] *Ibid.*, p. XIX.

rigid rules concerning the rhyme imposed by the schools of the Meistersinger.[79]

In discussing *Faustus* and what the marionette play might have learned from it, Arnim also makes some general remarks about the German stage. He complains bitterly that at present every German theater manager lacks the ability to discover good dramatic material especially suitable to the times. In Marlowe's day, he continues, a theater manager would have noted immediately Goethe's early Faust fragments and adapted them to the stage. Even Maler Müller's *Faust* deserves to be performed.[80]

Goethe did not take any notice of his young friend's letter and Faust studies nor of the questions he raised in the introduction. Nor did he answer Arnim's letter of the following year (1819) which accompanied the transmission of his play *Die Gleichen*.[81] The conservative classicist and cosmopolitan, who in 1818 had coined the expression: "Everybody ought to be a Greek according to his own fashion, but a Greek he must be,"[82] could not be pleased with Arnim's latest creations. A few years later he said characteristically of Arnim: "He is like a barrel, where the cooper forgot to fasten the hoops. Thus it overflows."[83] On December 4, 1820, Arnim paid another call on Goethe. He was struck by his physical appearance and reported on it to Wilhelm Grimm: "He looks well in spite of his age, and yet it is sad to notice the change since I saw him last, nine years ago. His lips are sunken in, the fire of his eyes is gone, his posture reveals his age, and it seems that a habit of angry concentration has taken the place of the benevolent, pleasant expression he used to have."[84] In spite of Goethe's obliging manners, Arnim felt that the regrettable incident of 1811 had not been forgotten and that their friendship could not be renewed. Perhaps also Arnim, now approaching his fortieth year, was no longer the enthusiastic disciple, but had developed rather his own ideas and principles and become more critical of others. He wrote to the Grimm brothers a month later that Goethe had not lived up to an "essential requirement." His writings, with the exception

[79] *Ibid.*, p. XX.
[81] *Schriften der Goethe Ges.*, XIV, 156.
[83] Goethe to Varnhagen, July 8, 1825.
[80] *Ibid.*, p. XX.
[82] *Idem.*
[84] Bettina-Goethe, p. 237.

of the "Morphologische Hefte," lack harmonious unity and betray an irreligious soul; they strive too much for opposition and display. He adds that this lack is also apparent in many of Goethe's followers and has led them astray, particularly in matters of art.[85]

Now also publicly, in journals, Arnim begins to expose what he considers weaknesses in Goethe's personality and writings. When in 1822 the fifth part of Goethe's *Aus meinem Leben. Auch ich in der Champagne* appeared, Arnim reviewed it for Adolph Müllner's *Literatur-Blatt* in a frankly critical manner. In this review he discussed Goethe's work in connection with the memoirs of Casanova and Lauzun.[86] The first two pages of this comparison do not lack an ironical note, which is, however, touched with genial humor.

The Italian allies himself with the German in disgust for everything political . . . the German through the dangers and privations of his military environment is stimulated to ponder on the laws of color (*Farbenlehre*). . . . It is unusual to find that the German in this book writes no tender and loving words, for it is he who has given to Germany for nearly a century the most attractive expressions of beautiful sensuality. . . .[87]

Arnim also points out that, unlike the Frenchman and Italian, Goethe is very discreet in relating his adventures, compromises nobody, is candid only about the dead, never about people still living, so that his memoirs actually appear less comprehensive than one would expect. One also gains the impression that although known and beloved by high and low, Goethe still keeps a wall around his inner self and the work that absorbs him. As was to be expected, the review, while supposedly dealing with all three men, tends to neglect Casanova and Lauzun in favor of Goethe.

Arnim was no longer the blind admirer. On the other hand, he

[85] Arnim-Grimm, p. 483.
[86] Arnim's review of Goethe, *Aus meinem Leben*, II, 5; of *Aus den Memoiren des Venezianers Casanova, Nach dem Manuskript bearbeitet von Wilh. von Schütz*, I. und II, Bd. (Leipzig, 1822), and of the Duke of Lauzun's Memoirs (2nd ed., Paris: Barrois, 1822), II. Vol., in the *Literatur-Blatt*, hrsg. von A. Müllner, 1822, pp. 262-3. This review led to disagreeable arguments with the editor, Müllner, and the publisher, Cotta, who objected to the disrespectful comparisons. Goethe ignored everything completely. Comp. *Goethe Jahrbuch*, XXI, 279-31.
[87] *Ibid.*, p. 262.

did not become spiteful and antagonistic, but sought to pay due tribute to Goethe's greatness as he saw it. He declares that he received this new book joyfully because here negations and inconsistencies are less apparent than in Goethe's later works. In fact, Arnim finds here only one instance of an unjustified attitude of negation, Goethe's disparagement of the art treasures at Treves. Among Goethe's inconsistencies Arnim counts his moody and irritating personal attitude, which he knew from his own experience. Only too often he would encourage, advise, and protect people, and then suddenly neglect them, as in the case of Plessing. In this particular instance Goethe gives a partial explanation when he says that he found Plessing's constant attentions and obtrusiveness too tiresome. But Arnim found contradictions not only in Goethe's personal relationships, which on some grounds are excusable, but also in his ideas. Thus he points out that in his *Westöstlicher Divan*[88] Goethe attacks the virtue of modesty, and on the contrary praises it highly in his "Morphologische Zeitschrift." Arnim wonders whether such inconsistencies have become habitual with Goethe as a result of peculiarities in his style which sometimes expresses unimportant things with great seriousness and emphasis.

Arnim takes this opportunity to set forth again his opinion of Goethe's studies in natural science. A year earlier he had stated that he found these studies more interesting than Goethe's poetical writings.[89] In the present review, his summary of Goethe's scientific achievements lacks the appreciative note. Speaking as a contemporary scientist, who is well acquainted with the controversies in question, he draws the general conclusion that with the exception of the mineralogists, none of the scientific scholars,

[88] *Ges.* (1819), pp. 801-7. Arnim's essay, "Otto Brüggeman, ein Beitrag zu Goethe's *Westöstlicher Divan.*" Here Arnim protested against Goethe's denial of Brüggeman's definition of modesty, which reads, "Das Wenige, was der einzelne Mensch leistet, in seinem abhängigen Verhältnis gegen das große Weltleben zu erkennen und sich dessen nicht zu überheben." This essay on "Otto Brüggeman" (or Brughman, as Goethe wrote), who accompanied Olearius on his good-will trip to Russia and Persia, consists of anecdotes and adventures. Cf. Bettina-Goethe, p. 238.

[89] Bettina-Goethe, p. 238. Arnim wrote to the Grimm brothers, January, 1821: "Unter allen seinen jetzigen Arbeiten sind mir die 'Morphologischen Hefte' das Liebste, da ist er bei weitem weniger auf Schein and Opposition."

neither anatomists, botanists, nor physicists have much use for Goethe's contributions. The mineralogists recognize him because his work shows knowledge and a proper scientific humility before a vast field. The anatomists think that Goethe has given undue emphasis to certain details; the botanists consider his work *Die Metamorphose der Pflanzen* as unimportant. Above all the physicists are much annoyed by his controversy with Newton, and they find his *Farbenlehre* useless, obscure in theory, and unimaginative in the experimental part. If Goethe were not a master of rhetoric and an admirable poet carried away by the beauty and flow of words, his scientific writings might have been clearer, and he might have also given simple reports on questions arising and on doubtful experimental results, instead of omitting them. He might thus have made a really valuable contribution to science.[90]

In conclusion Arnim also discusses at length Goethe's description of the "Kanonenfieber" from which he suffered when he was at the front with the German army in 1793.

The review gives public utterance to Arnim's disgust with what he considered unattractive traits in Goethe's character and work. He makes it quite plain that not only his personal feelings had been deeply hurt, but that his opinions with regard to Goethe's rôle in Germany's cultural endeavors had undergone a fundamental change. One must admit, however, that this criticism can scarcely be called unbiased. He was more than doubtful of Goethe's fame as the greatest German poet of the present and future. He was now more eager to keep in touch with the Grimm brothers than with Goethe. He was doubtful of the merits of Goethe's works, for he himself got little enjoyment from reading them. This is his sincere reaction, even though ironically phrased, when Bet-

---

[90] *Literatur-Blatt,* hrsg. von A. Müllner, 1822, p. 262. Here Arnim writes: "Diesen Vorwurf einer seltsamen Dunkelheit über einfache Gegenstände möchte auch wohl das Schwerste sein, gegen welchen die Farbenlehre zu verteidigen; er möchte jedoch ganz schwinden, wenn Goethe aufrichtig das Ahndungsreiche, aber auch das ganz Schwankende, Unausgebildete seiner Anschauungen mitgeteilt hätte. Die Freude am Gelingen versteckt ihn aber, wo es nicht fort will, die Worte runden sich, alles scheint sich darin zu umfassen und zu beschließen, die Rhetorik wird Herr über den Gegenstand aber nicht der Verstand, geschichtliche Einsicht schmückt ihn und doch ist nichts geschichtlich verbunden und begründet."

CLASSICISM

tina writes him of her brief visit to Goethe in July 1824.[91]

Shortly before Arnim's death in January, 1831, Bettina visited Weimar twice, in the late summer and the fall of 1830, and tried to call on Goethe, but according to Goethe's diary, "Frau von Arnim's obtrusiveness was rejected."[92] Thus Arnim died unreconciled with the man whom he once considered his great master and rejecting him as Germany's spiritual leader. After Arnim's death the old bonds of friendship between Goethe and Bettina were not renewed. In 1832 she wrote him humbly: "Don't you know me any more? If you only knew how much your silence hurts me!"[93] However, Bettina had at least the satisfaction of knowing that Freimund, her son and Arnim's, was hospitably received by Goethe as the last visitor before his death.[94]

The other great poet in Weimar, Schiller, had died half a year before Arnim paid his first visit to Goethe in November, 1805. Reinhold Steig has emphasized that, unlike the early Romanticists, the Heidelberg circle, including the Grimm brothers, understood and appreciated Schiller. Jacob Grimm especially was full of admiration for Schiller's objective, aesthetic point of view. In young Arnim, however, one cannot discover much interest or understanding for Schiller's poetry and philosophy. On reading Schiller's *Wilhelm Tell* he wrote to Brentano: "Schiller's *Tell* is unworthy of both, Schiller and Tell; I feel a better 'Tell' striving for expression in myself."[95] In asking whether Schiller's chorus was received without applause in Weimar, he declares: "Such choruses are unsuitable to the present stage of musical development, and the ancients had never spoken choruses."[96]

Arnim's and Schiller's conceptions of poetry were indeed entirely different. Arnim wished to cultivate the simple natural

---

[91] Bettina-Goethe, pp. 263-4. We read here: "Von den Grimms schreibst Du wenig oder nichts, und doch hörte ich von ihnen lieber als von Goethe, von dessen künftiger Seligkeit bei mir nicht die Rede ist (er mag es sich wohl nur einbilden, daß sich die Leute darüber bekümmern), dessen jetzige ich aber schon lange bezweifle, seit mir selbst bei seinen Arbeiten nicht recht wohl wird."

[92] Bettina-Goethe, pp. 284-5.

[93] *Ibid.*, p. 286. [94] *Ibid.*, p. 287.

[95] Arnim-Brentano, p. 115. Arnim's letter to Brentano, October 3, 1804. A critical reference to the *Braut von Messina* occurs in an earlier letter.

[96] *Ibid.*, p. 94.

poetry of the people (*Volkspoesie*), and he appreciated Goethe chiefly as the poet of popular songs (*Volkslieder*). Schiller, on the other hand, raised the people to an unreal poetic height and put words into the mouth of the masses which were unnatural and incompatible with their lives and surroundings. Whether peasant, burgher, or aristocrat, all spoke and acted on the same high aesthetic and poetic level. What applied to poetry, applied also to the theater; and this explains Arnim's criticism of Schiller's *Wilhelm Tell*. Schiller could never be a poet of the people (*Volksdichter*) and thus, in Arnim's eyes, merit the highest possible fame. It was only E. M. Arndt among contemporary poets who could, in his opinion, almost claim this distinction.

A few years after Schiller's death, however, there appeared in the *Zeitung für Einsiedler* a belated sign that Arnim had some appreciation for him. He published extracts from Schiller's letter to a young poetess,[97] praising them as excellent examples of constructive criticism, confidentially carried on between a master and a hopeful disciple. This publication, with Arnim's commentary, must be regarded as a rare admission by Arnim of Schiller's great rôle. Another, less emphatic, came a few years later in a review of Zacharias Werner's *Attila, König der Hunnen*. Here Arnim makes interesting comparisons between Werner's and Schiller's dramas, praising the latter. He calls attention to Schiller's diligence and precision. *Die Braut von Messina* he considers the best drama; in *Die Jungfrau von Orleans* the supernatural element is overdone.[98] Unfortunately Arnim did not follow Creuzer's suggestion to write a review of Schiller's "Theater" in the *Heidelbergische Jahrbücher*, though he took it under consideration.[99] A study of the correspondence between Goethe and Schiller which he began in 1829 remained also an unpublished fragment.[100]

About two other German classical writers, Lessing and Wieland, Arnim never wrote anything critical. Most likely their interests and personalities were still more foreign to him than Schiller's.

[97] *Tröst Einsamkeit*, pp. 196-9.
[98] HeidelbJbb., I, 1810, p. 11: "Doch sind die Ahndungen und höheren Empfängnisse in der 'Jungfrau von Orleans' zu stark überhäuft." Cf. p. 102.
[99] NHeidelbJbb., XI, (1902), pp. 195-6, 199, 204.
[100] Cf. Karl Henrici, "Auktions-Katalog," 149, Nr. 41, p. 7.

One is justified in the deduction that criticism in the wider and modern meaning of the term was not considered worth while by Arnim. He regarded it as his task to write critically only about such poets as he considered interesting, important, and constructive for him, and as furthering art for the people.

VII
NATIONALISM

Arnim's poetic life was nurtured in the ideas and activities of the Heidelberg circle. His interests as a critic were naturally very much concerned with all the writings of this group of friends. In this circle young Arnim held a distinctive position, on the one hand, because he enjoyed the special friendship of Goethe, and on the other, because he was the only North-German and aristocrat, and as such was able to take a broader view of affairs in Germany than, for instance, Brentano. Strong patriotic feelings drew him to participate actively in realistic political problems and the center for such activities was his native Berlin. Heidelberg remained the oasis of idealistic poetic pursuits.

At the beginning of the year 1809 Arnim returned again to Berlin, where people had just begun to breathe more freely after evacuation by the French army. With the return of the royal couple at Christmas, 1809, the metropolis was again the center of social and political activities. The founding of the university became the most important factor in the cultural life of the city. Men like Fichte, Adam Müller, and Savigny joined the faculty of this new institution, and the Prussian capital now became the meeting ground for all those who worked for the liberation of Prussia from the Napoleonic yoke. Arnim, too, was heart and soul for this cause. His political and national sympathies came into the foreground during this time until the tragic internal political situation of Prussia after the War of Liberation showed him the hopelessness of all further endeavors in the political field. The most productive period of his career encompassed these first years in Berlin; the same was true of Heinrich von Kleist, who was then his close associate.

As happens often in times of political restlessness, literature and literary journalism forsook the principle of art for art's sake and turned to the realistic questions of the day. In those days the questions foremost in the mind of intellectuals were such as these:

Should Prussia become permeated with the new spirit of the French Revolution, or should she pursue a policy of national development in which the historic state evolves organically? Should one adopt the political philosophies of Rousseau and Montesquieu or that of Edmund Burke? Finally, should Prussia open her gates to industrialization, following England's and France's example and the preachings of Adam Smith, or should every effort be made to have Prussia remain an agricultural country?

For the defence of tradition and a conservative policy Arnim founded the "Christlich-deutsche Tischgesellschaft," which counted among its members leading aristocrats, nationally minded intellectuals, poets, and scholars. Their voices were heard in the *Berliner Abendblätter*, the new journal founded by Kleist, devoted to a policy faithful to the king and Prussian tradition, and counting among its contributors Kleist himself, Adam Müller, Arnim, and Fouqué. The object of their attack was the policies and attitude of Chancellor Hardenberg. The sharp antagonism of the Kleist-Müller-Arnim group lasted through the entire period of Hardenberg's rule. As late as 1816 Arnim complained in a letter to Görres that with the beginning of the war of 1813, when he learned that Stein had not taken Hardenberg's place, he had immediately abandoned all hope for any permanent and thorough reforms within the state.[1] All documents of the "Christlich-deutsche Tischgesellschaft" that have come down to posterity, and likewise the topics discussed in the *Berliner Abendblätter*, attest this bitter struggle between the national conservative group and Hardenberg and his clique for supremacy in the cultural and political affairs of the state.

Arnim, well versed in all these controversial questions, a prolific reader, of quick perception and intelligence, now became in the field of economics and politics a valuable collaborator for both the *Berliner Abendblätter* and later the *Preussische Correspondent*. In these journals his witty, critical pen did valiant service for the development of a national program. One will search in vain for any strictly literary-historical criticism from Arnim's pen in either of these newspapers. None of the philosophers, poets, writers, or

---

[1] Josef von Görres, *Gesammelte Briefe*, hrsg. von Marie Görres, VII, 483; Arnim's letter to Görres, January, 1816.

artists who breathed the new political atmosphere in Prussia could escape the powerful currents of the time or fail to reflect political ideas in their writings. When Steig says, *"Des Knaben Wunderhorn* marks the beginning of this new Berlin movement," he does not exaggerate.[2] One might justly call Arnim the prophet of Prussia's national rise. This is shown by an examination of his program for *Der Preusse,* a weekly he had intended to publish in 1806, but the plans for which never materialized.[3] In his essay "Von Volksliedern," Arnim prophesied that "a time will come when tedious military service will become a source of great honor and joy."[4]

Nevertheless, history does not rank Arnim among the outstanding leaders of this period, such as Stein, Hardenberg, Fichte, Arndt, and Jahn. Among his contemporaries Fichte also lacked popular appeal, but his teachings and ideas began to meet with wide approval shortly before the War of Liberation.[5] On the other hand, Fouqué, a poet less know today, became very popular with the publication of his *Sigurd* in 1808. In spite of all Arnim's endeavors and the mission he felt called to undertake, namely, to speak the language of the people and to bring to them "their" poetry (*Volkspoesie*), he failed in popular appeal, partly because he lacked the opportunity, and partly because he could not surmount the barriers interposed by his aristocratic birth and thoroughly romantic character.

From 1809 till 1814 Arnim collaborated closely with most of the leading patriots. With greater maturity and confronted by different circumstances, he revised his earlier attitude toward Arndt and Fichte and his judgment of these men. They too had changed their outlook in accordance with the more urgent political needs and now believed that Prussia could play an important rôle in leading Germany to better days. A really close friendship grew up between Arnim and Heinrich von Kleist during the brief period before Kleist's suicide. Like Arnim, Kleist was an eccentric, ro-

---

[2] Reinhold Steig, *Heinrich von Kleists Berliner Kämpfe,* Berlin and Stuttgart, 1901, p. 3. Cited below as *Kleists Berliner Kämpfe.*

[3] The forthcoming publication of *Der Preusse* and Arnim's program as future editor for this weekly were announced in *Der Reichsanzeiger,* II, 1806, Sp. 3291-3293.

[4] DNL, CXLVI, 1, 67.

[5] *Kleists Berliner Kämpfe,* pp. 307-8.

mantic personality. He also lacked popular appeal and did not succeed in establishing any real contact with the masses.

Arnim's literary and patriotic influence first became noticeable in Berlin in the "Nordstern" circle, a group of young writers including Chamisso, Neumann, Varnhagen, and Bernardi. Fouqué also was connected with this group. These men regarded *Des Knaben Wunderhorn* as the realization of their own endeavors. On his arrival in Berlin in 1809, Arnim was enthusiastically received into this circle. Closer association, however, rather estranged him from it. Brentano even derided the "Nordstern" group.[6]

Neumann, Varnhagen, and Fouqué published jointly in 1808 the satirical novel, *Die Versuche und Hindernisse Karls,* which Arnim reviewed in the *Heidelbergische Jahrbücher* of 1810.[7] The critic had no very high opinion of the work nor of the circle from which it originated, as he plainly states in his review. An examination of the book shows that his attitude was abundantly justified. The satirical tone which marks it is, indeed, arrogant and mediocre. The authors not only ridiculed Johannes von Müller, Voss, and Jean Paul, but they also repeated the criticism of Goethe's *Wilhelm Meister* often heard in those days, namely, that all poetry is ruined in this novel. Naturally Arnim had to take issue sharply with this arrogant and satirical spirit, and impressed on the authors that they could learn much from *Wilhelm Meister,* its plot, style, etc. "The young men of the 'Nordstern' circle," he says, "should lay aside their supercilious attitude and desist from silly criticism of the work of so mature a writer as Goethe"; and he points out that the poetic element was not ruined when Wilhelm Meister entered real life and abandoned the career of an actor, as these young men had assumed. In short, Arnim had no use for a novel which was but a parody of other novels, and emphasized strongly that it was high time to begin to read original writers again instead of their critics and parodists. In comparison with *Wilhelm Meister,* he declares, *Die Versuche und Hindernisse Karls* is a novel that one can well shelve and forget, the sooner the better.

[6] Cf. *ibid.,* pp. 6-7.
[7] HeidelbJbb., 1810, pp. 347-9; Reinhold Steig in his *Heinrich von Kleists Berliner Kämpfe* does not mention this review of Arnim.

It is only for the chapters on war and military events, written by Fouqué, that Arnim has praise. These were permeated with a novel conception of the patriotic spirit and a new esteem for the soldier, which coincided with Arnim's ideals.[8]

The relationship between Arnim and the members of the "Nordstern" circle did not grow more intimate as the years passed. Their names did not appear in the list of the "Christlich-deutsche Tischgesellschaft" when its first meeting was called by Arnim on January 18, 1811. But among the members of the new organization was Heinrich von Kleist, who had become in the preceding year Arnim's closest collaborator and friend. It is most regrettable that these two idealists of early nationalism did not meet before and that fate terminated their association so soon. Even though they happened to be in Königsberg at the same time, in 1806 and 1807, there exists no evidence that they met before 1810 in Berlin.[9] From February 4, 1810, until his death on November 21, 1811, Kleist lived in Berlin; except for a brief trip to Frankfort-on-the-Oder. Strictly speaking, Kleist's and Arnim's acquaintanceship lasted only a year and a half, for Arnim and his young wife went on a trip to South Germany in August, 1811, and did not return till after Kleist's death. Kleist's regard for Arnim is expressed in a letter written in the summer of 1810. Here he remarks that of all his friends, Arnim is the one of whom he is most fond, although he has not seen Arnim so often since the latter's marriage.[10] Few documents except their joint journalistic productions remain to testify to this friendship. In the Heidelberg circle Kleist and his works found little mention. To be sure, Arnim had been asked by the *Heidelbergische Jahrbücher* to review Kleist's *Penthesilea*, but unfortunately for posterity, he did not comply with this request.[11] While the bonds between Kleist and Arnim grew closer, Brentano remained aloof. Jacob Grimm recognized Kleist as an outstanding poet; young Ferdinand Grimm exulted in him.[12]

---

[8] Cf. *Kleists Berliner Kämpfe*, p. 56.
[9] Reinhold Steig, *Neue Kunde zu Heinrich von Kleist*, pp. 37-8.
[10] *Ibid.*
[11] Alfred Kloss, *Die Heidelbergischen Jahrbücher der Literatur in den Jahren 1808-1816* (Leipzig, 1918), p. 55.
[12] Reinhold Steig, *Neue Kunde zu Heinrich von Kleist*, p. 122.

When he was editor of the *Zeitung für Einsiedler* Arnim had taken favorable notice of Kleist's *Phöbus*.[13] One is justified in assuming that the fairy tale *Das Märchen von der langen Nase*, published anonymously in the *Phöbus* (June, 1808) was a contribution of Arnim's to this periodical.[14] Arnim met Kleist soon after the latter's arrival in Berlin in February, 1810, and wrote in that month to Wilhelm Grimm of the newcomer as a very odd personality, of a sort that is apt to appear when talent breaks through the old Prussian forms. He characterizes Kleist as the most simple human being he has met in a long time, though he has, to be sure, an inclination toward cynicism. There is an uncertainty in his speech that approaches stammering, a reflection of which, Arnim declares, can be found in the constant erasures and corrections in Kleist's manuscripts. He leads a queer life, often stays in bed for days, smoking his pipe, in order to work undisturbed. His novel *Kohlhaas* Arnim regards as excellent.[15] In a letter to the Grimm brothers, September 3, 1810, Arnim calls Kleist the "best fellow," yet one who has talent to become a second Dante because he enjoys so much tormenting his poetical characters.[16]

In the same letter he announces the appearance and purpose of the *Berliner Abendblätter*, inviting the Grimms to send contributions. For the present the *Abendblätter* were to entertain the reader rather than be serious, or make attempts at instruction, or include literature. One can hardly take this statement of Arnim seriously, nor another, saying that he did not enjoy his collaboration on the *Berliner Abendblätter*. As a matter of fact, the journal was on a high level from the very beginning, containing serious discussions of political and literary events. It afforded Arnim an opportunity to criticize important personages and ministers, and this is his only reason, he states,[17] for continuing as an active collaborator. In spite of his pretended indifference to the *Abendblätter*, Arnim contributed no less than seventeen articles and reports,[18] and submitted ten others which did not pass the censorship.[19] This is certainly an impressive number for one writer, in view of the fact that the paper was published for only half a

[13] *Tröst Einsamkeit*, June 25, 1808; p. 35.
[14] Mallon, p. 35.   [15] Arnim-Grimm, p. 84.   [16] *Ibid.*, p. 70.
[17] Arnim-Grimm, p. 84.   [18] Mallon, pp. 42 f., 48.   [19] Arnim-Grimm, p. 96.

year, beginning October 1, 1810, and ending March 30, 1811.

Most of the articles written by Arnim were on political and economic topics. Those not passed by the censor are of greater interest because they touch upon local questions of literature and the theater. In these articles Arnim wanted to submit to the public and especially to Iffland the reforms and requirements for a new stage for the romantic drama, and thus pave the way for the production of Kleist's and Tieck's plays. The current discussions and quarrels about the theater Arnim raised to a more general and impersonal level. Apparently he was very optimistic of his rôle as a mediator, since he was on a better footing with Iffland, producer and director of the Berlin theater, than Kleist was.

Arnim demanded first of all a hearing for local playwrights. They have a greater right on the stage of their fatherland than foreign writers. It must be humiliating, he continues, for men like Kleist and Tieck as well as for the entire nation, to be neglected in favor of Contessa, Robert, and other similarly mediocre dramatists.[20] Of course, personal interest also motivated Arnim's efforts. For years he had studied and collected old German plays, and intended to edit them. He also hoped for a production of his drama *Halle und Jerusalem*, completed in 1810. His ideal was to have the old German and romantic plays dominate the German stage, and to continue and extend the Shakespeare revival, already begun by the early Romanticists.[21] However, Iffland did not react favorably to Arnim's endeavors as a mediator and made no concessions to the Berlin group of romantic playwrights. For this Iffland blamed the stubbornness and lack of cooperation of local poets.[22]

Arnim wrote to his friend Dorrow in April, 1811, about Kleist's and his own discouraging experiences: "Kleist with his *Abendblätter* had felt the severe pressure of the government. Half of the articles intended for publication had been suppressed by the censorship of the Berlin police. No free discussion of the local theater was permitted. Iffland and Hardenberg stuck together like grease to a wheel."[23]

[20] *Kleists Berliner Kämpfe*, p. 96.
[21] *Ibid.*, pp. 242-3.   [22] *Ibid.*
[23] Wilhelm Dorrow, *Reminiscenzen* (Leipzig, 1842), p. 457.

As stated above, Arnim was in Frankfort-on-the-Main at the time of Kleist's death. From here he wrote to the Grimm brothers, December 6, 1811, of his friend's suicide:

> The poor fellow, I feel sorry for him. His stubbornness was not very pleasant, but he was honest in his work as few others. His short stories are good, and for his dramatic talents he only lacked a worthy stage which was interested in him. A series of unfortunate circumstances probably drove him to this unhappy act. There was the fiasco of the performance of his *Der zerbrochene Krug* in Weimar during Kleist's absence; the failure of his *Phöbus,* an excellent journal; the destruction of his *Berliner Abendblätter* by a government afraid of it, and finally poverty added to the strain.[24]

Kleist's tragic end caused considerable comment, but even now his opponents were not silenced. The attacks of the *Morgenblätter* assumed ugly personal forms, which made the indignant Arnim write to this paper in defence of Kleist. In this protest Arnim praises Kleist's exemplary life as an army officer and as a government official, the two callings he had abandoned in order to dedicate his life to poetry:

> Perhaps only a few poets may boast of such sincerity of character and severity of standards in their work as the deceased. Instead of reproaching him for adherence to a new school, one should rather regret that he did not recognize any school and only in rare instances yielded to tradition and the judgment of his artist friends. With great stubbornness he rather gave way to the accidental, which may have misrepresented often the depth and beauty of his feelings. He ruled his destiny with a firm hand, and his persistence, increasing with the vicissitudes of his life, is explainable, for he carried his burden, realizing his inner powers.[25]

Throughout his life Arnim took Kleist's part, like a faithful friend. Brentano's comment that the poetic cloak of poor Kleist had been too scanty, he rebuked with the remark that that of Brentano was too ample and in the hurry had not received a good fitting, so that it covered his eyes.[26] In 1825 a poor performance

---

[24] Arnim-Grimm, p. 172.

[25] The *Morgenblätter* did not pay any attention to Arnim's protest, a copy of which is in the Varnhagen collection at the Staatsbibliothek in Berlin. Cf. *Kleists Berliner Kämpfe*, p. 684.

[26] *Ibid.;* Arnim-Brentano, p. 297, cf. Brentano's criticism of Kleist's *Penthesilea:* "Es ist doch in allen Arbeiten dieses unglücklichen, talentvollen Menschen eine ganz merkwürdige scharfe Rundung, eine so ängstliche Vollendung und wieder Armut, und es wird mir immer äußerst peinlich und doch macht es mir Freude, etwas von

of *Käthchen von Heilbronn* moved Arnim deeply and reminded him of all the noble talents that had been misunderstood in their time and killed by cold criticism. Then he wrote to Wilhelm Grimm that he was convinced Kleist would still be alive if he could have witnessed one performance of his play in Berlin, no matter how poorly done.[27] It is of interest that Arnim as a critic lavished praise on two men who were not appreciated by their contemporaries, and were equally tragic in their lives, Kleist and Hölderlin. Both were, in his opinion, great poets of the German people, and of the utmost sincerity in their poetic work.

Arnim's connections with nationalistic groups in Berlin were manifold. They brought an acquaintanceship with Ernst Moritz Arndt, who was secretly in Berlin from Christmas 1809, till Easter 1810. Speaking of this period in Berlin in his *Erinnerungen aus dem äußeren Leben,* Arndt says that he met there a number of men and youths who had bound themselves together in the interest of patriotic work, among whom was Arnim.[28] Arndt supported Arnim eagerly in his collection of folksongs for another volume of the *Wunderhorn.*[29] As mentioned earlier, Arndt's major book on national topics, *Geist der Zeit,* had not been received very favorably by Arnim. He objected to its general pessimistic outlook for Germany and the reproaches it voiced against Prussia. Seven years later, at the end of the great war year, in 1813, when he wrote his review of Arndt's *Das preussische Volk und Heer 1813,*[30] Arnim referred to the general impression which the book had made on him, recalling that the author evidently did not formerly have "a very high opinion of our people," that is, the Prussian people. However, Arndt had now changed his opinion and had made a study of Prussia and its army which led him to recognize the important rôle of Prussia in the war of 1813. In his review Arnim gives due credit to Arndt and now speaks of him

---

ihm zu lesen"; *ibid.,* p. 302. Cf. also Brentano's criticism of Kleist's *Hermann, ibid.,* p. 344.

[27] Arnim-Grimm, p. 544.

[28] *Ernst Moritz Arndts Werke,* hrsg. von Wilhelm Steffens, II, 88-90.

[29] Arndt wrote to Reimer on November 27, 1810: "Hier mein lieber Getreuer, sind einige Sächelchen, die meine Freunde gesammelt haben, wovon einiges vielleicht für das *Wunderhorn* dienen könnte. Du magst es Arnim geben." E. M. Arndt, *Ein Lebensbild in Briefen,* hrsg. von Meisner und Robert Geerds, 1898.

[30] *Der Preussische Correspondent,* December 25, 1813, p. 4.

as an honest writer who is filled with ardor for his ideas and a love of the subject.

Arndt's treatment of history interested Arnim very much. His method was to emphasize individual episodes in the history of nations, in this case the year 1813 in which he himself had participated, rather than to generalize and to pass historical judgments. He considered this method the only correct one, for it gave a realistic and truthful picture of events. The other was much too vague and difficult for a contemporary, and such a procedure should be left to future generations. Arnim also agreed with Arndt that it was solely the respect for spiritual freedom that had led Prussia to victory, and that therefore spiritual freedom, above all, should be preserved and treasured in the future. As a romanticist, historian, and collector, Arnim had still another wish at heart, namely the preservation of literary and historical documents and time-honored institutions. Thus, in the now abolished kingdom of Westphalia he wished to see preserved the old Germanic system of justice which had been reintroduced by Napoleon, and also all the historical documents relating to the seven years of the kingdom's existence.[31]

Of greater literary value is Arnim's review of Arndt's *Der Rhein, Teutschlands Strom, aber nicht Teutschlands Gränze*.[32] First, Arnim discussed here in detail Arndt's personality as a writer and politician, and secondly, the topic he had chosen for this book, which was one of a delicate political character. Arnim ranks Andt as one of the best contemporary writers, for Arndt's discussions of burning questions of his time reveal deep under-

[31] The passage is as follows: "Auch in dem untergegangenen Westfalen hatte sich bei aller Verderblichkeit und Fremdartigkeit des Ganzen im Einzelnen manches Gute entwickelt, was bewahrt zu werden verdiente. Manche Einrichtung wie die Friedensrichter und die Geschworenen, die vielleicht aus Deutschland stammen, nach weitem Umlaufe wieder als fremde Einrichtung dahin zurückkehrten, verdienten allgemeiner eingeführt zu werden, ebenso die mündliche kürzere Verhandlung, die Öffentlichkeit der Gerichte, usw. Eine Pflicht der Bibliothekare wäre es jetzt insbesondere alles, was auf jene unseligen sieben Jahr bezug hat, zu sammeln, da der allgemeine Haß gegen die Gewaltsamkeit jener Einrichtung auch den gedruckten Denkmalen so gefährlich ward. . . . *Der Westfälische Moniteur* wird künftig in der Geschichte eines der abenteuerlichsten Denkmale sein. Literarische Sammler werden aber unserer Zeit immer wesentlicher und leider immer seltener. . . ."

With regard to the Westphalian system of justice, cf. also Arnim's review of Jacob Grimm's *Deutsche Rechtsaltertümer*.

[32] *Der Preussische Correspondent*, January 28, 1814, p. 4.

standing and are marked by clarity of treatment. He has covered his field completely, and his manner of presentation does not lack appeal and energy. Arndt, indeed, comes close to being Arnim's ideal of a perfect writer, but he has one great defect:

> He has become a beloved poet of the people (*Volkschriftsteller*), yet not a genuine one. Whenever he tries to be really popular, he fails, for being popular (*volksmäßig*) is a talent and gift and does not depend upon the artist's endeavor. If it were possible to compare periods, one might liken him to Hutten—but our time does not have a Luther, of whom Hutten said, "Whatever comes from me is human and is bound to fail, but whatever comes from you is divine and will exist forever!" Luther as a political writer deserves the highest attention, but he has never received it, as far as we know.[33]

Men like Arndt and Hutten have the desire to present their opinion to the public, but Luther, like Frederick the Great, was driven by spiritual forces. Out of inner necessity such men say and do unconsciously what they must.

In this connection Arnim also expressed his opinion of Edmund Burke, then regarded by many as a great and fascinating political leader, like Luther in his age. Arnim disagreed with this view. He admitted that Burke was a political leader of great sagacity and of some prophetic foresight, but at the same time he was too rhetorical and affected, and lacked "unconscious divine directness."

With regard to the political topic of Arndt's book, the river Rhine and Germany, Arnim avoided statements regarding the contemporary situation and discussed the problem historically and in general terms. Arndt was concerned with the physical and cultural separation of the German-speaking people on both sides of the Rhine, and the question as to how, after Napoleon's defeat, they could be reunited. Arnim did not accept Arndt's rather romantic reasons for this separation; he also rejected geographic causes for it and differences in the character of the people, and ascribed it rather to the indifference of the population and mistakes in constitutions and in legislation. He believed that such a long historical separation could not be bridged over easily, and

---

[33] Arnim's review of Arndt's *Der Rhein, Teutschlands Strom, aber nicht Teutschlands Gränze*, in *Der Preussische Correspondent*, January 28, 1814.

preferred to build on the slogan: "Germany extends as far as the German language!" Arndt's idea of strengthening the German element by the formation of an order of knights, he rejected as artificial. He trusted that the future would solve the question of the political education of the population. If the people have high ideals, then education also will improve among them.

These reviews of Arndt's two books appeared in *Der Preussische Correspondent,* the outstanding patriotic political newspaper in Berlin during the War of Liberation. *Der Preussische Correspondent* had been founded by Niebuhr and supported by Scharnhorst. Its first issue appeared on April 2, 1813. The original intention was to enlarge it into a national journal. A number of outstanding men were its chief contributors: Niebuhr, Göschen, Schleiermacher, Arnim, Arndt, and Ludwig Jahn. Arnim served as editor from October 1, 1813, till January 31, 1814. His contributions to the *Correspondent* fall chiefly into this period and are very numerous. He notes in the farewell address to his readers of January 31, 1814:

> I have written all articles, sketches, announcements, anecdotes, and poems, unless they are signed otherwise, or unless they are news dispatches by correspondents. . . . I have endeavored to add to all of my writings something of value for our people. This may have been disliked by the highly intellectual, but has pleased people of culture.[34]

Just as earlier in the case of the *Zeitung für Einsiedler,* Arnim tried to use the *Preussische Correspondent* as a means of serving the people and bringing national ideals before them in a popular form. From the literary point of view, the *Correspondent* falls behind both the *Zeitung für Einsiedler* and the *Berliner Abendblätter.* Arnim's contributions consisted mostly of short anecdotes and episodes from the battle-fields and from home. The only valuable literary reviews, besides those of Arndt's works noted above, are his discussion of Fouqué's poems, Zacharias Werner's *Die Weihe der Unkraft,* and of the anonymous publication *Der Frau von Staël Verbannung aus Frankreich.* To these must be added a eulogy on Fichte at the time of his death. During his editorship Arnim obtained the collaboration of the Grimm brothers and of

[34] Cf. DNL, CXLVI, 1, p. CXXI.

Brentano. These friends sent him anecdotes and news; Brentano from Vienna, Wilhelm Grimm from Cassel, and Jacob Grimm from France.[35]

Arnim's experience as a newspaper editor was only the short-lived adventure of a romanticist in the field of practical realities. Several reasons may be cited for his resignation. He himself attributed it to the annoying censorship: "Articles were cut to such an extent that finally only a lie remained".[36] Even in his farewell note to the reader, the following passage was eliminated by official direction:

> The restrictions are so severe that they suppress all desire to express even that which is permitted. Nations cannot learn any longer by mutual experience because they hear nothing truthful from each other.[37]

Differences of opinion between Niebuhr and Arnim may also have been a factor. Even though they were friends, their literary tastes differed, and they disagreed on some general policies.[38]

As noted above, one of Arnim's reviews in the *Correspondent* was that of Fouqué's poems.[39] Fouqué was a very prominent person in the literary and political circles of Berlin in those days. Arnim liked the poems because they were well written and incorporated the real war experiences of the poet. Arnim hoped, indeed, that the stirring days of the war would bring a revival in poetry:

> Time teaches and will do so more in the future, that poetry should bring not only tales of a lost paradise, but also prophecies of one to come, to which all heroic deeds point, so that this aspect of poetry will flourish again. Let us hope that the wealth of subject-matter during this year will arouse poets, for never in past decades has there been such an abundance of heroic material for German singers.[40]

Arnim's literary relationship with Fouqué had begun in 1809, when

---

[35] Cf. Arnim-Grimm, p. 288. The Grimm brothers originally intended to publish their own journal.
[36] Arnim-Brentano, p. 325; Arnim's letter to Reimer, November 18, 1813.
[37] *Ibid.*, p. 324.
[38] DNL, CXLVI, 1, p. CXX: Niebuhr's letter of January 11, 1814; also Arnim-Brentano, p. 334: "Die Ängstlichkeit der Censur, die Borniertheit und das Einreden von Niebuhr gestattete mir auch nur den kleinsten Teil des Möglichen. Sorgen und Besorgnis der eigenen Geschäfte raubte mir viel Zeit, die Verbindungen waren bei der allgemeinen Unruhe sehr schwer anzuknüpfen, ausländische Zeitungen fehlten."
[39] *Der Preussische Correspondent*, October 15, 1813, p. 4.
[40] *Ibid.*

Arnim returned to Berlin. As mentioned above, he reviewed in the *Heidelbergische Jahrbücher Die Versuche und Hindernisse Karls* by the "Nordstern" group of writers, among whom was Fouqué. On the appearance of *Sigurd, der Schlangentöter*, the work which made Fouqué famous, Arnim suggested to Wilhelm Grimm that they review it jointly, and in particular compare this new version with the original saga.[41] As it happened, Wilhelm wrote most of the review, which was published in the *Heidelbergische Jahrbücher* in 1809. Arnim added only a few words to soften Wilhelm's severe criticism, which had charged that Fouqué had been superficial in his treatment of old poetic treasures and had failed to reach a high poetic level in his version. As Arnim wrote to Wilhelm, Fouqué's chief mistake was that he alternated in a queer manner the unconscious mechanism of old poetry with that which had been evolved in modern poetry; in other words, that he put on the same string imaginary, unobtainable desires with actual fullfillment.[42]

While Arnim was in close contact with all circles of poets and writers of his day in Berlin as well as with many leading men in university and political circles, he did not seem to care for a closer acquaintanceship with the Berlin philosophers. His natural inclinations, his inherent romanticism, did not tend toward abstract philosophical thinking. In his youth he expressed strong disgust for speculative thought, he "despised all philosophy."[43] This may explain why his relations to Fichte and Schleiermacher in Berlin were rather superficial, even though both supported the "Christlich-deutsche Tischgesellschaft."

Fichte had taken a courageous position in his *Reden an die deutsche Nation* in the winter of 1807-8. Nevertheless, Arnim and the Berlin patriots remained rather cool. As a teacher at the university Fichte was not popular, a fact well known to Arnim, who repeated Fichte's words in a letter to Wilhelm Grimm: "Although I have lectured for fifteen years, students don't understand me."[44] In the *Phöbus*, Adam Müller said of Fichte that in spite of all good intentions, he could not attain any popularity because "he had no understanding for those (the students) who should under-

[41] Arnim-Grimm, pp. 30, 41.
[42] *Ibid.*, p. 83.
[43] Arnim-Brentano, p. 53.
[44] Arnim-Grimm, p. 83.

stand him."[45] Other reasons may have contributed to Fichte's unpopularity; the Berlin Romanticists would have preferred to see a professor of natural philosophy in the chair at the university, Arnim having in mind his old acquaintance Steffens.[46]

However, the beautiful eulogy which Arnim wrote at Fichte's death in 1814 corrects the impression we might derive from his earlier remarks on the philosopher. "In the morning of January 29," he writes, "our highly esteemed Fichte passed away. His death aroused something more than sadness, and compels us to meditate on how quickly the great spiritual leaders of Germany are vanishing, before the nation herself is rebuilt."[47] He goes on to praise Fichte's strength of character, his harmonious mentality, his determination, which almost might be called pride, his sincerity as a philosopher, his masterly power of polemic. As the greatest disciple of Kant, he created a new and very stimulating philosophical school of his own, without realizing it until Kant called attention to it. Arnim declares that he does not feel competent to pass judgment on Fichte's writings, but that the effects of Fichte's pen are obvious. In contrast with what had seemed to be the earlier opinion of himself and others regarding Fichte's popularity, he now calls Fichte "the sun on the students' heaven in Jena." Fichte did not give his students any formula or prescriptions, he gave his whole personality. He was worried often lest his students could not understand him, and this led him to attempt to express himself in a more popular language and made him an even better writer. Arnim also extols Fichte's "insight into the corruption of his time". In public lectures he gave advice to all classes of the German people and set forth the severest admonitions in a peculiarly good-natured tone. With great courage he stigmatized French corruption in its influence on the German nation. Furthermore, in 1813 he did not merely talk about the duties of a German, but volunteered for the Reserve Corps of the Army, in spite of ill health. In Arnim's opinion it would be a self-rewarding task to write a biography of this unusual man. The biographer must not overlook apparently insignificant events and utterances.

[45] Johannes Bobeth, *Die Zeitschriften der Romantik,* pp. 243-4.
[46] *Kleists Berliner Kämpfe,* pp. 307-8.
[47] *Der Preussische Correspondent,* January 31, 1814, pp. 1-2.

Fichte's manner of expression was "frank and uncouth, he did not shrink from the extraordinary, the shocking, and the ridiculous."

Like Fichte and Fouqué, Arnim volunteered to serve his native country in the army. However, his wish to go to the war-zone was never realized, for his Reserve Corps was dissolved early.[48] Perhaps if he had gone, we might have had from him at that time patriotic, lyrical poems, like those of Körner, Fouqué, and others. To fight as a journalist in Berlin, behind the front lines, brought him disappointment and humiliation, and too soon, as noted above, he resigned as editor of the *Preussische Correspondent*. He had hoped that with the war a new epoch for Germany would dawn, in which he himself might serve his fatherland in an important political position. So much the greater then was his disappointment over the prevalence of reactionary forces in Germany and Hardenberg's continued leadership. He had no choice but to retire to the quiet of his estate Wiepersdorf and to consecrate himself once more to his literary mission. Only the letters to his friends still spoke of his shattered aspirations and ideals. To Brentano he wrote in 1814:

> Even though no important activity was allotted to me, I nevertheless sacrificed devotedly my time and thought, desires, and mentality to the serious call of this important year for our fatherland. But now I shall shake off all cares.[49]

Also in other letters to his romantic friends Arnim's disillusionment is noticeable, particularly those to Görres during the years 1814-1817 were written in this mood: "Almost by force a hand from above seems to push me away from all public life", he declares in 1816, "and at times intuition tells me that my love and ideals for the welfare of the nation are not appreciated now, but will be in a better, purer future, when greater mutual confidence reigns."[50]

---

[48] Arnim-Brentano, pp. 310-15.
[49] *Ibid.*, p. 337.
[50] Josef von Görres, *Gesammelte Briefe,* hrsg. von Marie Görres, VIII, 481-4; Arnim's letter of January 23, 1816. Cf. also Arnim's letter of June 4, 1814, p. 416.

VIII
THE DRIFT TOWARD REALISM

Arnim survived the War of Liberation by only a few years, dying in January 1831. The years following 1815 appear in the history of Germany as a period of general fatigue, of indefinite searching for something new. This feeling of emptiness and lassitude, especially in the political life of Prussia, was the result of Hardenberg's rule, and the élite of the time watched the developments with resignation. Unfortunately intellectual life did not escape the same fate. The German poets and writers of the postwar days were depressed and disgusted. A fear to speak freely, a dread of the unbelievably strict censorship made new creative work impossible. Of the powerful romantic intellectual and political life which had dominated Berlin about 1810, only a timid remnant had been rescued for the aesthetic salons of the metropolis.

Gradually, however, a change became perceptible. The year 1815 brought a new phase in the history of German civilization. Time was bringing about the collapse of the systems of the old world, the world of the rights of small sovereign states, the world of absolutism with its strong individualism and its romanticism. The younger generation of 1815 would no longer look on with resignation. It soon began to prepare the ground for the events of 1848.

Arnim's mind was divided between these tendencies. His previous training, his own inclinations, and whole personality made him adhere to the traditional and romantic outlook, but events, and in particular his personal circumstances, forced him to a change of attitude. But thirty-four years old in 1815, he still had an open mind, could perceive the new trends and experience transformations in his spiritual life. His writings during the years immediately following, especially his contributions to the daily papers, reveal a stronger tendency toward realism. Significant for this change of attitude is the termination at this time of his relationship to the *Heidelbergische Jahrbücher* and the *Preussische Correspondent*, as well as to Görres' *Rheinische Merkur*. He had to abandon his hope for closer collaboration with Görres. Instead of these typical romantic periodicals, he contributed now to *Der Gesellschafter oder Blätter für Geist und Herz;* to Brockhaus' publications, like the *Literarische Conversationsblatt* and the *Blätter für literarische Unterhaltung;* or to pseudo-romantic journals, like Fouqué's *Berlinische Blätter für deutsche Frauen;* and to Adolph Müllner's *Literatur-Blatt*. These are only a few of the more important periodicals for which Arnim wrote. To these must be added his numerous contributions to various "Almanacs," a type of periodical which reveals still more distinctly the transitory character of this literary period.

Toward the end of the war, out of necessity, he had to abandon his restless romantic wanderings and to settle down at his country estate Wiepersdorf to earn his daily bread as a farmer. Such a radical change in his life separated him from his restless friend Brentano. The romanticist had to become a realist if he wished to retain his family estate and support his family,[1] for the French occupation, war contributions, and high taxes had reduced his holdings considerably. Like Wilhelm Meister he had to resign from the great world of art and dedicate himself to the chores and routine of a gentleman-farmer. He did not fail in his new duties, but accepted the situation with admirable vigor and good humor. For the rest of his short life he carried himself like a typical "märkischer Junker," so much so that a youthful visitor to the "Literarische Mittwochsgesellschaft" in Berlin in 1824 was astonished when he was introduced to the romanticist Arnim and beheld a stout gentleman who was engaged in a discussion with Fouqué regarding wheat prizes, sheep-shearing, manure, etc.[2] He even came to like the rural solitude and the novel labor, as may be gathered from a letter to Wilhelm Grimm.[3]

[1] Arnim-Grimm, p. 327: ". . . aber so ist mein Verhältnis, daß ich gewissenlos gegen die Meinen würde, wenn ich meine Angelegenheiten nicht durchführte. So wird nun Lehmacker verteilt, Kohl, Salat und Selleri in Reihen gepflanzt statt Soldaten. . . ." Letter to Wilhelm Grimm, May, 1815.
[2] DNL, CXLVI, 1, p. CXXIV.
[3] Arnim-Grimm, p. 327: "Ein größeres öffentliches Leben war mir unerreichlich, ein kleines Mitlaufen gestattet meine Lage nicht, so ist mir die Einsamkeit will-

It is surprising that in spite of his manifold duties Arnim could continue his literary activities. However, he complained often that he could devote little time to poetry. As noted above, his changed circumstances brought a touch of realism into his writings. In the *Kronenwächter* in 1817 he showed far more respect for form and clarity than in previous works. Here he followed Goethe's example. The precise local and historical descriptions in the *Kronenwächter* foreshadow the historical novel as it evolved under other hands in the next decades. During this time also he turned more to the short story as a medium of expression, very much as Tieck was doing. In 1818 Arnim's *Der tolle Invalide* was published; in 1820, *Die Majoratsherren;* and in 1826 his collection of short stories entitled *Landhausleben*. These stories, like Tieck's, are purged of fantastic caprice and tend to bear the imprint of realism.

In his daily journalistic activities Arnim's changed outlook became still more apparent. The reason for this was that he now wrote chiefly for the pseudo-romantic literary circles in Berlin, the salons, aesthetic-tea societies, and Almanacs. He was attracted by the financial compensation offered by the Almanacs, and also enjoyed reporting realistically on the events of his time, contemporary situations in politics and economics. At first national political articles predominated in his contributions to the journals from Wiepersdorf, for the experiences of the war of 1813-15 were still fresh in his mind. During 1815 he was collaborator on the *Rheinischer Merkur,* for which he wrote eight articles, all more or less of a political nature, regarding the question of greater Germany and the constitutions of the single states. In 1817 he made political contributions to the *Deutscher Beobachter,*[4] of Hamburg, and to the Jena periodical *Nemesis*.[5] He displayed also keen interest in the outstanding personalities of Prussian political life, such as Hardenberg, Blücher, and Scharnhorst, and in what was

---

kommen und das mühevolle Erhalten dessen, worauf doch endlich das Ganze mitberuht, verliert von seiner Verdrießlichkeit."

[4] "Über Aushebung zum Kriegsdienst in Preußen," p. 522; "Über das Legen der Bauern," p. 543; cf. Otto Mallon, *Arnim-Bibliographie*, Nr. 92.

[5] "Betrachtungen über die Verfassung des vormaligen Königreichs Westfalen," pp. 441-467; cf. *ibid.*, Nr. 93.

written about them. In addition to this he liked to write about his travels, an interest in which he anticipated the *Jungdeutschland* group. In his "Memoirs of a Traveller" he wrote of a trip to Halle,[6] of the October festival in Munich in 1829,[7] of a visit to the "Teutoberg,"[8] of Prenzlau, Dresden,[9] Cologne, Bonn, Vienna, Antwerp.[10] These reports had little of romantic or fantastic color, but rather a modern, realistic tone. They must be conceived of as fragments of a greater book on travels on which Arnim was working just before his death.[11] That he was much interested in many kinds of political, administrative, and economic questions is shown in his numerous contributions to the *Gesellschafter* and the *Literaturblatt*. His reports of current art activities and exhibitions belong in a separate group. The *Blätter für literarische Unterhaltung* in 1830 alone contain five such articles.[12]

In comparison with these varied interests, Arnim's writings on purely literary questions fared rather badly. In his literary articles also realistic and factual-historical elements were dominant, such as one searches for in vain in his contributions to periodicals during the first decade of the century. It seems as if Arnim wanted to stem the tide of disgust and depression, to set up a countermovement to the censorship and the falsification of current events, the result of the strict censorship. His writings stand in strong contrast to the early *Biedermeyer* literature, the over-sentimental, aristocratic love-hero stories found in the Almanacs.

In this connection it may be mentioned that some of his unpublished literary productions in the years 1815 to 1831 relating to the Varnhagen group may have been destroyed by Varnhagen.

[6] *Literarisches Conversationsblatt*, pp. 117-18, Leipzig 1823; cf. *ibid.*, Nr. 124.
[7] *Blätter für literarische Unterhaltung*, pp. 157-9, Leipzig 1827; cf. *ibid.*, Nr. 141.
[8] *Berlinische Blätter für deutsche Frauen*, pp. 1-19, 107-138, Berlin 1829; cf. *ibid.*, Nr. 148.
[9] *Der Gesellschafter*, p. 719, Berlin 1817; cf. *ibid.*, Nr. 95.
[10] *Blätter für literarische Unterhaltung*, pp. 89-91, 93-94, Leipzig, 1831; cf. *ibid.*, Nr. 158.
[11] Joseph von Görres, *Briefe*, III, 361; Arnim's letter to Görres, October 7, 1829.
[12] "Ältere Nachricht vom Maler des Danziger Bildes"; "Ausstellung und Versammlung des Vereins der Kunstfreunde im preußischen Staat"; "Besprechung von A. Hirt, 'Kunstbemerkungen auf einer Reise'"; "Genrebilder, Staffage"; "Besprechung von T. H. Schuler, 'Beschreibung des Straßburger Münsters'"; cf. Otto Mallon, *Arnim-Bibliographie*, pp. 84-5.

According to Steig, Varnhagen did away with all of the letters of Arnim and Brentano in which he found disparaging remarks about the Varnhagen group and about Rahel in particular.[13] It is, however, to be emphasized, that Arnim and Brentano were on friendly terms with Rahel, due to Varnhagen's mediation. Between the widowed Bettina and Rahel a hearty and sincere bond of friendship existed. It was due to this that Bettina turned over to Varnhagen Arnim's unpublished papers for organization.

When Arnim formed his association with the *Gesellschafter*[14] he had at last found a paper for which he could write with enjoyment, for the *Gesellschafter* was, in Arnim's words, "not malicious and ignorant like most other papers, and only once in a while a little stupid, which one has to take for granted in this world."[15] The publisher, F. W. Gubitz, showed a full appreciation of his collaboration, and Arnim continued to write for the paper until his death in 1831. Altogether he made more than fifty contributions on subjects from all fields of human interest, using many forms of literary and poetic expression: reviews, essays, poems, and short stories. What flowed from the pen of the busy gentleman-farmer was indeed a variegated medley. That he was conscious of this is revealed by a letter to Görres in 1822,[16] where he expresses his chagrin that his writings have to suffer because of the diversity of his plans and the interruptions caused by business.

Gubitz called Arnim's work, "German from a varied panorama" (*Deutsches aus vielseitiger Umsicht*).[17] We have further information from Gubitz about Arnim's relationship to him and his paper. They were friends professionally and personally. A mutual confidence united them. They stimulated each other, although they had their quarrels and agreements.[18] Differences resulted only when Arnim submitted to the practically minded Gubitz romantic,

---

[13] *Kleists Berliner Kämpfe*, pp. 612, 623; Arnim-Brentano, p. 295.

[14] The history of the *Gesellschafter* or *Blätter für Geist und Herz* has not as yet been written. This periodical was not included by Houben and Walzel in their bibliography of Romantic periodicals, where it was supposed to appear in a later volume. Cf. p. XI of the introduction in Volume I of the *Die Zeitschriften der Romantik*. L. Geiger in his *Unbekannte Aufsätze A. v. Arnims* publishes twenty-seven of Arnim's fifty-seven contributions to the *Gesellschafter*.

[15] Joseph von Görres, *Briefe*, II, 520; Arnim's letter to Görres, October 21, 1817.

[16] *Ibid.*, III, 62 (1822).   [17] F. W. Gubitz, *Erlebnisse*.   [18] *Ibid.*, p. 104.

pseudo-scientific essays like that on Jung-Stilling's *Theorie der Geisterkunde* (cf. above). On the other hand, Gubitz had no objections to Arnim's political views; he found his essays always marked by clarity of thought and noble conviction. As the editor recalled in later years, Arnim presented his ideas in a definite, understandable manner, unprejudiced by class or social differences, with an impartiality and directness "which never left him when he traced the historical phenomena of the world" (*im Verfolg weltgeschichtlicher Erscheinungen*).[19]

Most of Arnim's critical writings which were published in the *Gesellschafter* have been discussed in the foregoing chapters. Here we shall confine ourselves to those which reveal best his critical attitude in later years and his relationship with the literary circles of Berlin in the days following the war. Thus in "Über eine Theater-Kritik" Arnim gives his opinion of Dorothea Schlegel's criticism of Oehlenschläger's *Ludlam-Höhle* and of the tasks of criticism in general. With bitterness he scourges the absurdity and vanity of this type of ignorant, destructive criticism, in which a number of his contemporaries indulged. These critics lack a genuine feeling for art, which Arnim defines as the "splendid intuitive knowledge how to grasp at once the essential, the inner urge of the artist, and to judge how far he succeeded."[20] They object to everything new and modern, and to everything traditional. Praise they consider superfluous, and in the end they discuss with great glee that which they can blame and deplore. The more such evil criticism increases, the more vanity and boredom will increase and the more hopeless and senile the state of society will become. Arnim closes his epistle with a poem entitled "Literargeschichte" on the theme, "Formerly people only talked and gossiped, but now most of them write, and writing promotes audacity, for one cannot contradict ink." The accord is given in the first two stanzas:

> Sassen sonst die alten Basen
> Bei dem Kaffee rings im Kreise,
> Dünkten sie sich auch schon weise,
> Und vergassen drein zu blasen;
> Doch wenn sie verbrannt die Zungen,

[19] *Ibid.*, p. 106. [20] *Unbekannte Aufsätze*, p. 35.

Kam Vernunft im Widersprechen;
Rächte alle Mißhandlungen,
Sonst da blieb es noch beim Sprechen.

Statt Gesellschaft kommt jetzt Zeitung,
Wird beim Kaffee still gelesen
Und es stäubt der krit'sche Besen
Jede voll in der Verbreitung,
Bis nun jede eingesehen:
Daß sie dies auch könne leisten,
Ohne etwas zu verstehen,
Jetzt ach! schreiben schon die Meisten.[21]

Another attack on modern criticism was his review of Müllner's *Ährenlese neuerer Kritik*. Arnim entitled this discussion "Ährenlese auf dem Felde älterer Kritik,"[22] for he considered Müllner's attempt to collect abstracts of new criticism as unnecessary. It would be more important by far to collect critical writings from older periodicals, which cannot be found so easily in libraries and may completely disappear. Thus he called attention to the fact that Goethe in *Aus meinem Leben* had mentioned that he used to contribute to Schlosser's *Frankfurter Gelehrte Anzeigen* of the year 1772. It is, says Arnim, most important that these superior essays and reviews be saved for posterity, for they illustrate that criticism undergoes few changes throughout the ages and is always excellent whenever a great mind applies itself to it.[23] As examples he quotes from the *Frankfurter Anzeigen*, Goethe on "Klopstock's Oden"[24] and Goethe's opinion of translations.[25]

These two essays of Arnim, of the year 1818, "Über eine Theater-Kritik" and "Ährenlese auf dem Felde älterer Kritik," show

---

[21] *Ibid.*, pp. 35-7.
[22] *Ges.*, p. 335; 1818 (not in Geiger's collection).
[23] *Ibid.*, p. 335; 1818; "Ährenlese auf dem Felde älterer Kritik."
[24] *Idem*, and Goethe in the *Frankfurter Gelehrte Anzeigen*, p. 57 (1772): "'Klopstocks Oden.' Bei einem Werke der Ewigkeit gilt weder Lob noch Tadel. Hier steht es! ist alles was der Liebhaber und Verehrer am Altare sagen kann. Weg also mit dem geschwätzigen Cicerone, der uns Gefühl an den Fingern herzählt und den Blitzstrahl des Genies mit der Hand greifen lehrt." Goethe's contributions to the *Gelehrte Anzeigen* have now been identified, and have been republished many times. Cf. Max Morris, *Der junge Goethe*.
[25] *Ibid.*, p. 766: "Es ist uns schon lange ein unerklärbares Phänomen gewesen, wie Leute, die so ganz ohne Geschmack die Alten lesen, sich einfallen lassen können, Übersetzungen davon zu machen."

that he had not abandoned his earlier views and principles in respect to criticism. In spite of the fact that he frequented the literary salons of the metropolis and contributed to many insignificant and second-rate journals and almanacs, he nevertheless did not lower his requirements or cease to raise a warning voice. He felt that the incongruities and excesses in criticism had taken on more dangerous forms and were more widely practised than a decade before, when he had struggled with the unhealthy conditions in criticism in his *Zeitung für Einsiedler.* His healthy realism now made him turn away from such literature as the *Theater-Kritik of Dorothea Schlegel* (cf. below), or the philistine literature Merkel was offering in his journal *Der Freimütige,* or the dramatic productions of Iffland and Ernst Raupach at the Royal Theater in Berlin. He left this branch of literature, which did not even attempt to ennoble and improve *belles lettres,* and delved more deeply into realistic topics, political and economic questions, short stories, travelogues, and biographical reviews.

The scope of his writings on literature for the *Gesellschafter* reflects very well the breadth of Arnim's interests in his later years. In one issue he published hitherto unknown letters of the Karschin, praising highly this poetess of the people and stating that many, like himself, wished that the first and original versions of her poems had been preserved rather than later ones which show the imprint of artificial improvements by her scholarly friends. Truly, he adds, natural poetry like hers is something rare in Germany.[26] In another number he discusses the willful and absurd destruction of valuable documents, such as happened, for example, around 1800 through the closing of the monasteries and their libraries: this at a time when people should have known better than to destroy such literary treasures.[27] Or again, he relates interesting incidents from Otto Brüggeman's life because it touched upon Goethe's *Westöstlicher Divan.*[28]

[26] *Unbekannte Aufsätze,* p. 56: "In einem Volke wie das unsere, wo diese Fertigkeit nicht, wie in Italien, künstlich anerzogen und ausgebildet wird, setzt es allerdings eine Eigentümlichkeit voraus, des Besten gerade auf diesem Wege, in dieser Art überraschender Begeisterung—als plötzlicher Einfall fertig ausgesprochen—sich bewußt zu werden."
[27] *Ibid.,* p. 95.
[28] *Ibid.,* p. 43.

Not until he began making contributions to the *Gesellschafter* did Arnim take cognizance of Sir Walter Scott in the form of essays and reviews. Henriette Schubart translated in 1817 the third volume of Scott's *Minstrelsy of the Scottish Border*. As early as July, 1803, while on his "grand tour" in England, Arnim had become acquainted with this collection, soon after its first publication.[29] It proved to be one of the stimulating influences which called forth the *Wunderhorn*.[30] Arnim now confirms this in his discussion of the Schubart translation. He goes on to say that in the revival of interest in poetry of the people it is to the credit of Scott that he made these old poems more intelligible by means of his historical introduction, and also brought them closer to his contemporaries by adding his own ballads from Scottish legendary material.[31] He speaks also of Shakespeare's relation to Scottish subject-matter and the similarities in art and spirit where the peoples of Europe touch each other, pointing out that the most tragic of Shakespeare's dramas, *Macbeth,* was based on Scottish history. He finds it surprising that Shakespeare did not write more Scottish tragedies, and also that he did not utilize more in his *Macbeth* the strong family inter-relationships and traditions prevalent in Scotland. The similarities in the spiritual and artistic life of the people of Europe (*Volksgesinnung*) could be revealed by a comparison of the German with the old Danish heroic legends made available in Grimm's translation. Kinship could also be traced with the modern-Greek robber tales, which had been collected by Freiherr von Haxthausen, though not yet published.[32] Arnim regarded Scott as the man who had given voice to the English-Scotch *Volksgesinnung,* who had therefore accomplished precisely the same as he, Arnim, had tried to do for the German *Volksgesinnung* with the publication of the *Wunderhorn*.

Scott's *Waverly* appeared in 1814 and the first part of Arnim's *Kronenwächter* in 1817. In its well-rounded, realistic portrayals, this work shows that Arnim was not Scott's, but rather Goethe's apprentice. This he emphasized in a notation to his short story *Die Ehrenschmiede. Novelle aus den Denkwürdigkeiten eines Naturforschers*. Here he states that as a poet he had stepped on the

---
[29] Arnim-Brentano, p. 95; Arnim's letter to Brentano, July 5, 1803.
[30] *Unbekannte Aufsätze*, p. 80.   [31] *Ibid.*   [32] *Ibid.*

THE DRIFT TOWARD REALISM

fertile soil of natural poetry before Scott discovered the Scottish Highlands.[33]

In 1822 Arnim wrote an extensive review of a series of Scott's publications.[34] They included translations of Scott's *Waverly* (Leipzig, 1822) and *The Pirate* (three translations, Berlin, Leipzig, Berlin, 1822), the original *The Pirate* (Edinburgh, 1822), and a novel by K. H. L. Reinhardt, *Die Circe von Glas-Llyn. Ein Roman nach Walter Scott,* which was one of the numerous contemporary imitations of Walter Scott in subject-matter and style. This discussion differs from all of Arnim's previous reviews in its precision, severity, and its approach to modern, critical standards. It is surprising to note how carefully Arnim discusses details of these translations, and with what assurance he appraises the endeavors, successes, and failures of the translators,[35] revealing an intimate knowledge of the English language and of Sir Walter Scott. Whereas he has nothing but praise for Scott the lyric poet, he criticizes him vigorously as a writer of prose.[36] He compares his work with Goethe's and condemns Scott for wordiness and for repetition in the construction of plots. Arnim finds that his later novels are devoid of new themes and that they lack suspense. This applies in particular to the *Pirate*. Here Arnim finds no confirmation of Virgil's "Nova progenies caelo demittitur alto,' for several characters in *The Pirate* are reminiscent of similar ones in *Waverly* and *Kenilworth*. The plot is neither novel nor interesting, and the whole is successful only in its portrayal of local *mores*. To be sure, *Kenilworth* is also unduly long, but it is full of interest, has suspense in the plot, and an interesting character-development, all of which *The Pirate* lacks. In *Die Circe von Glas-Llyn; Ein Roman nach Walter Scott,* the author, K. H. L. Reinhardt, has caught nothing worth while from the Scottish master. It lacks style and suspense, it is not romantic but obscure, and is much like a mediocre play acted by ordinary comedians.

Arnim's lively interest in English literature continued. We have

[33] Werke, II, 3.
[34] *Literatur-Blatt,* hrsg. von Adolph Müllner 1822, pp. 250-2.
[35] *Ibid.;* Arnim reproached severely the translator of *Waverly* for inexcusable mistakes in his mother tongue; but he praised all three translations of *The Pirate,* that by Spiker being perhaps the best because he preserved very carefully the style and explained unknown words and objects.
[36] *Ibid.;* cf. also Arnim's *Landhausleben; Werke,* XIX, 11-12.

evidence of this in 1829, in a study *Hamlet und Jacob*,[37] published in Fouqué's *Berlinische Blätter für deutsche Frauen*. This journal affords a typical picture of the decline of Romanticism. Its name and still more the articles it contains suggest that one treads here the slippery ground of aesthetic rodomontades (*ästhetisierendes Geflunker*).[38] Arnim's article is, however, a notable exception. His other contributions to this journal consisted of travelogues.[39]

In this study our critic attempts to show that Shakespeare's motivation in writing *Hamlet* lay in the English political problems of his time. The question of succession to the English throne after the death of Queen Elizabeth was uppermost in everybody's mind. The queen herself gave the solution during the last days of her life. According to Arnim's interpretation, this painful question, which dominated for years the political life of English as a "to be or not to be," as well as the doubts which tore at the soul of James I and his sinister fate, made a great impression on Shakespeare. The duty to avenge his mother and father created a severer problem for James than was Hamlet's. The theory that *Hamlet* was an acute, timely problem explains in Arnim's opinion why this great tragedy is so unusual and so entirely different from all others by Shakespeare. The poet has given expression here to all the anxiety for England's future under the reign of a doubtful successor like James I, as well as to the ease of mind that followed many years of watchful waiting, when the successor turned out to be better than his reputation. At the same time, Shakespeare voices the apprehension that an ill fate may trouble this successor, who is given to contemplation rather than action at a time when ruthless action was demanded of a ruler. Thus the Danish fable was but the core around which Shakespeare built the greatest of his dramas.[40]

This theory about the origin of *Hamlet* had suggested itself to

---

[37] *Berlinische Blätter für deutsche Frauen*, I, 1-12. This study is not found in Mallon's *Arnim-Bibliographie*, but it is assigned to Arnim by Houben and Walzel in *Zeitschriften der Romantik*, Vol. I.

[38] Houben and Walzel, *Zeitschriften der Romantik*, I, p. XIII.

[39] *Berlinische Blätter für deutsche Frauen*, IX, 1-19, 107-138.

[40] *Ibid.*, pp. 1-12: "Die dänische Fabel ist ein Schiff, Shakespeare ist der Steuermann, aber der Sturm, der es treibt, gehört weder den Dänen, noch dem Shakespeare, sondern der englisch-schottischen Geschichte."

Arnim during his studies of Mary of Scotland. He wanted to write a drama *Maria Stuart;* but, unlike Schiller's, it was to include not only the last events of her fateful life, but also all the earlier ones, such as the death of Rizzio and her husband Darnley, the murder of Bothwell, the strange life of her son James, his knowledge of the plot of Essex, the death of Elizabeth, and James' coronation in London. Now, however, after discovering and studying *Hamlet,* Arnim abandons his plan, for it would, he says, be "like writing the Iliad after Homer."[41]

Like Goethe, Arnim recognized Hamlet's complicated character. He was a highly gifted youth who was not at the mercy of his strong emotions, but rather examined and weighed them before reaching a decision. When two equally strong motives and waves of feeling pulled him in opposite directions, he might delay action, but was not weak-willed. In passing, Arnim also mentions that Shakespeare possibly portrayed other contemporaries in *Hamlet,* Essex perhaps as Laertes. This, however, he regards as unimportant. It is not his intention to analyze *Hamlet* by tearing it to pieces, but rather add to its interpretation and understanding by showing its close relationship to the age of the poet.

A year earlier, in 1828, Arnim had published in the *Monatliche Beiträge zur Geschichte dramatischer Kunst und Literatur* a somewhat similar study, an attempt to investigate the relationship between the stage and the courts or ruling houses of Germany and to determine how far the latter influenced the German stage. It was his intention to show the effect of the much admired foreign art on German stage life during the Eighteenth Century, and how the stage was "Germanized" under Frederick the Great. He called this extensive study "Sammlungen zur Theatergeschichte"[42] and wrote to Wilhelm Grimm that he had labored hard on it. He had had to look through many business papers of his father, the late "directeur des spectacles" in Berlin. The study had been received

---

[41] *Ibid.,* "Ein unbequemes Gefühl, als ob ich mich schon in einem bekannten Theaterstück befände, das ich nur halb vergessen, störte mich bei der Ausführung, bis mir endlich Jakob, wie ich ihn mir dachte, wie er geleibt und gelebt, als Hamlet im schwarzen Kleide erschien."

[42] *Monatliche Beiträge zur Geschichte dramatischer Kunst und Literatur,* hrsg. von Holtei, 1828, pp. 1-42.

by the public with great curiosity and interest, for he had given a picture of Frederick the Great as it evolved from the documents, not simply a generalization.[43] This study, indeed, reveals Arnim in a new role, as historian of the Berlin stage at the time of Frederick the Great. The work is also noteworthy as a romanticist's criticism of the stage and its management.

A decade earlier, in 1818, German stage management had been criticized by Arnim and Brentano in a series of notes, "Briefe über das neue Theater,"[44] in which they attacked the theater of Iffland and Kotzebue. Arnim's "Sammlungen zur Theatergeschichte" in its critical aspects must be regarded as an outgrowth and continuation of these fragmentary "Briefe." He took great pains to analyze and emphasize the importance of proper stage management, in which, he says, the German stage had failed completely in the past. The evil was not completely remedied on the contemporary stage. The fault lay with the stage manager, in so far as this poorly defined office demanded the impossible or that which only a genius could fulfill. Hence there were few or no good stage managers in Germany.

A three-fold task was demanded of this individual. First, he must serve art and therefore be artistic and imaginative, must possess "den freiesten Kunstaufschwung des Geistes." Secondly, he must be a business manager and therefore be economical and practical. Third, too often he must be a polite courtier who has to pretend compliance and still carry through artistic plans of a high order. Naturally such a "dreiartiger, dreieiniger and dreibeiniger Musenvorsteher"[45] is seldom found, and for this reason too often the princes were their own stage managers, which proved to be a "happy" solution, for now the stage manager no longer needed to be a courtier! Even the second requirement could be dispensed with, for the prince was wealthy. Only the first, artistic talent, was necessary. Arnim goes on to show ironically how under these circumstances criticism is silenced, for everybody feels in duty bound to display enthusiasm; the decline of the theater is cer-

---

[43] Arnim-Grimm, p. 574.
[44] *Wünschelrute*, hrsg. von H. Straube und F. P. von Holmthal, Göttingen, 1818, pp. 89-90, 93, 123, 128, 134-135.
[45] *Monatliche Beiträge zur Geschichte dramatischer Kunst und Literatur*, p. 12.

tain, even if the whimsical prince does not throw aside his "stage duties" like a tiresome toy. With indignation Arnim asks whether the theater has now to remain in a subordinated position, like a whist party, like a barrel-organ.[46] To this must be added another deplorable factor, namely, that there was a lack of good German plays during the Eighteenth Century. There was no poetic freedom, and nothing novel ever arose to create a furor. Nobody thought of encouraging the development of national talent, but the theatrically inclined princes resorted to foreign plays and called on French actors and Italian singers, not realizing that the foreign examples might smother native art and talent,[47] native taste and language. Arnim admits, however, that foreign artists are not always detrimental to native art, and as examples mentions that Gluck and Mozart had raised French and Italian opera to a higher level. One may assume, therefore, that Arnim had the feeling that real genius is not smothered by "foreign influences" and that art is mutually stimulated.

Frederick the Great, Arnim continues, like other German princely sponsors of the theater, gave his support only to the foreign stage. But the wars and victories during his reign and the internal governmental policies of this great Prussian king awakened national feeling among the Prussians in their own worth, and this in turn wakened an interest in native art and opposition to the French theater. These forces grew silently in spite of the fact that Frederick continued to support only the French theater in Berlin. Several stage managers put on German plays, disregarding financial sacrifices. Friendly criticism encouraged them and called attention to weaknesses in the French stage and praised the English drama. Only the fact that the public, of its own inclination and initiative, began to frequent the German theater more and more, can explain that the latter in 1775 in Berlin became more of a financial success than the French theater, which had

[46] *Monatliche Beiträge*, p. 23: "Soll nun ein Schauspiel etwas Untergeordnetes sein und bleiben wie eine Whistpartie, soll es wie eine Spieluhr das Wohlbekannte ableiern, ohne durch neue Strebungen Herz und Geist zu beunruhigen?"

[47] *Ibid.*, p. 33: "Daß jene fremde Richtung eigenen Geschmack und Sprache verderben, großen Talenten den Raum zu ihrer Entwicklung verschließen konnte, war jener Zeit fremd, jene Fürsten meinten wohlwollend, gute Vorbilder zu eigener Entwicklung aufgestellt zu haben."

the support of Frederick the great and the large French colony.[48] Yet, in spite of this victorious power of national interest on the part of the common people, the Prussian king did not change his personal attitude towards the German theater, as Arnim notes with some embitterment, yes, he even declared all its actors incompetent. On the other hand, during these years the king very rarely visited the very excellent French theater. Arnim doubted that the reason was solely disgust with the petty quarrels among actors and actresses; he thought rather that the king must have felt an unconscious weariness of the French theater.

Providence spoke the last word. The Bavarian war of succession in 1778 threatened to become dangerous for Prussia. Expenses had to be retrenched and Frederick decided to cut considerably the allotment for the French theater in the budget. This had a slow but deadly effect. Eight years later the German theater, by that time a state-sponsored enterprise, was able to move into the new royal opera house. In the end, Arnim concludes, providence and fate, or rather the will of the people decided, and Frederick the Great, who was but a tool, had to carry out his predetermined mission.[49] Not out of love for the German stage did he send away the foreigners, but because he had become tired of the expenses and monotony. Thus "Sans Souci," the name of Frederick's favorite palace, applies here also: we can be without care, for the German theater will live, Arnim concludes optimistically.

When one looks back over the writings discussed in this chapter, one notices above all the increased attention which Arnim pays to facts and minute details. He is no longer the roaming romanticist who can afford to disregard reality. In the Walter Scott review he even pointed out minor mistakes in translation, some-

[48] *Ibid.*, p. 37: "Während das deutsche Theater über 21,000 Rthlr. jährlich einnimmt und viel mehr noch einnehmen könnte, wenn das Haus Raum gewährte, sinkt die Einnahme im neuen französischen Schauspielhause von 17,000 Rthlr. auf 11,000 Rthlr., und doch muß jeder eingestehen, daß es nie so wohl besetzt mit ausgezeichneten Talenten, so dekoriert, so bekleidet erschienen sei."

[49] *Ibid.*, p. 41: "Über Friedrich dem Großen als Stifter und als Vernichter des französischen Theaters waltete der gute Genius seines Volkes wie über alle großen Führer der Völker, er aber mußte hier wie in so vielen Fällen tun und erfüllen, wozu er bestimmt war, ohne diese seine Bestimmung zu kennen."

thing a romanticist would not bother about, one can rest assured. Again, in the essay last discussed he furnishes figures and data about the theaters in Berlin which he has collected, and he incorporates documents of his father, the "directeur des spectacles," all of which goes to prove that here a romanticist's path leads at history and literature from an entirely different angle. Arnim had been interested in recording historic events concerning the arts, but his approach had been a different one. In his *Zeitung für Einsiedler* and in *Halle und Jerusalem,* for instance, he looked at history and literature from an entirely different angle, Arnim now feels that the censored literature and press of the day could not be regarded as historically reliable, and that it was therefore his task to give a more faithful—and thus more realistic—treatment of the past. Repeatedly he emphasized this point in the reviews of Blücher and Scharnhorst to be discussed below.

Prior to the politically restless days of 1830, literary societies and aesthetic-tea circles, the "discutier et debatier cliques," gained great popularity. Such a "Biedermeyer" group had gathered around Varnhagen von Ense. Arnim and Bettina were occasional guests there. While Arnim, the Prussian aristocrat, and Bettina with her background of Frankfort and Italy, already showed marked differences in personality, Arnim and the strict, pedantic Varnhagen, and even more the restless, extravagant Rahel, were opposite poles. Yet all four came to know each other very well during the last years of Arnim's life, and later, the widowed Bettina and Rahel, the two most prominent women of the intellectual society of Berlin, became close friends, so close indeed, that Bettina, as we have seen, asked Varnhagen to organize Arnim's literary remains. Varnhagen's opinion of Arnim in his memoirs must be taken with a grain of salt, however, for he was biased in favor of Rahel and did not do justice to Arnim and Bettina. Varnhagen was a very prolific writer, yet without originality or poetic imagination; he was a typical representative of the insipid, lifeless literature in Berlin after the Wars of Liberation. To write biographies was his predilection. Most of them were published in a series of *Biographische Denkmäler.*

Arnim, his friend, was also interested in biographical works and reviewed three of Varnhagen's sketches.⁵⁰ These reviews are not of particular value as literary documents because Arnim, in most cases, only summarizes the contents, emphasizing the historical importance of the hero and neglecting all questions relating to the literary value of the book in question.

His first review, "Fürst Blücher von Wahlstadt," could still be published in the *Gesellschafter*. Here he voices in the very first lines his strong indignation at the censorship of the press in Germany, which distorts history, and he points to England as the only ideal country, where everything that is published in newspapers and current journals is true and can serve future generations as reliable documents.⁵¹ Varnhagen's biography of Blücher Arnim finds incomplete because of the censorship, and he hopes that some day a biography of Blücher will be written which will become a valuable folkbook, like that of the knights of King Arthur's table, and which will expose freely all the sins of politics and the forces which brought so much suffering to Europe and tried to destroy the brave, freedom-loving German nation. Blücher, as Varnhagen in his introduction has emphasized, was the hero of the people, in whom the demoniacal forces of the masses found expression at that crucial moment when the fate of whole nations was at stake and civilization grasped desperately at blind forces of nature for salvation.⁵²

In his review he elaborates this conception of Blücher. He calls attention to the fact that the biographer, perhaps because of the censorship, has told too little of the discontent of Blücher's soul in later years, discontent that the noble hopes of the titanic age were not fully realized after the victory of arms. Outwardly the

---

[50] *Ges.*, 1826, pp. 144-148: L. A. von Arnim, Besprechung von K. A. Varnhagen von Ense, *Biographische Denkmäler* III, Fürst Blücher von Wahlstadt. *Blätter für literarische Unterhaltung*, Nr. 197, 785-6. 1830: L. A. v. Arnim, Besprechung von K. A. Varnhagen von Ense, *Denkwürdigkeiten des Philosophen und Arztes Johann Benjamin Erhard*, Stuttgart, 1830. *Ibid.*, Nr. 213, 849-851. 1830: L. A. v. Arnim, Besprechung von Varnhagen von Ense, *Biographische Denkmäler* V, *Leben des Grafen von Zinzendorf*, Berlin, 1830.

[51] *Ges.*, 1826, pp. 144-8: "In England mag es leicht genug sein, über Zeitgenossen zu schreiben, denn alles Bedeutende, von allen freundlichen und feindlichen Gestirnen beleuchtet, stellt sich in seinen frischen Schöpfungen unverhüllt dar; die Zeitschriften sind die Jahrbücher der Weltgeschichte."

[52] Karl August Varnhagen von Ense, *Biographische Denkmäler*, III. Fürst Blücher von Wahlstadt. Einleitung, 3.

hero was very reserved, severe and abrupt, but this coldness covered a highly sensitive, emotional, and religious soul. He was very intelligent, and knew how to handle people. Arnim felt called upon to add a few personal observations to Varnhagen's excellent description (page 588) of the hero's external appearances. Thus, for instance, he read in Blücher's face, in the expression of his eyes, an unusual, secretive attraction which arrested the attention of everybody, even of those who did not know him. It was as if his eyes knew of the final victory.[53] This expression was entirely different from the abysmal, desperate depth noted in Napoleon's eyes, even at a time when no one could yet surmise his final fate. Perhaps it was strange also that Blücher's whole external appearance was so singular. Nobody resembled him in the slightest, as if, Arnim says, nature had created such a man only once and then broke the mould.

Arnim's other reviews of Varnhagen's biographies were published, as noted above, in Brockhaus' *Blätter für literarische Unterhaltung*. This periodical was a typical "Biedermeier" product. In fear of censorship, practically all articles and reports were printed anonymously under *chiffres*. The collaborators are today considered rather mediocre. Arnim began to contribute to the periodical after 1826, when he had become convinced of the intellectual impartiality of the editorial board.[54] Recently Mallon's researches have established the total number of his contributions to this journal[55] as thirty-one. It had been founded by Kotzebue in Weimar as the *Literarisches Wochenblatt*. After his death the publisher, W. Hoffmann, became editor. With the sixth volume it was acquired by the publisher Friedrich A. Brockhaus in Leipsic, and continued to be issued by that firm until 1900. Soon after this transfer to Leipsic difficulties arose with the censor and the journal was prohibited in Prussia, but shortly thereafter it was permitted again under a new title, *Literarisches Conversations-*

---

[53] *Ges.*, 1826, pp. 144-8. "Es erschien uns nämlich in seinem Antlitz ein geheimnisvoller Reiz, wie eine Ahnung, daß diese mächtigen bedeutsamen Augen durchaus nicht im gemeinsamen Laufe der Dinge untergehen könnten."

[54] Arnim-Grimm, p. 544; Arnim's letter to Wilhelm Grimm, January 16, 1825.

[55] Otto Mallon, "A. v. Arnim's Beiträge zum 'Literarisches Conversations-Blatt,' und zu den 'Blättern für literarische Unterhaltung' (1823-31)," *Preuss. Jahrb.*, 1931, Bd. I, 44-68.

blatt. A second conflict with the censorship in 1826 brought still another and final title, *Blätter für literarische Unterhaltung.*

Arnim reviewed for this periodical the biography of another Prussian hero, Scharnhorst,[56] of anonymous authorship. As in the Blücher review, the critic deplores the evils of the censorship, which alone is responsible in this case for the anonymous biographer's giving only a very general picture of the unusual Scharnhorst. He has touched only very briefly on Scharnhorst's relationship to other generals and contemporaries and to the unhappy events of the year 1806. Hardly anything is included of Scharnhorst's notes, diaries, letters, or concerning the motives which would explain his personality and influence.

Another more extensive review of Varnhagen which Arnim wrote for the *Blätter für literarische Unterhaltung* is that of the biography of Graf Zinzendorf.[57] This review is rather interesting, because here Arnim makes his own observations on Zinzendorf as educator and on the literary and cultural activities of his religious sect and community, the Herrenhuter Gemeinde, which had been founded by Zinzendorf. Arnim praises Varnhagen's biography as a valuable addition to existing books about Zinzendorf, because it describes him very admirably as a statesman. Varnhagen had compared Zinzendorf as a religious personality with Lavater and Stilling. Arnim in turn draws a parallel with Pestalozzi, with regard to education, and emphasizes that Zinzendorf started a new, milder, and more humane movement, which no longer looked on learning as the only aim.[58] He discusses a few more characteristics of this unusual man. Zinzendorf was always a great philanthropist, in spite of the fact that he did not possess great wealth. Perhaps it was because he gave people faith and self confidence, Arnim thinks.

Like his contemporaries, the critic also found it extraordinay that Zinzendorf after his visit to America renounced all his titles and privileges. This does not appear to meet with Arnim's approval. Even though he recognizes the noble religious motive, the brotherhood of mankind, similar to the equality of men that had

---

[56] *Blätter für literarische Unterhaltung*, Nr. 303-4, 1830, 1209-10, 113-14.
[57] *Ibid.*, Nr. 213, 1830, 849-851.
[58] *Ibid.*, p. 849.

been fought for in revolutions, Arnim thinks that both, Zinzendorf and the political revolutionist, lost sight of the past in the dream of a future which can never be brought to reality. Examining the literary and cultural activities of the Herrenhuter community, the critic comes to the conclusion that of the many good hymns which originated there, none is really excellent, and that the community has thus far made no really original contribution to art and literature. Only the dissolved communities which settled in the Wetterau have made a remarkable approach to poetry with their emotional hymns, an outgrowth of Zinzendorf's "Morgenländische Spielerei mit Lieblingsliedern des Glaubens."[59]

The last review which was published before Arnim's death was that of Houwald's *Seeräuber*.[60] As if he had a premonition that the days of his own life were numbered, Arnim in this review takes account of the failures and successes of Houwald's life, and perhaps of a poet's life in general, including his own. Here he comes to dwell on the bitter fact that the world always denies the recognition due to greatness.

What he has to say about *Die Seeräuber* may be briefly mentioned first. The subject-matter of Houwald's tragedy abounds in highly dramatic moments and theatrical effects, such as stealing of the brides, the fire and seizure of the pirate's castle, the return of the brides, the excitement of the masses at the death sentences, and so on. But Houwald did not make use of these dramatic moments; they are not enacted on the stage, but only described in monologues and otherwise. One asks why? Because the discouraged Houwald knew that he probably would not be able to find a producer; he therefore adapted this dramatic material only for the reading public. The dictators of the stage resort almost exclusively to translations; foreign plays with foreign customs and ideas, foreign characters and foreign riots, are performed. Arnim mentions still another point in explaining why the dramatic moments are not more fully exploited. The author in this play shows a certain tendency towards moralizing and generalizing (*moralische Casuistik*) in emotional scenes. This philosophizing is, how-

[59] *Ibid.*, p. 851.
[60] *Blätter für literarische Unterhaltung*, 1830, Nr. 361, pp. 1441-3. *Die Seeräuber. Ein Trauerspiel in 5 Aufzügen von Ernst von Houwald* (Leipzig: Göschen, 1830).

ever, a natural outgrowth of the plot and action; he did not set out deliberately to write a moralizing play.

Houwald's fate as a poet had been a very unhappy one, sadder than Arnim's, who as we have seen, after the War of Liberation had to retreat to the country in order to earn a livelihood. When, therefore, in this review the writer with bitter irony arraigns the world and Germany in particular for injustice to its poets, he is most likely voicing resentment at his own disappointments. Embittered complaints like the following recall those of the "Jungdeutschen":

> While in France it has become customary only since the Revolution, in Germany it is an old custom that poets are exploited for labors which others could do. To give examples: Wieland had to become a tutor for princes; Lessing, a librarian in a small town; Goethe, a minister of state; Schiller, a teacher of history".[61]

Arnim complains that there is always money for superfluous buildings, fashions, acrobats, singers, etc., but never for poets; poetry is a breadless art. There may be some truth in the argument that the material cannot affect the spiritual, that there must be "art for art's sake," and that the poet finds his own satisfactions independent of the world, as Houwald expresses it so effectively:

> Die Rose will nur blühen,
> Der Vogel singt nur sich,
> Drum blühe du und singe,
> Ist's auch allein für dich![62]

But Arnim warns that indifference towards the poets will have a detrimental effect on the nation as a whole. There is dire need that publications and copyrights be better protected so that literary creations may remain the poet's and the people's own; that the stage do something to encourage native talent, so that most playwrights may not have to adapt their plays for only a *reading public*. Should there not be room for every talent and capacity in a well ordered human society, Arnim asks, so that it may drive roots and bear fruit?

[61] *Ibid.*, p. 1441
[62] *Ibid.*, p. 1442, cf. also *Berliner Musenalmanach*, 1831.

THE DRIFT TOWARD REALISM

Arnim had not found such a well ordered human society among his contemporaries. His best years he had spent performing the duties of a farmer, which left him little time for concentration on poetic and literary subjects. Yet his spirit was unbroken and in the numerous essays, reviews, and literary notes of his spare time he continued to preach on his old text: Back to an intuitive approach to art, and art based on the historical and national wealth of the people. Now, a few days before his death, still in a challenging mood, he concluded this, his last review, with Houwald's bold words:

> Ich brauche kein Gebet von fremder Lippe,
> Denn mein Gedank' ist schon Gebet, ich brauche
> Den Priester nicht, denn ich bin selbst dein Priester,
> Mein Will' ist rein! Du hast ihn, Herr, geläutert.
> Und im Vertraun, daß ich dich ganz verstanden,
> Weshalb du mich die dunkle Bahn geführt,
> Glaub' ich, er muß dir wohlgefällig sein![63]

[63] *Blätter für literarische Unterhaltung,* 1930, p. 1443.

IX
ARNIM'S POSITION IN THE HISTORY OF CRITICISM

Literary critics may be divided into two groups. The members of one of these, through their vast range of information in the historical field, their clear and logical reasoning, and their brilliant style, have been able to guide contemporary poets and prose writers into new paths and to make important contributions to the theory of literary genres and the methodology of criticism. Such were Lessing and August Wilhelm Schlegel, who formulated successively the ideas of rationalism and romanticism in Germany. It is in another direction that we must seek the importance of the second group of critics. This includes many writers whose chief importance was in the creative rather than the judicial office. Such critics are idealists and their attitude is an outgrowth of genius ruled by emotion. Their opinions on literature have their greatest value as interpretations of the writers' personalities and of their contributions in other fields of production. As idealists they project their view of life into their discussions of literature, thus making a fuller revelation of themselves and of the struggles and aspirations of the generation to which they belong.

Goethe and Herder were outstanding representatives of this type of critic and it is to this group that Achim von Arnim must be assigned. His impulsive, idealistic *Weltanschauung,* which found expression in a long series of productions in the field of romantic poetry and fiction, could not adapt itself to processes of analytical reasoning and logical categorizing which are necessary for the establishment of theories of general validity. Arnim was first and foremost a *Dichter* and his judgment of literary sources and achievements flowed from the same fountain of intuitive genius as his *Dichtung*. His critical style, even in the later, more realistic years, bears everywhere the stamp of romantic imagination. This makes his work at times difficult to understand, and it may be added, none too easy to translate into English. Often his meaning must be *felt,* and certainly a part of the importance of his contribution lies in the enthusiastic and fanciful manner in which his ideas are presented.

Nevertheless, Arnim has a significant place in the history of German criticism. A younger son of the great idealistic generation, he came very early under the influence of Goethe and Herder, with whose work he became well acquainted as a student, through the comradeship of Clements Brentano, and while on his "grand tour." How strong the influence of Goethe's personality and writings was, has been shown in the foregoing pages. While we have abundant evidence of this dependence on Goethe, specific references to Herder are almost entirely lacking. Nevertheless, like others of the younger romantic group, he was strongly affected by the ideas of this great philosopher of the humanistic age. It can hardly be denied that the conceptions which guided the editorial work of young Arnim on *Des Knaben Wunderhorn* and his critical attitude throughout life were deeply rooted in Herder's spiritual and historical approach to literature.

In his early critical writing Arnim shows himself a progressive. This appears first in his essays on physical science, where we have seen him to be a protagonist of a dynamic, monistic view of nature's processes. Later, it reveals itself in his attitude toward art. Here he supports the Schlegel brothers and Tieck in the fight against the wretched state of contemporary criticism, the same struggle against cliquish narrowness, pedantry, and shallow gossip that had been waged a little earlier by Schiller and Goethe in their *Xenienkampf*. Arnim's concepts of art, then, developed, as we have seen, under the influence of the political events of the first decade of the new century. His national feeling was fanned into flame when Prussia's glory was annihilated at Jena and Germany lay prostrate under Napoleon's heel.

This enthusiasm becomes outspoken with the establishment of the *Zeitung für Einsiedler* in 1808. Here he voices emphatically the idea that art must be an expression of the creative genius of a people, for only that literature is truly great which is imbued with a national, popular spirit. Arnim is now firmly convinced that literary schools, such as classicism and romanticism, have outlived their day and that the need now arises for a literature that voices a unified German spirit. Imitation of Hellenistic culture must cease, for Germany can attain to the artistic heights of the ancients only if she becomes conscious of the native resources in her glorious past. Arnim now assigns to literary criticism the task of making the reader acquainted with the best creations of this popular spirit, of unearthing and making known the treasures of a mighty past, of re-creating the "remote and unknown." Only when the critics shall have fulfilled this great mission can Germans expect a great national literature.

This is the doctrine that underlies the critical work of Arnim in the years that followed. While these ideas were in the main those of the younger generation of romanticists, Arnim has nevertheless a peculiar and striking position. To be sure, certain similarities with his romantic contemporaries are obvious. In family background and the force of the national ideal one may group him most closely with Heinrich von Kleist. With Tieck he shared the romantic idealization of the German past. He has much in common with Görres and Brentano, but stands apart from these, his personal friends, in his North German militant Protestantism and Pan-Germanism, which were an organic outgrowth from the experiences and ideals of the race of Brandenburg aristocrats from which he sprang. Undoubtedly he learned much from the Schlegels, and he confesses it. He certainly uses a very similar method of approach to literature to that which marks A. W. Schlegel's general critical procedure, especially in the latter's famous series of Berlin lectures, *Über schöne Literatur und Kunst,* 1801-1803, a programmatic criticism which seems to foster new ideas by means of a critical evaluation of a work of *belles lettres.* However, he differed from Schlegel in important respects. Arnim's criticism is programmatic, but for him the "program" is not an exact system or a set of dogmatic rules. It is rather an enthusiasm and a hopeful vision of an ideal artistic future.

This serves Arnim as a basis for a highly emotional approach. He scarcely ever analyzes single traits and features, but reacts to the work as a whole. His programmatic spirit prefers to select for consideration works which are in conformity with its conception of the purpose of literature and makes these constructive for the world of art as the critic envisions it. Thus, it is noteworthy that Arnim rarely writes about works that do not interest him personally. The writings of the physicist Ritter, the poems and dramas of the Schlegels, and other productions of romantic spirits, formed, as we have seen, welcome material for the exposition of his own ideas on nature and art.

As was noted in the introduction, many of the most interesting views of Arnim respecting poetry found expression in his correspondence with friends like Brentano, Goethe, and the Grimms. Here he is intensely serious in pressing his point, and although informal in style, his remarks are put in a form that is worthy of the dignified subject-matter. His reviews and critical essays, published and unpublished, are very uneven in quality. As is the case with his stories and plays, brilliant productions are at times succeeded by those that are hasty and superficial. In its entirety, however, the material that we have traversed is of much greater value to the student of literature for a knowledge of Arnim's spiritual personality than could have been supposed. It is surprising both in quality and quantity, and might well be supplemented by an examination of his writings on painting, sculpture, history and social questions, themes which did not fall within the range of this investigation.

Judged by quality of content and vigor of style, the contributions to the *Berliner Abendblätter* and the *Preussischer Correspondent* rate lowest among the material that has been examined. Of highest rank are the reviews in the *Heidelbergische Jahrbücher*. Here we see Arnim, the critic, at his very best. He was writing primarily for two groups—the romantic sympathizers, for whom his ideas, as he hoped, would become a stimulus and a program for the development of national poetry; and his opponents, such as Johann Heinrich Voss, to whom he and his romantic associates were anathema and who, he felt, must now recognize the strength and beauty of the new literary garb which was to replace the outworn garment of dry classicism. After 1815 we have noted a change in Arnim's critical style. The drift toward realism brings an increasing clarity of ideas and a more careful and finished form.

Finally, it must be stressed again that the literary-critical writings of Arnim are the expression of a thoroughly poetic soul. Bettina likened them to a *fermata* in a musical composition, the prolonging of a tone or measure from the work itself.[1] In Arnim's case this prolongation of the tone of the work under consideration is often better than the original. All of the diverse and scattered writings that have been brought together for our examination flow organically from one unique personality. His literary criticism, even more than his correspondence, reveals the noble idealist.

[1] Arnim-Bettina, p. 380.

BIBLIOGRAPHY

Reviews, essays, and notes by Arnim are not listed in this bibliography. With a very few exceptions Arnim's published writings are given in their chronological order in Otto Mallon's *Arnim-Bibliographie* (Berlin, 1925). Details regarding them will be found in the footnotes. Some of the unpublished material discussed is listed in Karl Ernst Henrici's *Auktions-Katalog* 148 (*Bettine von Arnim*) and in *Auktions-Katalog* 149 (*Arnim und Brentano Des Knaben Wunderhorn*). Unpublished material in the Goethe-Museum in Frankfort, to which references are made in the present work, is to appear in the *Jahrbuch des Freien Deutschen Hochstifts*.

Arnim's Works

Ludwig Achim's v. Arnim sämtliche Werke. XXI Bde. Neue Ausgabe. Berlin, v. Arnim's Verlag, 1857.

L. A. von Arnim, Unbekannte Aufsätze und Gedichte. Hrsg. von Ludwig Geiger, Berlin, 1892.

Arnims Tröst Einsamkeit. Hrsg. von Fridrich Pfaff, Freiburg i.B. und Tübingen, 1883 (*Zeitung für Einsiedler*).

Arnim's Letters

Görres, Josef von. Gesammelte Schriften, Vol. VIII-IX. Hrsg. von Marie Görres, München, 1874 (twenty-seven letters of Arnim).

Holtei, Karl von. Briefe an Ludwig Tieck. Breslau, 1864 (three of Arnim's letters).

Schüddekopf & Walzel. Goethe und die Romantik. Weimar, 1898 (nineteen of Arnim's letters).

Steig, Reinhold. Achim von Arnim und die ihm nahe standen, 3 Bde. Stuttgart, 1894-1913 (Arnim's letters to Clemens Brentano, Bettina Brentano, Jacob und Wilhelm Grimm).

Steig, Reinhold. Zeugnisse zur Pflege der deutschen Literatur in den Heidelberger Jahrbüchern. *Neue Heidelberger Jahrbücher*, 1902 (ten of Arnim's letters).

General

L. Achim von Arnim

Becker, Hermann. A. von Arnim in den wissenschaftlichen und politischen Strömungen seiner Zeit. Leipzig, 1912.

Bottermann, Walther. Die Beziehungen des Dramatikers Achim von

Arnim zur altdeutschen Literatur. Diss., Göttingen, 1895.
Darmstaedter, Ernest, "A. v. Arnim und die Naturwissenschaft." *Euphorion*, Vol. XXXII, 1931.
Geiger, Ludwig. "A. v. Arnims Beiträge zum Literaturblatt." *Zeitschrift für vergleichende Literaturgeschichte*, Vol. XII, pp. 209-29, 1898.
Gundolf, Friedrich. Romantiker. Bd. II, Berlin-Wilmersdorf, 1930.
Kayser, Rudolf. Arnims und Brentanos Stellung zur Bühne. Berlin, 1912.
Koch, Max. Arnim, Klemens und Bettina Brentano, J. Görres. "Deutsche National-Literatur," CXLVI.
Mallon, Otto. Arnim-Bibliographie. Berlin, 1925.
Mallon, Otto. "A. v. Arnims Beiträge" zum 'Literarischen Conversations-Blatt' und zu den 'Blättern für literarische Unterhaltung' 1823-31." *Preussische Jahrbücher*, 1931.
Müller, Johann, Ed. Arnims und Brentanos romantische Volksliedforschungen; ein Beitrag zur Geschichte und Kritik des "Wunderhorns." Hamburg, 1906.
Rieser, Ferdinand. "Des Knaben Wunderhorn" und seine Quellen; ein Beitrag zur Geschichte des deutschen Volksliedes und der Romantik. Dortmund, 1908.
Rudolf, Wilhelm. Achim von Arnim als Lyriker. Straßburg, 1914.
Schönemann, Friedrich. L. Achim von Arnims geistige Entwicklung an seinem Drama "Halle und Jerusalem" erläutert. Leipzig, 1912.
Schulze, Friedrich. Die Gräfin Dolores: Ein Beitrag zur Geschichte des deutschen Geisteslebens zur Zeit der Romantik. Leipzig, 1904.

Romanticism

Arnim, Bettina v. Sämtliche Werke. Hrsg. v. Waldemar Oehlke, Berlin, 1920.
Blochmann, E. "Die deutsche Volksdichtungsbewegung in Sturm und Drang der Romantik." *Deutsche Vierteljahresschrift*, H.3, 1923.
Bobeth, Johannes. Die Zeitschriften der Romantik. Leipzig, 1908.
Borries, Kurt. Die Romantik und die Geschichte, Studien zur romantischen Lebensform. Berlin, 1925.
Czygan, Paul. Zur Geschichte der Tagesliteratur während der Freiheitskriege. Berlin, 1911.
Eichendorff, J. von. Geschichte der poetischen Literatur Deutschlands. Bd. II, Paderborn, 1857.
Gubitz, F. W. Erlebnisse. Berlin, 1868. Berlin, 1922.
Gundolf, Friedrich. Shakespeare und der deutsche Geist. Berlin, 1920.
Gundolf, Friedrich. "Schleiermachers Romantik." *Deutsche Vierteljahresschrift*, H.3, 1924.
Houben & Walzel. Zeitschriften der Romantik, Bibliographisches Repertorium, I. Berlin, 1904.
Houben, Heinrich, Hubert. Verbotene Literatur von der klassischen Zeit

bis zur Gegenwart; ein kritisch-historisches Lexikon über verbotene Bücher, Zeitschriften und Theaterstücke, Schriftsteller und Verleger. Berlin, 1924-8.
Kloss, Alfred. Die Heidelbergischen Jahrbücher der Literatur. Leipzig, 1918.
Lettow-Vorbeck, M. von. Zur Geschichte des Preussischen Correspondenten von 1813-14. Berlin, 1911.
Levin, Herbert. Die Heidelberger Romantik. München, 1922.
Meinecke, Friedrich. Das Zeitalter der deutschen Erhebung, 1795-1815. Bielefeld, 1906.
Nadler, J. Die Berliner Romantik, 1800-14. Berlin, 1921.
Poetzsch, Albert. Studien zur frühromantischen Politik und Geschichtsauffassung. Leipzig, 1907.
Steig, Reinhold. Heinrich von Kleist's Berliner Kämpfe. Berlin, 1901.
Steig, Reinhold. Neue Kunde zu Heinrich von Kleist. Berlin, 1902.
Steig, Reinhold. Clemens Brentano und die Brüder Grimm. Stuttgart, 1914.
Steig, Reinhold. Bettinas Briefwechsel mit Goethe. Berlin, 1922.
Steig, Reinhold. "Goethesche Handschriften erhalten durch Bettina and Achim von Arnim." *Jahrbuch des Freien Deutschen Hochstiftes,* 1910.
Stephan, Heinz. Die Entstehung der Rheinromantik. Köln 1922.
Stockmann, A. Die deutsche Romantik, ihre Wesenszüge und ihre ersten Vertreter. Freiburg, 1921.
Varnhagen von Ense, K. A. Denkwürdigkeiten und vermischte Schriften. Leipzig, 1843-59.
Weiss, Alfred. Die Entwicklung des Fühlens und Denkens der Romantik auf Grund der romantischen Zeitschriften. Leipzig, 1912.

Literary criticism

Bran, F. A. Herder und die deutsche Kulturanschauung. Berlin, 1932.
Elkuss, Siegbert. Zur Beurteilung der Romantik und zur Kritik ihrer Erforschung. Diss. Straßburg, 1918.
Günther, Hans. Romantische Kritik und Satire bei Ludwig Tieck. Leipzig, 1907.
Haack, F. Die Deutschromantiker in der bildenden Kunst des 19. Jahrhunderts. Erlangen, 1901.
Harnack, Otto. Die klassische Ästhetik der Deutschen; Würdigung der kunsttheoretischen Arbeiten Schillers, Goethes und ihrer Freunde. Leipzig, 1892.
Kircher, Erwin. Philosophie der Romantik. Jena, 1906.
Körner, Josef. Nibelungenforschungen der deutschen Romantik. Leipzig, 1911.
Lempicki, S. von. Geschichte der deutschen Literaturwissenschaft bis zum Ende des 18. Jahrhunderts. Göttingen, 1920.

Lempicki, S. von. "Über literarische Kritik und die Probleme ihrer Erforschung." *Euphorion*, XXV, 1924.
Lempicki, S. von. "Bücherwelt und wirkliche Welt. Ein Beitrag zur Wesenserfassung der Romantik." *Deutsche Vierteljahresschrift*, 1925.
Lichtenstein, E. "Die Idee der Naturpoesie bei den Brüdern Grimm und ihr Verhältnis zu Herder." *Deutsche Vierteljahresschrift*, H.3, 1928.
Matthias, Theodor. Der deutsche Gedanke bei Jacob Grimm. Leipzig, 1915.
Möller, E. von. "Die Entstehung des Dogmas vom Ursprung des Rechtes aus dem Volksgeist." *Mitteilungen der Zeitschrift für österreichische Geschichte*, Vol. XXX.
Müller, G. "Zur Bestimmung des Begriffes 'altdeutsche Mystik'." *Deutsche Vierteljahresschrift*, H.1, 1926.
Neumann, F. "Das Nibelungenlied in der gegenwärtigen Forschung." *Deutsche Vierteljahresschrift*, H.1, 1927.
Wolf, H. "Die Genielehre des jungen Herder." *Deutsche Vierteljahresschrift*, H.3, 1925.
Rothacker, Erich. Einleitung in die Geisteswissenschaft. Berlin, 1930.
Schlegel, A.W. Kritische Schriften. Berlin, 1828.
Unger, R. "Vom Sturm und Drang zur Romantik. Eine Problem- und Literaturschau." *Deutsche Vierteljahresschrift*, H.3, 1924; H.1-2, 1928.
Unger, R. Hamann und die Aufklärung. Halle, 1925.

INDEX

Allgemeine Deutsche Bibliothek, 93
Annalen der Physik, 21, 24, 32 ff., 35, 42
Archenholz, Johann Wilhelm von, 25
Arndt, Ernst Moritz, 13, 134, 138, 144 ff.; 147
  Das Preussiche Volk und Heer, 144
  Der Rhein, Teutschlands Strom, aber nicht Teutschlands Grenze, 145
  Geist der Zeit, 13, 25, 144
Arnim, Bettina von, (née Brentano), 8 n, 27, 34, 53, 73, 81 n, 100, 115, 116 ff., 133 ff., 156, 167, 178
  Frühlingskranz, 53
  Quarrel with Christiane von Goethe, 119 ff.
  Königsbuch, 8 n
Arnim, Joachim Erdmann von, 22
Arnim, Johannes Freimund von, 133
Arnim, Ludwig Achim von, 1 ff., 6, 8 f., 11 ff., 16 f., 19 ff., 32 ff., 40, 42, 48 ff., 56 ff., 72 f., 79 f., 105 ff., 118 f., 130 ff., 142, 147, 151, 153, 159 f., 163 ff.
  Aesthetics, 4, 16, 28, 99, 106 f., 152 f., 159, 167, 176
  Childhood, 19 ff., 22, 105
  ESSAYS:—"Anmerkungen zum Märchenbuch," 77 ff.
  "Briefe über das neue Theater," 80, 164
  "Erzählungen von Schauspielen," 24, 88
  "Hamlet und Jacob," 162 ff.
  "Introduction to Wilhelm Müller's translation of Marlow's Doctor Faustus," 127 ff.
  "Literarnotizen," 157
  "Otto Brüggemann, ein Beitrag zu Goethes Westöstlichem Divan," 159
  "Sammlungen zur Theatergeschichte," 10 n, 81, 163 ff.
  "Ueber eine Theaterkritik," 157 f.
  "Ueber deutsches Silbenmass und griechische Deklamation," 106 f.
  Grand tour, 2, 23 f.
  Interest in the natural sciences, 2 f., 21, 32 ff., 49 f., 106, 131
  Journalistic activities, 3 f., 22, 26, 57, 152 f., 154 f.
  Lebensplan, 37, 39
  Märkischer Junker, 19, 21, 26, 31, 109, 112, 153
  POEMS:—"Adel," 12
  "Der freie Dichtergarten," 114
  "Der Götter Adel," 12
  "Geschichte des Herrn Sonett," 60
  "Lehrgedicht an die Jugend," 10, 114
  "Rundgesang gegen Unterdrücker des Werdenden in der Literatur," 59
  "Träume," 10, 107 f.
  Weltanschauung, 2, 26, 104, 106 ff., 119, 149, 174
  WORKS:—*Alte Bühne,* 63
  Auch ein Faust, 127 f.
  Ariels Offenbarungen, 24, 27 n, 52, 88
  Ehrenschmiede, 160
  Gräfin Dolores, 12, 30, 67, 71, 117 f.
  Halle und Jerusalem, 48, 67, 71, 91, 97, 142, 167
  Holins Liebeleben, 24, 50, 52
  Kronenwächter, 10, 38, 96, 122, 154, 160
  Landhausleben, 154
  Metamorphosen der Gesellschaft, 107 f.
  Sämtliche Werke, 7
  Schaubühne, 67, 92
  Scherzendes Gedicht von der Nachahmung des Heiligen, 107 ff.
  Travelogues, 155, 159
  Versuch einer Theorie des elektrischen Erscheinungen, 32, 33, 36 f.
  "Von Volksliedern," 9, 16 f., 138
  Wintergarten, 9, 11, 67
  Wunderhorn, 15, 17n, 26, 41, 55 f., 57, 63, 66, 68 f., 82 f., 88, 112, 116, 138, 160, 175
  Wunder über Wunder, 25, 105 f., 125 f.
  Zeitung für Einsiedler, 3, 26, 29, 58 ff., 63, 65 f., 70, 88, 92, 94, 106 f., 111 f., 114 ff., 141, 147, 159, 167

INDEX

Art-poetry, cf. *Kunstpoesie*, 40, 68, 70 f., 84, 107
Athenäum, 89 ff., 96

Berliner Abendblätter, 3, 26, 137, 141 ff., 147, 177
Berlinische Blätter für deutsche Frauen, 155
Biedermeyer, 155, 167
Blätter für literarische Unterhaltung, 169 f.
Blücher, Fürst von Wahlstatt, 154, 167, 168 f.
Böckh, August, 43, 65
Brentano, Christian, 33
Brentano, Clemens, 1, 3 f., 6, 8, 12, 15, 17, 19, 23, 25, 28, 31, 35, 38, 41, 49 ff., 58, 64, 66, 68 f., 76 f., 78 f., 80, 82, 87, 111 f., 113 f., 116, 121, 133, 136, 140, 143, 148, 153, 156, 164, 175 f., 177
WORKS:—*Aloys und Imelde*, 78
Chronika eines fahrenden Schülers, 82
Godwi, 38, 54 f.
Gründung Prags, 67, 78 f.,
Lustigen Musikanten, 54 f.
Märchen, 75
Ponce de Leon, 54 f.
Romanzen vom Rosenkranz, 67
Viktoria und ihre Geschwister, 81
Budde, Heinrich Wilhelm, 28
Bürger, Gottfried August, 66 n
Burke, Edmund, 137, 146

Calderon de la Barca, Pedro, 94, 98
Casanova, Giovanni, 130
Aus den Memoiren des Venezianers Casanova, 130
Chapbooks, 69, 168
Christlich-deutsche Tischgesellschaft, 14, 66, 137 f., 140, 149
Classicism, 29, 105 ff., 110 f.
Creative spirit, cf. Geist, spirit, 7
Creuzer, Friedrich, 62 f., 64 f.
Critical method, 15 f., 28, 60, 63, 93 f., 137 f., 157 f., 171, 174 ff.
Criticism, 15 ff., 28, 54, 59 ff., 89 ff., 106 f., 157, 171
Erlebniskritik, 28, 60
Intuitive criticism, 16
Productive criticism, 15

Dante, Alighieri, 49
Divine Comedy, 49

Dorrow, Wilhelm, 142

Edda, 68
Emmerich, Anna Katherine, 82
Enlightenment, 7, 15
Esprit, cf. Geist, 8

Fate-tragedy, 100
Fichte, Johann Gottlieb, 5, 15, 32, 41, 66, 136, 138, 149 f.
Folklore, 6 ff., 25, 61, 67, 69
Fouqué, Friedrich Freiherr de la Motte, 74, 137 ff., 148 ff., 153
Berlinische Blätter für deutsche Frauen, 153, 162
Gedichte, 148
Sigurd, 138, 149
Frankfurter Gelehrte Anzeigen, 158
Frederick the Great, 10, 146, 163 ff.
Freimütige, (Der Freimütige), 113, 159
French Art, 24, 165 f.
French Revolution, 5, 13 f., 125, 137, 172

Geiger, Ludwig, 1, 156 n
Geist, 2, 8 ff., 8 n, 16, 38
Auslegergeist, 16
Eigentümlicher Geist, 9
Gemeingeist, 11
Volksgeist, 7 ff., 8 n, 10
Zeitgeist, 8 f., 11, 13 ff., 82
Genialität, 8 f., 18
Genius, cf. spirit and also *Geist*, 8 ff., 8 n, 16, 38, 175
Gerlach, Leopold von, 14 n
German art, 5 f., 29, 56, 66, 93, 105 f., 110
German literature, 57 ff., 94, 110 f., 176
Old German literature, 56 ff., 92, 108 ff., 116, 119
Gesellschafter, (Der Gesellschafter), 3, 13, 98, 153 f., 155 ff.
Gilbert, Wilhelm, 21, 32, 35, 43
Goethe, Christiane von (née Vulpius), 119 f.
Goethe, Johann Wolfgang von, 3 f., 6, 16 f., 20, 23, 25, 29, 31, 38, 40, 49 ff., 61, 68, 70, 73, 74, 89, 95, 97, 100, 104, 106, 111 ff., 116 f., 129 ff., 134, 136, 139 f., 154, 158, 163, 172, 174 f., 177
WORKS:—*Dichtung und Wahrheit*, 111, 121 f., 130 f., 158
Faust, 60, 127 ff.

INDEX

Farbenlehre, 52, 132
Herrmann und Dorothea, 52, 98
Iphigenie, 95
Metamorphose der Pflanzen, 132
Morphologische Hefte, 130
Wahlverwandtschaften, 65, 117 f.
Werther, 52.
Westöstlicher Divan, 10, 131
Wilhelm Meister, 30, 52, 55, 122 f., 139, 153
Wilhelm Meisters Lehrjahre, 124
Wilhelm Meisters Wanderjahre, 124 ff.
Xenien, 115, 175
Golden Age, 5, 12, 39
Görres, Joseph, 1, 4, 8, 13, 49, 57, 64 f., 66 f., 69, 72, 82 f., 137, 151, 153, 156, 176
Altdeutsche Volks- und Meisterlieder, 83,
Die teutschen Volksbücher, 68 f.,
Mythengeschichte der asiatischen Welt, 68, 72 f.
Greeks, ancient, 105 f., 108
Greek declamation, 106
Greek philosophy of life and art, 20, 105 ff., 119 f.
Grimm brothers, 66, 8, 57, 58 ff., 66 f., 69 f., 75, 78 f., 83 f., 104, 121, 129, 132, 140, 143, 148, 177
Deutsche Sagen, 67, 84 f.
Kinder- und Hausmärchen, 67, 75 ff.
Grimm Jacob, 1, 8, 17, 40, 57, 70 f., 74, 77 f., 82, 140, 148
Deutsche Grammatik, 83 f.
Deutsche Rechtsaltertümer, 84 f., 145 n
Ueber den altdeutschen Meistergesang, 67, 71 f.
Grimm, Wilhelm, 1, 10, 31, 57, 67, 70 f., 78, 83, 86, 116, 121, 140, 144, 148 f., 153
Altdänische Heldenlieder, 67, 116, 121
Gubitz, Friedrich Wilhelm, 3, 13, 43, 156 f.
Der Gesellschafter, 3, 13, 43
Günderode, Caroline von, 97

Hagen, Friedrich Heinrich von der, 67, 69
Haller, Karl Ludwig von, 14
Restauration der Staatswissenschaft, 14
Hamann, Johann Georg, 7, 15, 39
Hardenberg, Karl August Fürst von, 14, 137, 151, 154

Heidelbergische Jahrbücher der Literatur, 3, 26, 42, 62 ff., 139 f., 149, 152 f., 177
Heine, Heinrich, 31
Heinse, Wilhelm, 89
Hellenism, 18, 106, 176
Hensel, Luise, 81
Herder, Johann Gottfried, 2, 6 f., 13, 13 n, 15, 23, 39 f., 71 n, 74, 104 f., 174 f.
Ideen zur Geschichte der Menschheit, 100
Vom Geist des Christentums, 7
Zerstreute Blätter, 8
Herrenhuter, 170 f.
History, 7, 11, 107
History and literature, 101 f.
Hoffmann, Ernst Theodor Amadeus, 80
Hölderlin, Friedrich, 12, 39, 96 f., 104, 126, 144
Arnim's "Ausflüge mit Hölderlin," 98 f.
Hyperion, 98
"Patmos," 99 f.
Poems, 99 f.
Houwald, Ernst von, 171 ff.
Die Seeräuber, 171 f.
Humboldt, Wilhelm von, 14, 117
Hutten, Ulrich von, 146

Idealism, 31, 39
Iffland, August Wilhelm, 142, 159, 164

Jahn, Friedrich Ludwig, 138, 147
Jacobi, Friedrich Heinrich, 15, 63 f., 88
Ueber gelehrte Gesellschaften, 63 f.
Waldemar, 88
Jenaer Literaturzeitung, 28, 47, 93
Jung-Deutschland, 155
Jung-Stilling, Heinrich, 26, 42 f., 47 ff., 100, 157, 170
Theorie der Geisterkunde, 42, 47 ff., 157
Heimweh, 47

Kant, Immanuel, 9, 21, 33
Karschin, Die (née Anna Luise Karsch), 159
Kleist, Heinrich von, 3, 66, 80, 119, 137, 138, 140 ff., 176
Kätchen von Heilbronn, 144
Michael Kohlhaas, 141
Penthesilea, 140
Phöbus, 141, 149
Zerbrochene Krug, 143

INDEX

Klopstock, Friedrich Gottlieb, 100, 158
Körner, Theodor, 151
Kotzebue, August von, 164, 169
Kunstpoesie, 40, 70 f., 84, 107

Labes, Baron von, 26
Lavater, Johann Kaspar, 100, 170
Leibnitz, Gottfried Wilhelm, 39 f.
Lessing, Gotthold Ephraim, 15, 106, 134, 172, 174
Literarisches Conversationsblatt, 153
Literatur-Blatt, 49, 153
Literarische Mittwochs-Gesellschaft, 152, 153
Luther, Martin, 26, 146

Mallon, Otto, 1, 169, 179
 Arnim-Bibliographie, 1, 179
 "A. v. Arnim's Beiträge zum 'Literarisches Conversationsblatt' und zu den 'Blättern für literarische Unterhaltung' (1823-31)," 1 n, 169
Marlowe, Christopher, 127 ff.
 Doctor Faustus, 127 ff.
Mereau, Sophie, 82
Monism, 29, 39 ff.
Montesquieu, Charles de, 137
Morgenblätter, 143
Möser, Justus, 7
Müller, Adam, 66, 136 f., 149
Müller, Johannes von, 121 139
Müller, Wilhelm, 127
Müllner, Adolph, 158
 Ährenlese neuerer Kritik, 157
 Literaturblatt, 49, 153

Napoleon, Bonaparte, 5, 14, 26, 66, 85, 91, 136, 146, 175
National literature and poetry, 6, 16, 70 f., 111 f.
Naturpoesie, 40, 68,
Nemesis, 154
Nibelungenlied, 6, 67 f., 71
Niebuhr, Bartold, 147 f.
Nordstern-circle, 123, 139, 149
 Die Versuche und Hindernisse Karls, 123, 139
Novalis, 5, 32, 39, 96 ff., 100
 Heinrich von Ofterdingen, 96 f.
 Magical idealism, 5

Öhlenschläger, Adam, 157
Ossian, 68

Paganism, 18, 107 f., 112 f.

Pedagogy, 105 f., 122, 124 f., 170
Philistinism, 6, 114
Poetry, cf. *Volkspoesie*, 6, 11, 70 ff., 75
Preusse, Der, (Der Preusse, ein Volksblatt), 25, 114, 138
Preussische Correspondent, 3, 15, 26, 137 f., 147 ff., 151, 177
Priestley, Joseph, 21

Racine, Jean Baptiste, 93, 95
 Phédre, 95
Rationalism, 5, 7
Raupach, Ernst, 159
Reichardt, Johann Friedrich, 22 f.
 Musikalische Zeitung, 23
Reinhardt, K. H. L., 161
 Die Circe von Glas-Llyn, 161
Rheinische Merkur, 153 f.
Richardson, Samuel, 107
Richter, Jean Paul, 139
Riemer, Friedrich Wilhelm, 117
Ritter, Johann Wilhelm, 32, 34 ff., 42 ff., 106, 177
 Fragmente eines jungen Physikers, 42 ff., 48
Roman poets, 22, 94, 106, 110
Romanticism, 5 ff., 16, 18, 43, 51, 87, 105 f., 110 ff.
 Early romanticism, 5, 51, 87, 142
 Heidelberg romanticism, 6 ff., 53, 55 ff., 64 ff., 79 f., 105, 115
 Late romanticism, 29, 66, 176
 Romantic historical school, 7, 25, 40
 Romanticism versus Classicism, 5 ff., 29, 175
Rousseau, Jean Jacques, 5, 14, 137
 Contrat social, 14

Sachs, Hans, 6
Savigny, Friedrich Karl von, 8, 76, 114, 136
Schack, Adolf Friedrich von, 21 n
Scharnhorst, Gerhard Joh. von, 147, 154, 167, 170
Schelling, Friedrich Wilhelm Joseph von, 7 f., 17, 32, 36 ff., 41, 43, 69, 106
 Ideen zu einer Philosophie der Natur, 36
 System des transcendentalen Idealismus, 37
 Von der Weltseele, 36
 Zeitschrift für spekulative Physik, 36
Schiller, Friedrich von, 49, 61, 100 f., 102, 121, 133 ff., 172, 175

INDEX 187

Braut von Messina, 102, 134
Jungfrau von Orleans, 102, 134
Maria Stuart, 163
Wilhelm Tell, 133
Schlegel brothers, 17, 87, 106, 175, 177
Athenäum, 89 ff., 96
Schlegel, August Wilhelm, 56, 74, 87 ff., 92 ff., 105 f., 110, 174, 176
Jon, 95 f., 110
Poetische Werke, 92 ff.
"Ueber schöne Literatur und Kunst," 176
Tristan, 94 f.
Schlegel, Dorothea, (née Mendelssohn), 157, 159
Schlegel, Friedrich, 3, 5, 16, 24, 39, 87 ff., 105 f.
Alarkos, 89 n, 90 f.
Deutsches Museum, 91 f.
Gedichte, 89 ff.
Europa, 3, 24, 37, 88, 94
Roland, 89 n, 90 f.
Schleiermacher, Friedrich, 147, 149, 154
Schmidt, F. V. V., 79
Die Märchen des Strazarola, 79
Schubart, Henriette, 160
Schubert, Gotthild Heinrich von, 42, 46
Ansichten von der Nachtseite der Naturwissenschaften, 42, 46
Scott, Sir Walter, 25, 107, 160
Kenilworth, 161
Minstrelsy of the Scottish Border, 160
The Pirate, 161
Waverly, 160
Shakespeare, William, 69, 94, 98, 110, 142, 160, 162 ff.
Hamlet, 162
Arnim's "Hamlet und Jakob (James I)" 162 ff.
Macbeth, 160
Smith, Adam, 137
Spinoza, Benedictus de, 39
Spirit, 2, 7 ff., 11 f., 16
Absolute spirit, 8
spiritus familiaris, 11,
Spirit of the people, cf. *Volksgeist,* 6 ff.
Stäel, Anna Louise Germaine de, 13, 147
Considérations sur les principaux événements de la révolution française, 13
Der Frau Stäel Verbannung aus Frankreich, 147
Steffens, Henrik, 150

Steig, Reinhold, 1, 27, 138, 156
Stein, Karl Freiherr von und zum, 137
Storm and Stress, 9

Tieck, Ludwig, 29 n, 38, 49 ff., 57, 87, 96, 104, 105, 142, 175
Die schöne Magelone, 50,
Lovell, 50, 96
Niobe, 105
Phantasus, 104
Thibaut, Anton Friedrich Justus, 65 ff.

Urkraft, cf. monism, 40
Ursprache, 106 f.
Universe, 7, 11, 39, 121
Universal poetry, 5, 39, 75

Varnhagen von Ense, Karl August, 155 f., 167 ff.
Biographische Denkmäler: Blücher, 168
Graf Zinzendorf, 170 f.
Volk, 6, 11, 160
Volksdichter, 68, 74 f., 146
Volksgeist, cf. *Geist,* 7 ff., 8 n, 10 ff., 40
Volkspoesie, 6, 11, 18, 68, 70 ff., 74, 108 f., 116, 134, 138
Volta, Alessandro, 21
Voß, Johann Heinrich, 6, 15, 28, 57, 60, 64, 111, 115, 119, 139
Voß, Heinrich, 57

Wagner, Ernst, 122 f.
Willibalds Ansichten des Lebens, 123
War of Liberation, 1, 12, 136, 138, 152, 167, 172
Werner, Zacharias, 26, 42, 83, 100 ff., 134, 147
Attila, 100 f.
Der vierundzwanzigste Februar, 103
Kreuz an der Ostsee, 100 f.
Luther, 100 f.
Söhne des Tals, 100 f.
System der Liebe, 42, 100 f.
Weihe der Unkraft, 103, 147
Wieland, Christoph Martin, 134, 172
Wilken, Friedrich, 65
Winkelmann, August, 15, 34
Winkelmann, Johann Jakob, 7, 108
Wünschelrute, 80

Zeitgeist, cf. *Geist,* 8 f., 11, 13 ff., 82
Zimmer, Johann Georg, 76,
Zinzendorf, Nikolaus Ludwig Graf von, 170 f.

VITA

Herbert R. Liedke was born April 8, 1905, at Heiligenbeil, Germany. He received his secondary education at the Gymnasium in Oranienburg, Germany. From 1925 till 1929 he studied at the University of Berlin, and the following year he taught secondary school in Halle, Germany. In 1931 he entered the Graduate School of Columbia University, studying Germanics. At the same time he taught at the College of the City of New York, holding the position of tutor until 1934 when he was appointed instructor.